On the Way to Collaborative Psychological Assessment

This collection of articles by Constance T. Fischer represents many of her major contributions to Collaborative Therapeutic Assessment. Fischer's work on the conceptual foundations and practices for individualized/collaborative psychological assessment are assembled in this volume. Also included are her thoughts about how to teach individualized assessment to students. This monograph will serve mental health professionals interested in Collaborative Therapeutic Assessment and instructors and students in graduate courses on psychological assessment.

Constance T. Fischer, PhD, ABPP, retired as professor emeritus of psychology from Duquesne University. She is best known for pioneering an individualized/ collaborative/therapeutic approach to psychological assessment and for her contributions to the field of qualitative research. Dr. Fischer has authored or edited six books and authored over 125 chapters and articles on psychological assessment, qualitative research, and professional issues.

The World Library of Mental Health

The *World Library of Mental Health* celebrates the important contributions to mental health made by leading experts in their individual fields. Each author has compiled a career-long collection of what they consider to be their finest pieces: extracts from books, journals, articles, major theoretical and practical contributions, and salient research findings.

For the first time ever the work of each contributor is presented in a single volume so readers can follow the themes and progress of their work and identify the contributions made to, and the development of, the fields themselves.

Each book in the series features a specially written introduction by the contributor giving an overview of their career, contextualizing their selection within the development of the field, and showing how their own thinking developed over time.

Titles in this series:

Passions, Persons, Psychotherapy, Politics: The selected works of Andrew Samuels
By Andrew Samuels

Towards a Radical Redefinition of Psychology: The selected works of Miller Mair
Edited by David Winter and Nick Reed

Living Archetypes: The selected works of Anthony Stevens
By Anthony Stevens

Soul: Treatment and Recovery – The selected works of Murray Stein
By Murray Stein

A Developmentalist's Approach to Research, Theory, and Therapy: The selected works of Joseph Lichtenberg
By Joseph D. Lichtenberg

Existential Psychotherapy and Counselling after Postmodernism: The selected works of Del Loewenthal
By Del Loewenthal

Love the Wild Swan: The selected works of Judith Edwards
By Judith Edwards

Conscience and Critic: The selected works of Keith Tudor
By Keith Tudor

On the Way to Collaborative Psychological Assessment

The selected works of Constance T. Fischer

Constance T. Fischer

Routledge
Taylor & Francis Group
LONDON AND NEW YORK

First published 2017 by Routledge

2 Park Square, Milton Park, Abingdon, Oxon OX14 4RN
605 Third Avenue, New York, NY 10017

Routledge is an imprint of the Taylor & Francis Group, an informa business

First issued in paperback 2021

Library of Congress Cataloging in Publication Data
Names: Fischer, Constance T., 1938– author, editor.
Title: On the way to collaborative psychological assessment: the selected works of Constance T. Fischer / edited by Constance T. Fischer.
Description: New York, NY: Routledge, 2016.
Includes bibliographical references and index.
Identifiers: LCCN 2016012610 | ISBN 9781138892088 (hbk: alk. paper) | ISBN 9781315709338 (ebk)
Subjects: LCSH: Personality tests. | Psychological tests. | Psychodiagnostics. | Counseling psychologist and client. | Psychotherapist and patient.
Classification: LCC BF698.4 .F563 2016 DDC 155.2/8–dc23
LC record available at https://lccn.loc.gov/2016012610

ISBN: 978-1-138-89208-8 (hbk)
ISBN: 978-1-138-31096-4 (pbk)

Typeset in Sabon
by Out of House Publishing

CONTENTS

LIST OF WORKS

1 Fischer, C. T. (1970). The testee as co-evaluator. *Journal of Counseling Psychology, 17*(1), 70–76.

2 Fischer, C. T. (1972). Paradigm changes which allow sharing of results. *Professional Psychology, 3*(4), 364–369.

3 Fischer, C. T. (1973). Intelligence contra IQ: A human science critique and alternative to the natural science approach to man. *Human Development, 16*, 8–20.

4 Fischer, C. T. (1976). Undercutting the scientist-professional dichotomy: The reflective psychologist. *The Clinical Psychologist, 29*, 5–7.

5 Fischer, C. T. (1977). Historical relations of psychology as an object-science and subject-science: Toward psychology as a human-science. *Journal of the History of the Behavioral Sciences, 13*, 369–378.

6 Fischer, C. T. (1978). Dilemmas in standardized testing. In J. Mearig (Ed.). *Working for children: Ethical issues beyond professional guidelines* (pp. 115–134). San Francisco: Jossey-Bass.

7 Fischer, C. T. (1979). Individualized assessment and phenomenological psychology. *Journal of Personality Assessment, 43*, 115–122.

8 Fischer, C. T. (1982). Intimacy in Assessment. In M. Fisher & G. Stricker (Eds.) *Intimacy* (pp. 443–460). New York: Plenum.

9 Fischer, C. T. (1978). Collaborative psychological assessment. In C. T. Fischer & S. L. Brodsky (Eds.). *Client participation in human services: The Prometheus principle* (pp. 41–61). New Brunswick, N. J.: Transaction.

10 Fischer, C. T. (1994). Assessing Process. In *Individualizing psychological assessment* (pp. 85–107). Mahwah, NJ: Erlbaum.

11 Fischer, C. T. (1978). Collaborative, individualized assessment. In Fischer, C. T. & Brodsky, S. L. (Eds.). *Client participation in human services: The Prometheus principle* (pp. 41–61). New Brunswick, N. J.: Transaction.

12 Fischer, C. T. (2004). Individualized assessment moderates the impact of HIPAA privacy rules. *Journal of Personality Assessment, 81*, 35–38.

13 Fischer, C. T. (1994). Rorschach scoring questions as access to dynamics. *Journal of Personality Assessment, 62*, 515–525.

14 Fischer, C. T. (1998). The Rorschach and the life-world: Exploratory exercises. In L. Handler & M. Hilsenroth (Eds.). *Teaching and learning personality assessment* (pp. 347–358). Hillsdale, NJ: Lawrence Erlbaum.

FOREWORD

I still remember the day in 1986 when I discovered Constance Fischer's book, *Individualizing Psychological Assessment*. Several weeks earlier a friend had given me a copy of a 1982 Fischer chapter entitled "Intimacy in Assessment" (included in this volume as Chapter 8), and I had read it with great interest. I immediately began looking for other publications by Fischer. When I discovered that she had published a book on her approach to assessment in 1985, I went immediately to the library at the University of Texas and checked it out. That evening after dinner I began to read and was filled with a combination of incredible excitement and awe. I pored over Fischer's words until 4 or 5 a.m., sometimes with tears of joy running down my face, and I had difficulty falling asleep. The next morning over breakfast I eagerly told my partner Jim about what I had discovered: Fischer's work was consonant with but went *far* beyond my own fledgling ideas of what I then called an "interpersonal model of psychological assessment." Fischer described collaborative methods very close to those I was exploring with clients and students, and moreover, she had elucidated a coherent philosophy of science that grounded and justified an interventionist approach to psychological testing. I remember saying, "This book is 30 years ahead of its time!" and Jim's smiling, probably thinking, "There's another example of Steve's hyperbolic speech!"

When the volume you are reading is published, almost exactly 30 years will have passed since that day. I can see now that if anything, my exclamation was understated. Indeed, the world of psychological assessment has changed so that many readers are open to the ideas and techniques of Collaborative and Therapeutic Assessment (C/TA). Nevertheless, this collection of Fischer's previously published papers and chapters is still "cutting edge," even for those who are involved in the C/TA community, which is one reason I was eager to see it published.

In piece after piece, Fischer challenges us to go beyond the view so many of us were taught in our psychology training programs and that is still so prevalent in psychology today – of human beings as collections of traits, conflicts, "coping mechanisms," and abilities (or more recently, of brain structures, neurotransmitters, and neural networks) – to a vision of people as meaning-makers who are constantly "becoming," shifting, transforming, and being influenced in turn by the world and the people around them. On top of this, Fischer reminds us that just as in physics, observation inherently influences what is observed, and there is no reality to be discovered about human beings that is not perspectival. Or, as I once heard Connie say succinctly, "We can only know through our relationship with the world."

This is a view of reality that is alive, interactional, fascinating, and exciting – and also, potentially scary and overwhelming. As Stolorow and Atwood (1992) wrote, few of us can tolerate for long an awareness of the "unbearable embeddedness of being," because it leads us to feel more vulnerable, less in control, and more unsure of ourselves (Finn, 2007). As much as we may try, we keep falling back into a vision of ourselves as separate and all powerful and of our tests as measures of who our clients "really *are*." Fischer models a way to deal with this complex awareness through a combination of humility and common sense. Inevitably our psychological assessments are "snapshots" of our constantly evolving clients, she says, but this does not render them useless nor mean that they are inherently disrespectful of human complexity (as many humanistic psychologists asserted in the 1960s). Rather, it is only by acknowledging the limitations of our psychological tests and the particularity of our perspectives and by inviting our clients into dialogue about our ideas and perceptions that we can help them find new perspectives that lead them to other ways of being in the world.

I believe this view of psychological assessment is as needed today as when Fischer first wrote about it, and given the recent push towards "evidence-based assessment" (e.g., Hunsley & Mash, 2010) her critiques of "scientism" in psychology (see Chapter 4) are as relevant now as they were during the age of behaviorism. A psychology graduate student recently asked me, "Now that there is so much work on mapping brain-behavior relationships, do you think psychological assessment will eventually disappear?" To me, this question reflects a new version of the fantasy that if we can discover the "Truth" about our clients, we will not have to interact with them to understand and help them. Fischer cogently explains in these pages why this will never be true. Furthermore, Fischer gives us the tools to avoid swinging to a polarized point of view, i.e., that since "Reality" can never be truly defined, all perspectives are equally valid and useful. Intersubjectivity (or a phenomenological worldview, as Fischer would likely term it) does *not* mean that we must devalue empiricism. In fact, Fischer's methods and techniques are highly empirical; they simply aim to include the observer and the person observed in making sense of the data that are collected. Incidentally, Fischer applied this approach not only to psychological assessment, but also in pioneering and spreading rigorous, empirical methods of qualitative research (cf. Fischer, 2006).

Like many influential innovators, Fischer's unique contributions stem in part from her having immersed herself in one field (phenomenological psychology as it was explored at Duquesne University in the 1960s and 1970s) and then applying her insights and knowledge to a completely new area (psychological assessment). In the previously unpublished autobiography comprising the introduction to this book you can read about this heady and exciting time in Fischer's life. You will also get a sense of the personal courage, professional conviction, and determination it took for Fischer to persevere in writing about and teaching her paradigm of psychological assessment. Professional journals resoundingly rejected her initial papers, and even at Duquesne, it took years for her colleagues to stop referring to her "testing course" and to use the term "psychological assessment." How many of us could have persevered in that context? Very few, I believe. Yet, Fischer did and was enormously prolific in her writing. The current interest in Fischer's work is evidence that her years of labor are bearing fruit and will, I believe, continue to do so for a long time. This book will help ensure that we do not forget what she has to teach us.

Before closing I wish to express my gratitude not only for Connie's ideas and writings, but also for her "personhood." In addition to her determination and brilliance, Connie is warm, generous, open, and humorous. She has been exceedingly kind to me over the years, and one of the things I am proudest of is that we are friends. I believe Collaborative/Therapeutic Assessment as it is now practiced is permeated not only by Fischer's ideas and worldview, but also by what one colleague (Bernstein, 2014) called her "Connie-ness." I hope this book gives those of you who do not know Connie or her work a window into who she is and what she has given to psychological assessment.

Stephen E. Finn
Austin, TX, October 15, 2015

References

Bernstein, L. (2014, September). *An open letter to Connie Fischer*. Paper presented at the Inaugural Conference on Collaborative and Therapeutic Assessment, Austin, TX, as part of a symposium, "We Can Only Know Through Our Relationship with the World: Constance T. Fischer and Collaborative Psychological Assessment," S. E. Finn, Chair.

Finn, S. E. (2002, March). *Challenges and lessons of intersubjectivity theory for psychological assessment*. Paper presented at the Society for Personality Assessment annual meeting, San Antonio, TX, as part of a symposium, "Concepts of the Self: Implications for Assessment," M. L. Silverstein, Chair. Reprinted as Chapter 17 in Finn, S. E. (2007). *In our clients' shoes: Theory and techniques of Therapeutic Assessment* (pp. 243–252). Mahwah, NJ: Erlbaum.

Fischer, C. T. (2006). (Ed.). *Qualitative research methods for psychologists: Introduction through empirical studies*. San Diego: Academic Press.

Hunsley, J., & Mash, E. (2010). Evidence-based assessment. In Barlow, D. H. (Ed.), *The handbook of clinical psychology* (pp. 76–97). New York: Oxford.

Stolorow, R. D., & Atwood, G. E. (1992). *Contexts of being: The intersubjective foundations of psychological life*. Hillsdale, N.J.: Analytic Press.

PREFACE

As I'm entering the close of my career, it is a great pleasure to have colleagues and a publisher express interest in seeing that a volume of my work on individualizing psychological assessment be made available to the profession and to graduate students on the way. The selections that appear here are anticipated to be useful both to colleagues who have long practiced in similar ways and to those who just now are learning about this approach. These selections were written between 1970 and 2013, and include the first article that was accepted for publication on my approach to assessment as well as a previously unpublished autobiography that provides a personal context to my work. These chapters may be read in any order, but are grouped into three sections. The first section illustrates the development of my approach to assessment; the second addresses realms of practice; the third provides examples of teaching.

A comment on the term "collaborative assessment," which for many has come to stand for my overall approach. I originally described five assessment principles: collaborate; describe; contextualize; respect complexity, holism, and ambiguity; and intervene (Cf. Chapter 11) with no particular order or ranking. However, colleagues quickly referred to my approach as "collaborative;" I think that may have been because that quality was what was so radically different from what we had been taught. Indeed I've come to realize that once collaborating with the client, one finds oneself in effect respecting the other principles.

I appreciate the decades of students who have contributed to the development of this approach. Steve Finn, my dear friend and longtime colleague, encouraged me to put this collection together. Moreover, he offered considerable assistance in choosing the selections and in seeing the book through the publication process. I also appreciate George Zimmar, Publisher at Routledge, for his enthusiasm about publishing this volume and for guidance along the way.

And to all of you who are taking collaborative work forward, as I often wrote at the end of my positive comments on graduate students' work: "Carry on!"

INTRODUCTION

Carrying On Toward Individualized/Collaborative/ Therapeutic Psychological Assessment

During the 2000s the *Journal of Personality Assessment* published a series of autobiographies of assessment psychologists. The series editors, Bill Kinder and Steve Strack, asked if I would contribute. I was surprised, and imagined that the invitation was in part related to the fact that the series had included only one woman (Jane Loevinger). But upon reflection, I realized that I had served ten years on the Society for Personality Assessment (SPA) Board of Directors and on assorted committees, had delivered a Master Lecture on "Individualized, Collaborative Assessment" (Fischer, 2000– Chapter 11 of this volume), and was being told by colleagues that my contribution in pioneering that approach was now evident as the forward edge of a paradigm change in psychological assessment. In 2006 I was presented SPA's Bruno Klopfer Award for "outstanding, long-term professional contributions to the field of personality assessment." Along the way I had published 130-some articles, chapters, and books. I felt honored to be included in the autobiography series, but it took me more than six years to complete my submission and hence it was never published in the journal. As this current volume was taking shape it seemed fitting to include this account of my journey.

"Carrying on," in my title, implies many aspects of my continuing journey toward addressing those aspects of being human that our natural science tradition has not taken into account. "Carry on!" also turns out to be the comment with which for decades I often have closed celebratory remarks on student papers. Former students, with implicit grins, often sign letters and emails to me in like manner. The term can also mean slogging on, soldiering on, and carrying something with or to others. My journey has differed in two major regards from the autobiographies published in the *Journal of Personality Assessment*: (1) I have lived as a woman through the era in which psychology was dominated by men, and (2) my efforts to contribute to the development of qualitative research methods and to conceptual foundations and practices for individualized/collaborative psychological assessment occurred within a discipline that until the last 15–20 years or so has been largely opposed to practices that are not grounded in positivism. In describing childhood, college years, graduate school, and professional career, I have chosen events that illustrate those two themes and other events that at least retrospectively seem related to how I've gone about my pursuits, through happenstance and choice. I also have chosen events to illustrate for younger readers some cultural and professional contexts of earlier years.

The Beginnings of Individualized/Collaborative Psychological Assessment

During my graduate training and early professional life, psychological testing and diagnostics were only secondarily for the person who was tested; primarily they were for psychologists and psychiatrists to classify patients and then to make decisions about them. It seemed to me that our testing could become much more useful to all parties if we changed the process in which the testee was seen as emitting responses whose meaning was decided in terms of our theories and constructs. Indeed, it seemed to me that the latter process could be destructive: it often left the patient feeling as though only professionals could make sense of what was "making" him or her behave in particular ways. Fortunately, at the Lexington, Kentucky Veterans Administration hospital, supervisors (several being explicitly existential) allowed me (as a trainee) to go beyond standardized administrations, in order to try to be more helpful to patients. Although tentatively and inconsistently at that time, I talked directly with patients about their actual lives, and reflected about how test data might provide additional access to those lives. I shared these hunches with the patients, and we explored them together.

Later I thought of these practices as life-world exploration, which I pursued much more thoroughly while I was teaching "testing" courses at Duquesne. My goal became to tailor my explorations and the written report so that I could describe the individual client as a person. This *individualizing* was enhanced by collaborating with the client. The process itself turned out to be affirming and growthful for the person. At that time, except for readers of Carl Rogers' work, testers worked with "patients" and "subjects," not clients. I searched for a term with which to replace "testing" and "evaluation," and borrowed "assessment" from nonclinical settings. I liked that the word's Greek origins referred to sitting beside and representing. Gradually, "assessment" has come to be a broader term than "testing." Today, of course, "testing" appropriately is seen as a tool for, but not the outcome of, assessment. But for about 20 years, I urged my Duquesne colleagues to refer to my "testing" courses as "assessment" courses. From their own experience with testing courses, neither they nor other colleagues could imagine how I could be teaching standardized testing and also be exploring actual lives.

By now, many psychologists have in various instances engaged in at least some individualized/collaborative practices, especially as they have learned that the practices are therapeutic in process in addition to optimizing concrete suggestions. But until the past 20 or so years, these practices rarely occurred in institutional or agency settings and even more rarely appeared in formal reports. Occurrences were occasional and unsystematic. Fortunately, our society has come to expect accountability in everyday language, psychologists less often feel compelled to prove their scientific standing and now are free to "be relevant," and individualized/collaborative assessment is seen as being "*commonsense*." At last it is increasingly becoming more *commonplace*. Especially with Stephen Finn's and his colleagues' workshops and innovations (more later), geometrically increasing numbers of psychologists are adopting and adapting this approach to assessment, and teaching and publishing their own innovations. I think that my contribution has been to name the practices, advocate for their consistent use, relate them to a philosophy of science (e.g., Fischer, 1977; 1998), present them in a broad range of journals, books, and symposia, and provide lots of concrete examples, for over 40 years – slogging on!

To my surprise and delight, as mentioned, many psychologists now are proclaiming that individualized/collaborative/transformative assessment has introduced a paradigm shift from regarding scores and classification as the goal of testing, to testing being a tool for exploring directly with people their experience, conflicts, and options. Please see Finn, Fischer, and Handler (2012) for chapters by the three of us and by colleagues, each illustrating collaborative and/or therapeutic assessment. Each chapter provides "teaching points." My chapter is "Collaborating throughout the Assessment."

My reports are descriptive, re-presenting the events we have come to understand. In regard to these events, once we have discovered the contexts and meanings for the client, no other level of explanation is required. My being grounded in a human-science orientation (see Fischer, 1998) has helped me to follow these individualized/collaborative practices more thoroughly and consistently, but of course colleagues grounded in other orientations have readily adopted, adapted, and expanded these practices.

Childhood through College

My mother, Irene Nelson Taylor, was the only one of four siblings born in this country, her parents having emigrated from Sweden. By the time she was eight, she was an orphan, and had moved with one of her sisters to live with an aunt and uncle in San Francisco. She left high school after tenth grade to attend a business school, and became manager of a Martha Washington candy store. For years I used mother's Drew Business School brown pamphlet on writing style and grammar.

My father, Milton Clay Taylor, grew up in Oregon. His grandfather "rode" with Wild Bill Cody, and had a street and a building named after him in Cheyenne. During high school Dad took great pride in devising a formula with which he won a contest for the most accurate estimate of the number of dried beans in a huge jar placed in the local drug store window. Dad became one of the first two Eagle Scouts in Oregon, earning badges that in one instance required felling a tree and carving it into a functional canoe. He delivered newspapers to legislators in the State Capitol building. I recall Dad making arrows (as in bow and arrows), building furniture, being a ham radio operator, and his teaching me to fire pistols on the range. (Dad was an alternate on the cancelled 1944 US Olympics pistol team.) Mostly I recall his pride in being a West Point graduate ("Country, Honor, Duty"), and his emphasis on order, loyalty, and teamwork. A familiar adage at home, from both parents, was "Anything worth doing is worth doing well." By the time I was in high school, Dad made a point to introduce me to (rare) women officers and administrators.

I recall mother's emphasis on family, her warmth and support, and her quiet competence and courage. For example, after World War II, Mother received printed orders to the Hudson Hotel in New York City from which we (she, my brother, Ron – four years old, and I, eight years old) would be shuttled the next day to a troop ship, and eventually be reunited with Dad, who remained in Germany at the end of the war. Upon arriving at the (to us) imposing Hudson Hotel, we were told that written orders notwithstanding, there were no available rooms, but that, yes, the shuttle would be there in the morning. Mom just gathered us with our luggage, sat on the lobby floor against a marble pillar, explained to be my brother and I that we would be "camping," and cuddled both of us throughout the night;

Ron and I felt completely safe. While we waited to disembark in Bremerhaven, Ron and I watched German youngsters dive 25 feet into oily water to retrieve orange peels that American mothers and children disposed of over the rail while eating the oranges; mother explained about hunger. When I was a high school freshman, we were stationed in Europe; I selected clothing styles from a Sears & Roebuck catalogue, and mother sewed everything from suits to dresses for formal dances. She grinned supportively at my escapades – from being the only girl to deliver movie schedules to residences at Fort Benning, Georgia, to my later declining to wear the requisite hat to post luncheons.

Our Frankfurt duplex (commandeered by the occupation army – Dad's) was pockmarked with waves of machine gun bullets. Ron and I discovered human bones and cockpit panels in the backyard. Our maid took us to her home outside the barb-wired compound via secret underground tunnels built to avoid body searches by the military police. We could smell rotting corpses when demolition equipment unearthed previously encased corpses. At a cocktail party, I (still eight years old) carried a tray of hors d'oeuvres through the room with wives and into the room where officers were socializing; there I heard an officer bragging loudly about how he had used a bayonet to "rip off that Jerry's balls." That incident became a magnet for my evolving impressions that: war is terrible, people get caught up in tides they don't choose, some people use war and power for their own purposes, and there ought to be ways to encourage people to respect their shared humanity despite differences.

Including graduate school, I had attended a dozen schools, because military families move on average every two–three years. High school was in Paris (Dad with the American embassy), in Göppingen, Germany, and in Alexandria, Virginia. I used to think that I'd never get married because I wouldn't know how to stay in one place. Besides, I believed that odds were against the Western world's surviving its wars. Yet I completed 46 years at Duquesne! I started college at Miami University of Ohio, my godmother's alma mater, and transferred to the University of Oklahoma at the suggestion of a love interest army captain now stationed in nearby Lawton; he was transferred out the next semester! Then when I feared I could not pass modern dance (phys. ed. requirement, despite previous credits in assorted sports, and having played on the junior varsity women's basketball team at Miami), I learned that if I transferred out and came back with 60 credits as a transfer student I could opt out of the dance requirement. So I attended the University of Connecticut for a semester and returned to Oklahoma. I posted my UConn grades on my door (I was Head Resident of a dorm) to refute any rumors about my six-month absence.

Back to earlier times and influential experiences: I was born at Schoffield Barracks, Oahu, Hawaii in 1938. (At the 2004 Hawaii APA convention it dawned on me that I was on the island of my birth on my birthday.) I attended grade school at West Point, New York; Salem, Oregon; and San Francisco. Sixth and seventh grades occurred at Ft. Benning, and then Atlanta, Georgia. At Fort Benning, walking back to school after lunch, we listened to news broadcasts as we passed open windows, mostly news of the Korean war. In the morning we dreaded the teacher's announcements: "Joanne Hackett will no longer be with us" (father was killed in Korea; family has to leave the post). I was on the softball team (otherwise all boys), but because girls were not allowed on the boys' bus, I could play only home games. Walking home across the parade grounds one Sunday, past the infantry weapons display (tanks, etc.), and with fighter planes zooming overhead, I reflected matter-of-factly that Western humankind likely would destroy itself before I became an adult. In 8th grade we were bussed from Ft. Benning to the Columbus public High School. I was surprised that unlike all my schools for military dependents (children of soldiers and officers), here there were no "colored" people (the terms "black," "Black," or "African American" had not evolved). At assembly we post kids, without consultation, stayed seated as the student body and faculty rose for "Dixie." The national anthem was not played.

Freshman and sophomore years (1953–54) were in Paris in a school for state department and military dependents, first in a former mansion where assemblies were held in an auditorium with silk-covered seats, and next in a warehouse along the River Seine, with tug boats blasting and warehouse steam pipes whistling. On my last day before moving to Germany, a valued social studies teacher called me in to the teachers' lounge. In a caring way he advised me to be cautious about letting males see how I think, lest I scare them off. He said that I thought with a masculine intellect, for example answering an essay question by systematically addressing economic, geographic, and political factors. I was a bit puzzled, but remembered. And in my junior year in high school I followed counseling to take typing and shorthand courses.

Other experiences in France figured in my continuing appreciation of multiple realities. When I was 14 (1953), the family visited the US cemetery in Normandy. After walking among the countless rows of crosses and stars (mostly of soldiers only four years older than I when they died), we were all tight-throated but proud of America. As we walked back to our car, Dad firmly but quietly instructed us to get in quickly and to lock the doors. As we drove out, farmers with handmade scythes threw stones at us. Dad later explained the United States' involvement with Algeria. On another occasion, our American car's hood, roof, and trunk were painted in red, "US Go Home." Walking through a subway station by myself one Sunday morning on my way to the Quai D'Orsay American Church, with my bobby sox marking me as an American, a thundering and repeated shout, "Les Americans en Amerique!!!," reverberated through the nearly empty tiled passage way, and through my soul.

Junior year was in Heidelberg, Germany, where weekdays I lived in a dorm for military dependents. My first morning in the dependents' mess hall, I encountered among my fellow students half a dozen kids I had known from earlier stations. Toward the end of the year, waiting with friends for a train home to Göppingen for the weekend, I rested a stack of books and my clutch purse atop my new yearbook on a car's bumper (the parking area was adjacent to the train track). When the train came, I realized that the car and all my possessions were gone. German law and tradition held that found property is stolen property if not returned. On Monday, my school's office staff said that three separate persons expressed pleasure to be able to return the items (which apparently had dropped onto the road over several blocks); no one left a name. This incident was especially uplifting in that of their own accord these citizens went out of their way to return strewn belongings of a dependent of a member of the military that not long ago had been an occupation army. In Spring semester a friend and I snuck out of the dorm each dawn, set a clock next to the net, and played nonverbal tennis on the officers' housing courts, and then snuck back into our dorms before the house mother arose. Much later we found out indirectly that she had known all along, but hadn't wanted to interfere with our adventure. Again, uplifting.

Senior year (1956) in high school was in Alexandria, Virginia, Dad having been assigned to the Pentagon. A "colored" girl friend from Heidelberg days spent the night with me and others who had known each other overseas. She had been fearful of traveling from Washington, DC into white Virginia. I met her in DC and we rode the busses together into and back from Alexandria. A couple of summers later, I was a waitress (now "server") at a Hot Shoppe where another white coed waitress asked me to double date with her so she could spend social time with a colored male cook. We women kept our heads below the car windows on the trip into and back from DC, so as not to be attacked by whites.

A different interracial experience at the same restaurant: at the end of a day's waitressing, I went into the freezer to pick up trays of butter pats for the dining room. I was vaguely aware that all the colored cooks watched me go down the stairs; at the bottom, the dozen all-colored prep staff had stopped their work and watched me go into the freezer. There, with butter trays frozen to my nylon sleeves, I found myself being stalked by a colored man about 6′2″ with only one eye, and evil it was. We moved among the shelves of sliced potatoes, onion rings, and the like, each pretending not to notice the other. Finally I saw an opening and ran, ramming the disc that served as doorknob, falling and spilling onto the floor of the prep room. Every one of about a dozen workers was standing with back to the workstation, watching the door. No one moved; I collected myself and the butter trays, and limped up the stairs, pointedly avoiding the manager's office, instead finishing my chores as I overheard whispered snippets of phone conversation between the cooks and the downstairs workers. I spoke to no one of the event, but I found that the fellow was no longer around, and from that day on the kitchen staff helped me with extraordinary good will to get all my orders out efficiently. In turn I found myself taking extra care in printing my orders legibly. These lessons in situation, context, and perspective found their way into my later professional conceptions and practice.

At the University of Oklahoma (1958), I majored in political science, with minors in history and economics. I took something like 20 extra credits to obtain a teaching certificate while maintaining my liberal arts degree. I was astounded when the woman who sat next to me in an economics class told me that during the last year she had been required, as a colored person, to sit outside of the classroom near the door. I was inducted into an education honorary society (all white). On my own I read Rousseau, Genet, Kierkegard, Camus, Fromm, Sartre (and *Peyton Place*!). One semester I regularly went fishing at sunrise with a friend, then went directly to geography class; another friend who sat near me later laughed when I confirmed that the odd smell was indeed of fish. On dates, we visited bootleggers (dry state except 3.2 beer), often driving through cornfields and dirt roads by moonlight. I waited in the car, heard the coded knock on a door and then the sound of shovel and creek gravel, and at last received the dripping bottle of Seagrams.

Student teaching in Oklahoma City turned out to be pivotal in my decision to apply to graduate school in psychology. I was teaching an honors course in world history when a student asked why the French had invented their class system (bourgeoisie, etc.). I explained that it wasn't designed, and said that I didn't know how it had evolved. We carried out an experiment in which I asked the class to say for one row what salad dressing each student's family preferred, then for the next row how many cars were in the family, and so on. Then I pointed to each student and asked the class if he or she was going to go to college (all were well qualified academically). The students immediately understood that we had an undesigned socio-economic class system. One girl raised her hand and commented that at least ours was not a caste system. She asked if, on my way to Oklahoma City from Norman, I had noticed some mud huts with the standard rocking chairs in the dirt yard (along with pecking chickens) and then told me that a certain one was her grandfather's home even now, but that her father was President of the city's largest bank. We were all quite excited about our ensuing discussion.

But the next day I was summoned to the Superintendent's office in Oklahoma City. With cowboy-booted feet crossed on his desk, which was graced by Civil War cannon balls and festooned with Confederate flags, he explained, "Missy, we don't have no classes in these here United States. And no regional differences neither. I've been hearing from parents, and I don't want you to do no harm to these children. Your job is to teach the facts. You aren't here to teach thinking." At the time, just below us Texas law prohibited the appearance of "United Nations" in public school books. He did acknowledge that I was said to maintain exemplary control of the notoriously unruly last period freshman study hall. I didn't tell him about my "initiation" in the first day of class: as I wrote an announcement on the blackboard, my flowing cotton skirt was suddenly pinned to the wooden chalkboard by a switchblade thrown from the back of the room. With my back to the class I had pulled the knife out, and closed and pocketed it, and continued writing. Later in the class, I quietly walked behind the knife's standing owner, pushed his chair firmly into the back of his knees, occasioning his immediately sitting down properly, and placed the knife on his desk in front of him. I did not report him, and the class and I had a fine understanding from there on out.

When the Social Studies department chair snuck in through the door at the back of the room to observe my student teaching, every student raised his/her hand to all my questions about homework reading. But students who did not want to be called on signaled that to me through eye-rolling or private hand signals. The chair told me later that he was amazed by full class participation.

I consulted with my supervising teacher, and decided that I would not accept any of the teaching offers I had received, and instead would go off to graduate school. My idea was that there I would find out if I could indeed be dangerous to children, and if not, I would have a master's degree that would give me more clout in the school system (in those days that was so). I decided on psychology for two reasons: (1) catalogues had many courses referring to learning (too late I discovered that those courses had to do with rats and pigeons!); (2) The two undergraduate psychology courses I had taken were about real people. One was a personality theory course in which we read Maslow's (1954) *Motivation and Personality* – his hierarchy of needs and his study of actualized persons. The other was a social psychology course taught by Muzafer Sherif. His field studies, like the Robbers' Cave experiment, were inspirational. Sherif had offered me an assistantship, but I was eager to move on. I applied, without guidance, to two universities because of their course offerings in learning, and was accepted by both: the Universities of North Carolina and Kentucky.

During the summer before graduate school, I worked as a waitress at a resort in Estes Park, Colorado. At one point our entire group went on strike between the tomato juice and salad course for the Tri Delta national convention. Contrary to contract, we had been provided with no meals other than soured gruel and white bread, and no salary for three weeks. One fellow had shipped a dry-iced sample of our sour gruel to a state health office, so we believed that we had that on our side. We had scant resources to get out of Estes Park if we were fired and the stream of applicants who appeared regularly were hired in our place. Fortunately, our strike was successful, and we were better fed after that. Following a picnic in my last month, I tripped crossing a stream, and then hiked with what turned out to a broken foot several miles into town to a doctor, short-cutting across meadows and streams because the manager refused to let me ride the tourist shuttle bus. I continued to waitress, and a month later I climbed Long's Peak in my cast. Earlier I found out from a friend who worked in the business office that my foot cast changed the plans of the Maître d' (a Miami gangster, with a shoulder-holstered gun) to move my sleeping quarters into a room that connected with his. These adventures, from waitressing, to working in dimes stores, laundromats, and movie theaters, provided a valuable supplement to my later professional training.

Graduate School in the 1960s

One reason I chose the University of Kentucky was that I was able to obtain a position as a residence hall director for the first year (1960–61). I had never taken an intro to psych course, and didn't think I should accept an offered assistantship to teach that course. During my second-through fourth years in graduate school, I worked as a Veterans' Administration psychology trainee in the Lexington Neuropsychiatric Hospital. Of my entering class of 22 at UK, only 5 were women, and of the class apparently only 5 eventually earned PhDs, which some faculty members cited as evidence of the program's rigor. Indeed, over the years after graduation, fellow graduates and I often have marveled that in comparison with colleagues from major universities we too had acquired a top-flight education. The program, like many others at that time, was a mix of psychoanalytic theory (of the old Fenichel sort), behaviorism (the cognitive part came much later), and experimental method. There was no training for private practice of psychology, which didn't exist outside of New York City; clinically trained psychologists were expected to work in mental hospitals, child guidance clinics, and other agencies.

Once involved with the study of psychology, I was no longer interested in returning to teaching social studies. Although there were numerous disadvantages to being a woman in psychology, my gender at that time allowed me to pursue my interests without worrying about preparing for a career. I knew I could always find work with my teaching credentials, shorthand and typing skills, and waitressing experience (I was missing two female credentials: nursing and social work!). My male classmates were understandably concerned about becoming head of a household, and being sure they could command a solid job; they worked hard to please professors, earn good grades, obtain research assistantships that would guarantee publications, and take courses that would make them more competitive in the market. In contrast, I felt free to read what interested me, to write term papers that took me more deeply into my interests, and to take challenging electives. I was most excited about social psychology. The *Handbook of Social Psychology* (in several volumes) contained many field studies – real life stuff, including Lewin's work. The issues were the ones that had earlier drawn me to political science – prejudice, patterns of affiliation, crowd behavior, effects of propaganda and of leadership styles, conditions of acquiescence, and so on. But after a while it dawned on me that the only setting in which I could later pursue social psychology would be as a professor, and I certainly didn't want to do that! So I shifted to clinical, not wanting to be a practicing clinician, but thinking that I might be able to pursue some sort of community preventative psychology (which in fact within his brief presidency, John Kennedy initiated and which became community psychology). So guess what I wound up doing for 46 years – being a professor and a practitioner of clinical psychology!

Much of the course work was engaging. One of our research courses included a major segment on philosophy of science – Peirce, Bridgeman, and so on. I spent many extra hours absorbed in finding more material in the library. Unfortunately, today students are not taught the difference between theory and underlying philosophy. Our sensation and perception course also was intriguing, and the professor encouraged reflection on the assumptions and distinctions being made in those days. I enjoyed Osgood's experimental psychology tome. Occasionally I earned extra money in my apartment, running statistical tests on a Monroe electric calculator. No LED displays; instead there were metal pop-up tabs similar to old cash registers. I recall being mesmerized as I entered measures of one variable in the left column, the others in the right column, pulled a crank, and kept going through hundreds of pairs. $2xy^2$ appeared in the middle panel, and sum x and sum y appeared on each side. My instructions were to repeat the entire procedure until I got the same statistics two out of three times, and then plugged the figures into the formula and did the calculations longhand to determine "*r*." After several nights of this process, as the Monroe clicked and clacked, I could tell pretty much whether there was going to be a statistically significant correlation; I was in touch with the uncanny mathematical orderliness of measured behavior!

We had excellent Rorschach courses (Beck's system supplemented with texts summarizing other systems) taught by adjunct faculty, but I was not favorably impressed with our other training in testing. One entire course was devoted to intelligence testing and research; we administered 60 Stanford-Binets, WISCs, WAISs, Ravens Matrices, Draw-A-Mans, and so on, all to standardize us into impersonal test administrators. At the VA Hospital, the Psychology Service received referrals from MDs on the same slips used for ordering x-rays, urinalyses, and so on, usually saying only "psychological evaluation" or "differential dx." We testers ("assessor" wasn't in our lexicon) were expected to remain blind to history and current issues and to draw conclusions only from test scores and patterns in order to demonstrate the objectivity and scientific merit of testing. However, in those days, our test impressions were one part of a case conference presided over by the psychiatrist, with social workers, nurses, occupational therapists, aides, and others also providing observations and impressions from their purviews. I continue to think that we should get back to talking with clients' involved others and integrate that information with our own data, and not just for custody evaluations.

In my last year of graduate school, for the final exam for an assessment course, I was assigned to test a patient admitted to the University Hospital's psychiatry unit. With three faculty members watching through a one-way mirror and making marks on a 6 x 6 grid, I was to interview the patient, and administer a Rorschach, a complete WAIS, selected TAT cards, and a DAP, all within three hours. The patient was 19 years old, admitted the night before after his first psychotic break; he was scared silly. When we heard the faculty members talking and laughing, I explained that I was learning to use these tests and that my teachers were watching me, not him, through what seemed like the mirror. He was visibly relieved, but I was docked points for interacting with the patient. I was also docked and indeed remonstrated with for not being efficient: even though I had indeed completed all of the tasks within the three hours, I had been observed taking rubber bands off the puzzle boxes during the session instead of in advance, and I had repeatedly crossed my body with my right hand to pick up my pencil on the left side. My practicum site supervisor that semester at the USPHS Prison and Hospital recommended an "A" for me, saying that I was the most competent of all the students he had supervised over the years (mostly due to my training at the VA hospital!). But the university professors assigned me a final grade of "C" because of the claimed inefficiency, and for talking with the patient.

Speaking of the Prison and Hospital, one day during my practicum there, I had had an especially meaningful second assessment session with an Hispanic woman who had been imprisoned for drug violations. After I shared my test-based advice with her, she smiled sadly and said she owed me something for my sincere efforts, and that she wanted to add to my training. She then explained that she would be given the proverbial one suit and $20 when she was released in a month, and that she would try to get a job away from her old haunts, save money, and get back to her three daughters. But she knew that she likely could not get a job with a prison record and being Hispanic, and that she probably would wind up prostituting again, which would in turn likely lead to drug abuse. I remain grateful to this woman and to many other early patients with whom I learned more fully the importance of going beyond test scores and constructs to explore life worlds.

A second memory of that day in 1963: I pushed a buzzer, and the guard with the classic ring of large keys came to escort us out of the testing room. There was an eerie complete silence, in sharp contrast with our entrance, which had been accompanied by clanking on the bars, cat calls, and the like. We looked to the guard in puzzlement; he said, "Oh, you don't know: President Kennedy has been shot." It turned out that inmates and mental patients across the land were as quieted as the rest of the country.

Another note about the times: When I began my VA traineeship in the Psychology Service, which was decidedly of high quality, hospital closets still contained straightjackets and ice packs for restraining agitated patients. One patient with remarkable dents in his frontal areas was known as the former medical doctor who was lobotomized by a patient who ripped off a piano leg in the day room and bludgeoned his skull. This former physician still helped staff physicians with medical exams. Neuroleptics had just come into use, and we were all awed at their serendipitous discovery and by the tremendous impact on symptoms of schizophrenia. On the other hand, we observed that this happening further medicalized the mental health field despite the so-called antipsychiatry movement (Ronald Laing, for example, spoke at the Lexington VA hospital).

At the VA I learned from other patients, also wanting to be honest with me and to help me to understand. One fellow who was in and out with acute psychotic breaks patiently explained to me that he could tell hallucinatory voices from others, but that they were so compelling that that discernment did not matter. That point turned out to be invaluable in working with many other patients. A tall, ramrod straight, chronic paranoid schizophrenic man explained to me as we walked across the grounds (he did not like to be looked at while we talked) that all that his doctors and I had learned about him was true, and that the medications did calm him, but that he would never basically change; whatever was wrong had been wrong since his teens and no insight made a difference. Patients and clients continue to teach me.

During my four-year traineeship with the VA, except for one woman who overlapped with me by six months, I was the only female trainee. There were no women psychologists or psychiatrists. Of course all the patients (military veterans) at that time were male. But I hardly noticed; it was never an issue. We trainees had wonderful camaraderie, and our supervisors provided excellent experiences and mentoring. It was at the VA hospital that I met William (Bill) Fischer; we married in my third year of graduate study. Bill had come to Lexington as a postdoctoral fellow to study with Dr. Erwin Straus, an accomplished phenomenologically oriented psychiatrist who had come to the United States to escape Nazi Germany. He was a colleague of numerous European existential and phenomenological psychiatrists, and wrote extensively on the human condition and on clinical matters. I sat in on some of the Straus seminars. Dr. and Mrs. Straus (a poet, violinist, and warm hostess) on several occasions invited Bill and me to their home for dinner parties, where a string quartet played and luminaries from the University and its Medical School engaged in animated discussion. The Straus home was filled with books and art (one wood carving dated to the fifteenth century) which a Gestapo officer patient of Dr. Straus's had shipped to him after arranging his and his wife's escape to the United States.

Back to my academic education: There were several instances of sexual ploys visited upon women students on the parts of a particular faculty member and of an eminent psychologist speaker. I believe that today such blatant use of power is much rarer. Likewise the following sort of incident: In one of my courses after a professor, standing with one foot on a chair, elbow resting on his knee, and gesturing broadly with the other hand, had gone on for about five minutes about how deficient we students were in clinical knowledge. I interrupted and asked him what he advised us to study. One hand became a fist, and with the other he pointed at me and angrily declared that, "I'll see to it that you never graduate!!" Although I was anxious for a while, I rightly assumed that he did not have that power. Later, when a senior faculty member asked me about other inappropriate conduct on this person's part, I confirmed what I knew directly and affirmed that I had heard the other accounts. The professor then asked me if I would be willing to describe all of this to the Department Chairman and allow my name to be used as a witness. I said yes. Then as an afterthought he mentioned that such action almost guaranteed that I would not graduate but that of course that probably did not matter to me since I was a woman and would not have a career anyway. I allowed my name to be used, but so far as I know neither the professor nor I experienced repercussions.

During my MA thesis defense, two faculty members grilled me on existentialism and its being "antithetical" to scientific psychology. I sidestepped most of these questions, saying that I couldn't imagine the relation to my research. I gradually realized that I was being associated with the VA philosophical group. Earlier, when I wrote a term paper for a personality theory course, the professor called me in to say that I had earned an "A" on the paper, but that he wanted to advise me that I should be more cautious, that bravery could get me in trouble. I was astounded; I had simply written a paper on the implications of some papers of James and Dewey for personality theory. From my perspective, I certainly had not challenged any positions. My dissertation defense taught me still more about vested interests in particular viewpoints. I had conducted a series of experiments that clearly showed that people perceive social meaning when making spatial judgments about silhouettes of humans (e.g., people facing each other are seen as being physically closer). A new faculty member whom I had not met was a perception expert and had been appointed to my defense committee. After the defense, I was kept waiting in a hallway for 40 minutes before being told that I had passed. Soon thereafter, my advisor, Al Lott, explained over manhattans with my friends and me in his home that the perception expert was adamant that I could not have obtained my claimed results without faking the data because they were contrary to all theories of perception! On the other hand, a year later, the *Journal of Personality and Social Psychology* accepted my dissertation-based manuscript for publication (Fischer, 1968). Moreover, the Editor, Wilbur McKeachie, helpfully typed on a manual typewriter (that's all there was then!) two-and-a-half single-spaced pages of notes and suggestions to me about how to convert my dissertation-speak writing into an article.

Academic Life: Joining a "Third Force" Department

In 1965 the Lexington VA sponsored a national symposium on "Phenomenology: Pure and Applied," instigated by Erwin Straus. Bill and I (married in 1964) were amazed when Amedeo (Andy) Giorgi, a psychologist from Duquesne University, told us during a coffee break that his Department was gathering faculty members interested in developing an existential/phenomenological approach as an alternative to the prevailing positivistic, behavioristic psychology. Father Adrian van Kaam, a Holy Ghost father (the order that founded Duquesne) had chaired the department and in 1966 published *Existential Foundations of Psychology*. The next year we moved to Pittsburgh, Bill as an Associate Professor at Duquesne. My internship was transferred to what was then the Leech Farm Road VA Neuropsychiatric Hospital. The next year I was invited to join the Duquesne faculty as an assistant professor. In my first year the Chair of the department was a woman, who left DU the next year, so I was again the only woman, although I didn't think much about that at the time. In my second year, our Chair arranged a leave for me the first semester, and Michael was born that October. The Chair approved a part-time appointment second semester, and for several years the Department agreed to teaching schedules that allowed Bill or me to be home with Michael. I planned to continue to teach at DU (and I did), but I found that some colleagues had assumed that I had taught that first year just to stay busy before starting a family. For example, crossing campus my first semester back, a colleague waved enthusiastically and asked what I was doing there. When I answered that I was teaching a class, he worriedly asked if the baby was all right. Later, Andy Giorgi (then Chair) told me that a Department representative to the College Graduate Council had casually reported to him that the Council Chair while guiding a discussion of applicants for graduate faculty status had held up my folder, mentioned my name, and laughingly put the unopened folder aside, saying, "Didn't she just have a baby? That's not the kind of productivity we're looking for." Andy instructed the representative to be sure my folder was opened next time. I was then approved, with the Chair's remark, "Well, she has indeed produced more than babies."

Actually, at the time I was unconcerned about credentials and promotion, instead blithely soaking up new learning. These were exciting years. I sat in on the graduate course in which Andy read draft chapters of his *Psychology as a Human Science*

(1970). Most of the faculty sat in on graduate courses on continental philosophy offered by the Philosophy Department. We brought in speakers of international acclaim such as David Bakan, Norman O. Brown, Victor Frankl, Paul Ricouer, and Jan van den Berg. We formed study groups to help each other read Heidegger, Husserl, and Merleau-Ponty.

Bill, well ahead of me in his study of phenomenology, explained a great deal to me in our home discussions. My current qualitative research on "being affected" and the ensuing "being emotional" (e.g., Fischer, 1996) owe much to Bill's early pursuits, including his book on theories of anxiety, as well as his own phenomenological research (W. F. Fischer, 1970). We sometimes hosted visiting professors from around the world for dinners in our home; the discussions were fantastic. In summers we sailed Chesapeake Bay. When Michael and I asked Bill what the fourth of a series of small boats should be named, he repeatedly replied, "Whatever." So Michael and I supplied the whimsical winner: "Whatever IV."

In the Department, we all had been impressed with psychology's advances in research method but felt strongly that psychology should develop additional methods suitable to humans' character as more than natural objects (see Fischer, 1977 – Chapter 5 in this volume). We all sacrificed financially to be at DU. For example, my starting full-time salary was $6,000, a reduction from my internship stipend. A classmate of mine was hired the same year at $500 more because, the Dean explained, he was a man and besides, I was married. One day, walking in Oakland near the University of Pittsburgh campus, I encountered a fellow I had known in Lexington. I congratulated him on his new position at Pitt, but I when told him where I was working, he earnestly replied, "Oh, I'm so sorry." This comment was occasioned not only by DU's being small and poorly funded, but also by the Psychology Department's growing reputation for being somewhat kooky (in the 1960s talking about qualitative research, basing our program on a philosophy that was unfamiliar to mainstream psychology, taking personal agency seriously, etc. was seen as unscientific).

By now, DU is well-funded, has a beautiful campus, and is ranked highly. Our clinical program is APA-approved, and we have an excellent reputation, even internationally. Indeed, our faculty and doctoral students are internationally diverse. Our program continues to pursue psychology as a human science, developing clinical and qualitative research methods that are grounded in hermeneutic philosophy. Our graduates are influential through their scholarship, social critiques, innovative community and professional service, and reputations for clinical soundness and caring.

My route to developing my approach to individualized/collaborative/therapeutic assessment was occasioned by both Bill's and my appointments at Duquesne and by a happenstance. No one else wanted to teach "testing," so the newest faculty member was stuck with that course. I was at first unexcited about the topic, but glad to be teaching graduate students. I soon found the course to be a wonderful opportunity to put human-science psychology into action. The bright students, who had come to Duquesne for its unique orientation, were open to my efforts, and I often learned from their creative ways of pursuing the assignments I devised. We found that developing the reflective/reflexive rigor required for understanding and for representing (re-presenting) qualitative research findings turned out to be ideal for learning to attend respectfully to assessment clients and to write truly individualized assessment reports.

It was from my notes for classes with these early students that I wrote my book, *Individualizing Psychological Assessment* (1985/1994).

Earlier, my late 1960s manuscripts had been tersely rejected by APA journals, with comments that I took as revealing that reviewers and editors had not read far enough to encounter excerpts of reports written so that clients could read them. I was told that my reports could injure patients who read about their pathology. I was also told that my writing was a danger to our profession in that if reports were written so that the public could understand them on its own, we would no longer be esteemed as experts. After the first acceptance of a journal submission about individualized assessment (Fischer, 1970 – Chapter 1 in this volume) by *APA's Journal of Counseling Psychology*, I cited that article in my later manuscripts, and found reviewers to be more open. Of course, I also wrote so that they could more readily grasp what these individualized assessments and reports were like. In 1978, Stan Brodsky and I published *Client Participation in Human Services: The Prometheus Principle*.

Under the initial leadership of Amedeo Giorgi, the Psychology Department developed an empirical phenomenological research method, which along with sociology's grounded theory method, was one of the first qualitative research methods practiced by North American psychologists. I decided to conduct a demonstration project on a matter of wide social concern, which resulted in half a dozen publications (see, e.g., "Empirical phenomenological analyses of being criminally victimized," Fischer & Wertz, 1979). A graduate student, Fred Wertz, and I had had no luck in acquiring participants through Pittsburgh and county police departments. So I donned a pale yellow suit with short skirt, wore heels, and wandered into my township's community building, where the Chief of Police agreed that he could be helpful. Carrying on. I have since edited a book on qualitative research (Fischer, 2006).

Along the way, Bill and I divorced; we remain close. Michael has continued to be a creative, discerning, reflective, compassionate, and philanthropic person of many interests. Self-taught in computer-programming, he formed his own consulting firm so that he can remain in his beloved NYC.

By the time I retired from Duquesne with Emeritus status, I had received the President's Awards for Excellence in Scholarship, and in Service, and was appointed the N. J. Dick Endowed Chair of Community Outreach for rendering academic material useful to the public nationally and locally. In regard to professional organizations, I have served as President of two APA divisions (Theoretical and Philosophical, and Humanistic), as President of the Pennsylvania Psychological Association and later as its Representative to APA's Council of Representatives. I felt honored to receive the Humanistic Division's Carl Rogers Award in 2005. I am most proud that in 2006, the Society for Personality presented me with its Bruno Klopfer Award for "unique and distinguished contributions to personality assessment." I doubt that my assessment work would have become particularly influential had it not been for opportunities to share with and learn from colleagues at SPA.

Society for Personality Assessment!

I had been a member of SPA since 1977, and a remote member of the Membership Committee. My organizational bases had been my state association and APA. Then at one of John Exner's Rorschach Workshops, at a break, I asked him and Irv

Weiner some questions. John was interested in the source of my inquiries, and after a while asked why I hadn't submitted a theoretical article to *Journal of Personality Assessment*. I replied that I didn't think that it published such work. Irv (then the Editor) indicated that the Journal received few such manuscripts. I submitted "Individualized Assessment and Phenomenological Psychology" (1979 – Chapter 7 in this volume), which was published as the lead article.

In about 1988, Ann O'Rourke, an industrial/organizational psychologist, invited me to present at what became my first SPA convention, on a panel entitled "The Sunny Side of the Street" – assessing for strengths and possibilities (at a time when presentations often focused on identification of pathology). A year or two later I was asked to participate in a panel on "Where are the Women in SPA?." At that time the only female Board member was Mary Cerney, In 1988, of the 40 persons on *JPA's* editorial board, only five were women. In my panel presentation, I answered the title's question in terms of (1) women students comprising at most one-fourth of doctoral programs, (2) women comprising an even smaller proportion of faculties (there had been one woman on the faculty at UK), and (3) women who did find faculty appointments often dropped out because of dislike for the aggressively competitive atmosphere – for grants, courses, co-authorship, promotion. Women found themselves opting for community service, raising their children, and clinical work. I pointed out that most SPA attendees had their expenses underwritten by their universities. Other psychologists had to pay their own ways, often (as now) at loss of private practice income or the family's bank account. At any rate, after my presentation (attended by about 35 members, but only one male), I was nominated to run for the Board, and I noted then that the Board continued to make significant, systematic efforts to involve women in SPA roles.

In 1993, Phil Erdberg sent me a preprint of a study demonstrating the usefulness of providing MMPI feedback (Finn & Tonsager, 1992). I was glad to see that such research was being published, but wasn't particularly excited about "feedback" (vs. collaborative discussion). But I dutifully dropped by the author's workshop room to meet and congratulate him. Steve Finn eagerly offered me a copy of his one-and-a-half-inch thick handout. That night, again dutifully, I flipped through the handout. As I later described in the Foreword to Steve's *In Our Clients' Shoes: Theory and Techniques of Therapeutic Assessment* (2007), I was still rereading in the wee hours of the morning, with eyes tearing. Steve had credited my work, and fully embodied its spirit in his moving examples. He also extended my work. We have learned from each other ever since. From that year on, we have set an evening for a dinner alone at SPA conferences, to catch up with each other's lives, and to share impressions of the status of collaborative/therapeutic assessment and of how we might serve its expansion. Along the way, Steve has formalized his Therapeutic Assessment approach, and has presented it hundreds of times across the US and in a dozen countries. Now, his colleagues from the Therapeutic Assessment Institute continue such presentations. Steve and I authored "Developing the life meaning of psychological test data?" (Fischer & Finn, 2008 – updated in 2014). At the 1999 meeting of the International Rorschach Society (now ISR), Steve organized a now regular panel presenting excerpts from collaborative/therapeutic Rorschachs. Early on, we discovered that Caroline Purves had been doing collaborative/interventional assessment with youngsters without naming her practices. Len Handler had taught from my textbook, and joined us in symposia where we shared developing concepts and practices. Of course by now many, many other colleagues are expanding

Collaborative/Therapeutic Assessment, culminating in recent years with the establishment of the Therapeutic Assessment Institute, which continues this work. SPA has established a C/TA interest group, and published a DVD on C/TA, with presentations by Steve Finn, Len Handler, and myself (see Fischer, 2009).

Now

In 2012 I retired (Emeritus) from the Psychology Department at Duquesne University, after 46 years of participating with faculty and graduate students in developing a viable human-science approach to psychology. I am fortunate to have been part of this meaningful undertaking, as well as to have found supportive and inspiring colleagues and dear friends within the Division of Humanistic Psychology and the Society for Personality Assessment.

I have joined friends in a nearby lively retirement community. I will continue part-time private practice and continue working on research and writing projects already underway – carrying on!

References

Finn, S. E. (2007) *In our clients' shoes: Theory and techniques of Therapeutic Assessment*. Mahwah, NJ: Lawrence Erlbaum. (Now available through Routledge.)

Finn, S. E., & Tonsager, S. E. (1992). The therapeutic effects of providing MMPI-2 test feedback to college students awaiting psychotherapy. *Psychological Assessment*, *4*, 278–287.

Finn, S. E., Fischer, C. T., & Handler, L. (Eds.) (2012). *Collaborative/Therapeutic Assessment: A casebook and guide*. New York: Wiley.

Fischer, C. T. (1968). Social schemas: Response sets or perceptual meanings? *Journal of Personality and Social Psychology*, *10*, 30–34.

Fischer, C. T. (1970). The testee as co-evaluator. *Journal of Counseling Psychology*, 17, 70–76. [Reprinted in (1971) A. Giorgi, W. F. Fischer, & R. Von Ecksartsberg (Eds.). *Duquesne studies in phenomenological psychology, (Vol. 1)* (pp. 385–394). Pittsburgh: Duquesne University Press.

Fischer, C. T. (1977). Historical relations of psychology as an object-science and subject-science: Toward psychology as a human-science. *Journal of the History of the Behavioral Sciences*, *13*, 369–378.

Fischer, C. T. (1985/1994). *Individualizing psychological assessment*. New York: Routledge.

Fischer, C. T. (1994). Rorschach scoring questions as access to dynamics. *Journal of Personality Assessment*, *62*, 515–525.

Fischer, C. T. (1996). A humanistic and human science approach to emotion. In C. Magai & S. H. McFadden (Eds.). *Handbook on emotion, adult development and aging* (pp. 67–82). Orlando: Academic Press.

Fischer, C. T. (1998). Phenomenological, existential, and humanistic foundations for psychology as a human science. In M. Hersen & A. Bellack (Series Eds.) & C. E. Walker (Vol. Ed.), *Comprehensive clinical psychology: Vol. 1: Foundations* (pp. 449–472). London: Elsevier.

Fischer, C. T. (2000). Collaborative, individualized assessment. *Journal of Personality Assessment*, *74*, 2–14.

Fischer, C. T. (2006). *Qualitative research methods for psychologists: Introduction through empirical studies*. San Diego: Academic Press.

Fischer, C.T. (2009). Individualized/collaborative psychological assessment; Excerpts illustrating collaborative discussion during assessment; Answers to some FAQs. *Pioneers of Collaborative/Therapeutic Assessment* [DVD disc 2]. Falls Church, VA: Society for Personality Assessment.

Fischer, C. T. & Brodsky, S. L. (Eds.). (1978). *Client participation in human services: The Prometheus principle*. New Brunswick, N. J.: Transaction.

Fischer, C. T. & Finn, S. E. (2008). Developing the life meaning of psychological test data: Collaborative and therapeutic approaches. In R. P. Archer & S. R. Smith (Eds.), *Personality Assessment* (pp. 379–404). New York: Routledge.

Fischer, C. T., & Finn, S. E. (2014). Developing the life meaning of psychological test data: Collaborative and therapeutic approaches. In Archer, R. P., & Smith. S. R. (Eds.), *Personality assessment, 2nd edition* (pp. 401–431). New York: Routledge.

Fischer, C. T. & Wertz, F. J. (1979). Empirical phenomenological analyses of being criminally victimized. In A. Giorgi, R. Knowles, & D. Smith (Eds.). *Duquesne studies in phenomenological psychology (Vol. 3)* (pp. 135–158). Pittsburgh: Duquesne University Press. Reprinted in Huberman, M.A. & Miles, M.B. (Eds.). (2002). *The qualitative researcher's companion*. Thousand Oaks, CA: Sage.

Fischer, W. F. (1970). *Theories of anxiety*. New York: Harper and Row.

Maslow, A. H. (1954). *Motivation and personality*. New York: Harper and Row.

van Kaam, A. (1966). *Existential foundations of psychology*. Garden City, NY: Doubleday.

PART I

THE DEVELOPMENT OF COLLABORATIVE/INDIVIDUALIZED ASSESSMENT

CHAPTER 1

THE TESTEE AS CO-EVALUATOR[1]

The basics of an existentially oriented view of man are proposed as the foundation for an alternative to the determinism and medical models of human functioning. This view is identified as implicitly underlying ethics codes, the movement toward greater client direction of clinical relationships, the social learning and reeducation conceptions, and the advocation of clinical work by nondoctoral persons. Recommendations arising from the existential position are made for psychological testing: coadvisement (client and tester discuss their perspectives on the testing situation), sharing impressions (about the client), writing everyday language, client's critique of the written evaluation, and client's designation of report receivers.

Criticism of the prevailing medical model of "mental illness" is articulate and widespread (e.g., Albee, 1968; Mariner, 1967; Szasz, 1960). However, the only thoroughgoing alternative seems to have been a general social learning model of the sort described by Bandura (Bandura, 1965; Bandura & Walters, 1963) or the behavior therapy learning model (cf. Eysenck, 1960). Where these have been posited as a framework for successful rehabilitation efforts in the field rather than in the laboratory, scrutiny reveals inadequate correspondence with rigorous learning theory (cf. Breger & McGaugh, 1965, 1966). The learning model, at least in its present form, which is rooted in animal research, has not been a convincing alternative. What is required is an explicit foundation for psychology as a uniquely human science. A systematic alternative to the medical model could then be developed from this foundation, to be followed by concrete recommendation for practice. In turn, the consequences of these practices would serve as criteria for research and subsequent validation, development, or refutation of the new model.

The present paper presents the rudiments of an existentially oriented view of man as the foundation for psychology as a human science. Concrete recommendations for psychodiagnostic psychology are then drawn. Most of these will be recognized as similar to ones now appearing in professional literature. However, there the justifications are given in terms of ethics, democracy, and the need to circumvent legislative regulation. The first two of these, at least, are not consonant with the prevailing emphasis on stimulus-response determinism and medical disease analogues. They are, however, singularly consonant with an existential perspective. Indeed, they reflect an implicit recognition of its validity. So also does the current reeducation analogue of psychological practice (Albee, 1968; Hobbs, 1964). Further, many individual clinicians actually work in greater accord with the existential view than with the theories to which they give lip service.

The existential perspective has implications for all the fields of psychology, and already has been actualized significantly in the area of psychotherapy and counseling, although often without systematic rationale. However, the recommendations proposed here are directed to psychological, especially psychodiagnostic, testing. The latter typifies use of determinism and medical assumptions. For example, the psychological tester usually has received a referral requesting a differential diagnosis, evaluation of a disorder's degree of severity, or a measurement of potential – in units of IQ, language skill, or whatever. The psychologist is as scientifically objective as is humanly possible as he examines the testee through complex, theoretically grounded, empirically validated instruments. He synthesizes the results in technical, professional idiom in a written report. This is sent to the referring psychiatrist, therapist, school official, or employment officer. The recipient may interpret the outcome to the testee. The report is filed permanently and marked "Confidential – Qualified Personnel Only." The above sequence usually flows undisrupted. But what of a testee who asks to read the report himself? Or who receives a verbal resumé, and insists that the psychologist is wrong? What of the person who requests that the report be available only to those whom he specifies, or that the report specifically be unavailable to, say, his child's teacher? What of the testee who refuses to pay for an evaluation he has not seen? All of these efforts are usually rebuffed by disclaiming psychology as either a business or as merely a personal service. Diagnostic psychology is instead said to be a science of the causes and signs of disordered behavior, humanely and judiciously practiced. Like medicine, its complex knowledge and skills simply must be trusted by the layman. The professional will tell him as much as he needs and is ready to know. The layman's responsibility is to try to accept and abide by professional judgment, although of course he may seek additional judgments.

Man as Co-constitutor of His Experience

The present paper posits that the above tradition is inadequate for man as more-than-body. Further, it holds that such practice impedes the client's positive growth. The basic assumption of an existential perspective is presented below as a constructive alternative, and as a source of concrete recommendations for testing practice.

Specifically, then, it is proposed here that (a) a person behaves in accordance with his own experience, that is, the meaning to him of his relationships with persons, objects, events. He is never a passive recipient in his relationships, but instead co-constitutes their meanings. That is, he can experience "things" only from his own perspectives. To put it another way, "things" cannot exist for a man outside of the way they are for him. His perspectives, of course, can and do change by narrowing or growing. It is also proposed that (b) a person can be capable of multiple perspectives, and that his openness to meanings is his uniquely human nature. To the extent that this relationship with the surrounding world is truncated, a person is less fully human. Relative fullness is psychological "health"; the various forms of constriction are "abnormality."

The general implications of the above position for psychological evaluation of a client is that to understand his past behavior, predict his future behavior, or identify feasible possibilities, the client's perspectives must be understood. They must be understood as closely as possible as *his* experience in *his* relationships. Preconceived constructs are inapplicable and irrelevant to the experiences in accordance with which he continues his living. Further, it is the client himself who is in the best position to confirm or clarify the evaluator's impressions.

There are also implications for an evaluation's effects on the client. If the evaluation is to facilitate positive change, the client must experience his limited possibilities for experience and behavior, as identified by the psychologist, as constrictions in *his* own way of living. And he must then experience any recommendations as desirable new variations of his own way of life, ones of which he feels at least minimally capable. Furthermore, if he is to grasp these suggested means of expanding his mode of life as feasible, he must experience them through positive relationships. The first of these should be his relationship with the evaluator, through which he can find himself as capable of further actualizing the perspectives which even now are broadening.

On the other hand, the psychological evaluation can have negative, narrowing effects. If the report is not directed to the client, but instead is received in various forms by, say, teachers, family, and administrators, then these persons may actively delimit his range of experience. For example, he may be classified as mentally retarded, and hence not be given a chance to attend regular schools and social functions, or to try to mow the lawn or play sandlot ball. As another example, the client might be classified as harboring unconscious hostility toward authority figures, and subsequently his complaints and critical observations would not be taken in their own right; he would not participate in authentic dialogue.

The client's relationships also can be limited indirectly through the ways in which the report receivers relate with him. He *is* his relationships with others. If he finds himself in these relationships as, for example, the inferior one, the crazy one, or the hostile one, then he is indeed at least partially these things. Further, these then become possible personal modes of relating with persons other than the report receivers.

The Testee as Co-evaluator

To the extent that the above view of man as co-constitutor of his experience is valid and is to be fruitful for clinical psychologists, a congruent, systematic revision of testing procedures must be attempted:

1. *Coadvisement.* If the client is to experience the testing situation as one through which he may come to expand his life then he must be actively involved to that end. On the one hand, the tester advises him of the referral's source and apparent reasons. In layman's language, he explains his role, the use of his tests, their merits and limitations, what sorts of information will go in the report, and finally, who might read the report. Subsequent agreement to be tested is an important affirmation of the mutuality of the testing endeavor. On the other hand, the tester asks the client to express his view of the purpose of testing and its possible outcomes. The significance of pursuant test responses is to be comprehended within this context. To repeat the key theme of this paper: The person behaves in accordance with his grasp of a situation; to understand that behavior the tester must be aware of that particular grasp. Also important, but difficult to ascertain directly, is the client's perception of the tester (cf. Leventhal, Gluck, Slepian, & Rosenblatt, 1962). Indeed, it has been established empirically that differences in such perceptions yield variations in performance (cf. Fiske, 1967; Sattler & Theye, 1967) – the client

responds not to objectively standardized materials and procedures, but through his co-constituted experience of them.

"The psychologist believes in the dignity and worth of the individual human being." It may be that the preamble to the American Psychological Association Code of Ethics (1963) expresses implicit recognition of the individual's co-constitution of his experience. Unless the validity of personally co-constituted experience is recognized, the person does not stand as an individual; his particular dignity and worth cannot be affirmed until he is understood from *his* perspectives. The same implicit recognition may be seen in Principles 7d and 8 of the Code: Testing proceeds

> ... *only after making certain that the responsible person is fully aware of the purposes of the interview, testing, or evaluation and of the ways in which the information may be used* [p. 57].
>
> *The psychologist informs his prospective client of the important aspects of the potential relationship that might affect the client's decision to enter the relationship* [p. 58].

These standards, too often ignored in practice, frequently are classified as "ethics," in a different realm from psychological theory. This nationally accepted code remains closer to universal experience – the original foundation of codes and theories alike – than do most of our overly reductive theories.

2. *Sharing impressions.* By the end of the testing session, the psychologist has begun to "make sense of" the client. But the latter behaves in accordance with what is real for him, and not with what the psychologist thinks is real for him; the tester must now dialogue rather than diagnose, in order to approximate the client's experience. This is not to say, however, that the person's experience is a reflected one, one of which he was or is conscious and able to articulate. Hence, the psychologist must ask himself such questions as, What sort of relationship must this person have with the kind of material on these Wechsler Adult Intelligence Scale subtests that these behaviors and levels of performance could emerge? Obviously, the narrower the psychologist's experiences and the more rigidly he adheres to them, the less competent he is to comprehend the other person's world.

A sample of the psychologist (P) and client (C) sharing impressions is given below:

P: Did you notice you didn't do as well on the arithmetic part and the part where you said numbers back to me? You know, on both those kinds of problems, you had to figure in your head. I wonder if you have trouble with those same things out in life, like on the job?

C: Well, yeah, that's right. But it doesn't matter about numbers – it's doing it in my head. I just always know that I can't get things to work out when I've got to keep numbers in my head, or like those block pictures.

P: I hadn't thought of that. I guess you did do better on the first half of the test where you were telling me answers about everyday things than you did on the last half where you had to quietly figure out the answers to abstract, new kinds of problems, and then tell me the answer.

C: Sure, I'm always at my best when I'm talking to people. It's like I know where I stand. Like in a business conference, I can talk up a really great idea, and everybody's impressed. But I'm sure not the guy to write it out by myself, or figure out a cost analysis. I just know I'm beat before I start – so I don't.

P: So when jobs call for you to work on your own you see that as equivalent to certain failure. Therefore, you never try to do them?

C: That's what I just said.

The psychologist would continue in a similar manner, bringing in observations from the other tests and techniques until mutual closure is reached. Presuming that by this time he has some familiarity with the client's life situation, he can now discuss possible new experiences through which the client might develop broader perspectives. For example, the above psychologist might offer, along with other suggestions, a programmed sequence of mathematics homework, beginning at a level where the client feels quite capable. In this way, he might gradually come to experience "loner," intellectual tasks in a light that permits positive challenge and confidence to emerge. Implied here is that insight is not necessarily requisite to broadening of perspectives; new experiences can be adequate.

At least one psychologist has published a test based in part on the above points. McMahon (1969) presents true-false "personality" items in couplet fashion, so that the person can qualify the significance of his response. Then, he and the counselor review the items together in a joint delineation of problems as the client sees them.

3. *Writing everyday language.* If the report receivers are to comprehend the client's world as he experiences it, then that is what the report should describe. Professional jargon reduces the client to predetermined categories, and despite their increasing popularization, they cannot encompass the person's experiences as his own. "Repressed hostility is displaced toward inanimate objects, and is released in impulsive outbursts" leaves the reader guessing as to the concrete referents of each term. He can do little more than guess at how such information could be helpful to the person; indeed, the implication of much such jargon is that only professional therapists are capable of "un-repressing" the patient. Nor are readers likely to know how to carry out esoteric recommendations such as "build self-esteem," or "provide releases for hostility." In addition, when jargon is employed, readers are uncertain of the grounds for, and validity of, the psychologist's conclusions and recommendations. If the report were written on a descriptive level, with clearly drawn inferences about the client's lived world, then the reader could judge its credibility for himself. Besides, he could better guess how to meet the tested person on his own ground, the most likely starting place for positive development.

Further, if report receivers are to relate to the person in a way conducive to further growth, it is best that they not have been presented a view of him as a passive object, a synapsing nervous system, a diseased organism, or a psychic hydraulic system. Similarly, it is critical that not only present deficiencies and difficulties be presented, but that the client's positive possibilities be specified.

Finally, if the psychologist writes in everyday, descriptive language, he is forced to examine his assumptions and decline the safety of established theoretical constructs. Fischer (1969) has discussed such an approach to clinical use of intelligence tests. Laing (1967; Laing & Esteron, 1964) and Lyons (1963) have written compelling commentaries on the arbitrary power of the professional, permitted by his status to veto the client's experience with his own criteria of what is real.

Nevertheless, there is a pragmatic need for acquaintance with personality theories. At present the psychologist must be able to communicate with fellow professionals who hear only the language of one orientation. Similarly, the psychologist must be aware of the loaded meaning of many terms in order to avoid miscommunication. In addition, knowledge of phenomena as identified by various systems alerts the psychologist to their existence even if he understands them differently. Finally, knowledge of theories allows dialogue with, and clarification and development of, his own approach.

4. *Client's critique of the written evaluation.* If the client is to experience himself as self-responsible, as capable of better fulfilling his human potential, he must do so not only prior to and during testing, but also following the psychologist's formal evaluation. He must read the report, dictate his addendum, clarification, or protest to be added to the report, and decide with which persons he is willing to share the written evaluation. This procedure also produces a beneficial side effect: Knowing that his client is going to read his report, the psychologist strives all the more to be true to him, to capture his world as well as words allow, and to avoid overstatements, unintended implications, and loose description.

The report receiver thus sees that the client has been regarded as a fellow being rather than an object of physicalistic measurement. He sees that psychological evaluation is an interpersonal encounter, a professional one to be sure, but unlike the physical sciences, undeniably interpersonal. He sees that the client's opinions are considered worth recording. Subsequently, the reader's relationship with the evaluated person will be one in which the latter's self-responsibility is respected. To the extent that this occurs, the client is – through this relationship – a responsible individual. To the extent that the report has conveyed the world as the client experiences it, the reader will know the ground where they can meet and then go forward.

The American Psychological Association's Ad Hoc Committee on Social Impact of Psychological Assessment has urged that more emphasis be given to research into methods and effects of communicating psychological evaluations (Berdie, 1965). The above procedure should be considered among such methods, and also should raise the issue of method's consistency with psychological theory, as well as with the goals of evaluation.

5. *Client's designation of report receivers.* Anastasi's (1968) third edition of her widely adopted psychological testing textbook advocates "informed consent" to be tested, but explicitly sees this as implying consent for release of information. In line with the above recommendations, the client should also be informed of the specific "information" to be released before he can make a decision as to whom he would trust with it. Brown (1961) makes similar suggestions for the case of the college student.

There may be specific persons to whom the client wishes the report to be sent immediately, and these he can name. Later, if other persons wish access to his records, they should be required to tell him personally of their concerns, and receive his permission, whether they be teachers, caseworkers, or whatever. Often as not, such direct discussion obviates need for referring to formal reports, and it certainly decreases the probability of reducing the person's behavior to theoretical constructs unrelated to the world he perceives and in which he lives.

Final Observations

In some cases, such as small children, prisoners, and acute psychotics, the above recommendations could not be carried out fully. Nevertheless, here too they should be actualized to the utter limits of practical circumstances. The focus should not be on (limited) insight and (suspended) rights, but on the necessity of the person's experiencing new relationships in order to expand his possibilities. Broad possibilities for relationships with himself, others, objects, and events is the psychologist's goal for his client – approximation of full humanity, given the confines of physiology, neurology, genetics, history, and present contingencies.

Objective test scores provide little information about the testee as an individual. They are, of course, useful for research, institutional decisions, and determination of relative standing along predetermined dimensions, but such data are of minimal aid in comprehending the world a person perceives and in accordance with which he behaves. Most projective techniques are similarly limited in that they are currently geared toward identifying equally predetermined traits, psychic processes, or diagnostic categories. Psychotherapists in particular often have despaired of using psychodiagnostic reports – they simply convey too little of the client's ongoing experience which the therapist seeks to share (cf. Breger, 1968). From the perspective of the present article, more pertinent testing techniques await, in large part, existential-phenomenological development of psychology as a science of man (cf. Fischer, 1970; Giorgi, 1970).

Finally, as mentioned, the explicit, foundational view of human nature presented here dissolves the apparent inconsistency between the preamble of the American Psychological Association Code of Ethics and psychology's status as a science. Besides serving as a basis for the recommended testing procedures, it also provides a rationale for the emerging social learning and reeducation efforts. Specifically, the "errors" of prediction in learning studies may be seen as failure to ascertain the meaning to the subject of the experimental variables. That is, the subject responds from his experience within the experimental situation, not to what the experimenter dictates as the "objective" nature of the presumed stimuli and reinforcers. Learning theorists, then, can both account for data better and reeducate clients more effectively by identifying the latter's co-constituted meanings.

The present perspective has supportive implications for the paramedical approach, for clinical work by persons with bachelor's and master's degrees, and for utilization of lay persons as therapists (Albee, 1968; Hobbs, 1964; Reiff & Riesmann, 1965). Specifically, those developments are consonant with the proposal that a primary qualification of competence in clinical work is ability to resonate to another's realm of experience, and to help him to broaden it through expanded relationships. Much of present training in esoteric, complex theoretical systems is irrelevant and obstructive to the extent that it cannot describe another's experiences as his, as the ones in accordance with which he behaves.

Note

1 The official citation that should be used in referencing this material is: Fischer, C. T. (1970). The testee as co-evaluator. *Journal of Counseling Psychology*, *17*(1), 70–76.

References

Albee, G. W. (1968). Models, myths, and manpower. *Mental Hygiene*, *52*, 168–180.

American Psychological Association. (1963). Ethical standards of psychologists. *American Psychologist*, *18*, 56–60.

Anastasi, A. (1968) *Psychological testing.* (3rd ed.) N. Y.: Macmillan.
Bandura, A. (1965). Behavioral modifications through modeling procedures. In L. Krasner & L. P. Ullmann (Eds.), *Research in behavioral modification* (pp. 310–340). N. Y.: Holt, Rinehart, & Winston.
Berdie, R. F. (1965). The Ad Hoc Committee on Social Impact of Psychological Assessment. *American Psychologist, 20,* 143–146.
Breger, L. (1968). Psychological testing: Treatment and research implications. *Journal of Consulting and Clinical Psychology, 32,* 176–181.
Breger, L., & McGaugh, J. L. (1965). Critique and reformulation of "learning theory" approaches to psychotherapy and neurosis. *Psychological Bulletin, 63,* 338–358.
Breger, L., & McGaugh, J. L. (1966). Learning theory and behavior therapy: A reply to Rachman and Eysenck. *Psychological Bulletin, 65,* 170–173.
Brown, D. W. (1961). Interpreting the college student to prospective employers, government agencies, and graduate schools. *Personnel and Guidance Journal, 39,* 576–582.
Eysenck, H. J. (Ed.) (1960). *Behavior therapy and the neuroses.* N. Y.: Pergamon.
Fischer, C. T. (1969). Intelligence defined as effectiveness of approaches. *Journal of Consulting and Clinical Psychology, 33,* 668–674.
Fischer, W. F. (1970). *Theories of anxiety.* N. Y.: Harper & Row.
Fiske, D. W. (1967). The subject reacts to tests. *American Psychologist, 22,* 287–296.
Giorgi, A. (1970). *Psychology as a human science.* N. Y.: Harper *&* Row.
Hobbs, N. (1964). Mental health's third revolution. *American Journal of Orthopsychiatry,* 34, 822–833.
Laing, R. D. (1967). *The politics of experience.* N. Y.: Pantheon Books.
Lang, R. D., & Esterson, A. (1964). Sanity, madness and the family. Vol. 1. *Families of schizophrenics.* N. Y.: Basic Books.
Leventhal, T., Gluck, M. B., Slepian, H. J., & Rosenblatt, B. P. (1962). The utilization of the psychologist-patient relationship in diagnostic testing. *Journal of Projective Techniques,* 26, 66–79.
Lyons, J. (1963). *Psychology and the measure of man.* London: Free Press of Glencoe.
Mariner, A. S. (1967). A critical look at professional education in the mental health field. *American Psychologist, 22,* 271–281.
McMahon, F. B. (1969). Psychological testing: A smoke-screen against logic. *Psychology Today, 2,* 54–59.
Reiff, R., & Riessman, F. (1965). The indigenous nonprofessional: A strategy of change in community action and community mental health programs. *Community Mental Health Journal,* No. 1.
Sattler, J. M., & Theye, F. (1967). Procedural, situational, and interpersonal variables in individual intelligence testing. *Psychological Bulletin, 68,* 347–361.
Szasz, T. S. (1960). The myth of mental illness. *American Psychologist, 15,* 113–118.
Walters, R. H. (1963). *Social learning and personality development.* N. Y.: Holt, Rinehart, & Winston.

CHAPTER 2

PARADIGM CHANGES WHICH ALLOW SHARING OF RESULTS[1]

Most of us feel uncomfortable when we keep information about a client secret from him. Yet professional standards have consistently upheld such secrecy. The present article addresses itself to this dilemma by illuminating the currently operative assumptions against an alternative paradigm. From there, concrete assessment practices that would allow impressions to be shared with the client are proposed.

Deleterious Effects of Secrecy

Imagine a client confronted with a mental health expert, one who presumably knows certain psychiatric facts about him, and who has probably recorded them in a file. Imagine further, that the client has no access to these facts for the purposes of questioning, correcting, or amending them, let alone for putting them to use himself. This person surely must experience himself as under scrutiny, as being evaluated by only vaguely known criteria. In this circumstance, he remains somewhat guarded in his relations with the professional; he is unable to flow with his own experience, to muse, or to explore its meaning openly (Fischer, 1971).

The effects of secrecy go even beyond the clinical relationship. The very fact that so many professionals regard their psychological findings as scientific data, as truths not requiring confirmation from the experiencing person, perpetuates general acceptance of a kind of causal determinism. That is, the existence of "factual" files supports a client's belief that his fate lies with his "traits" and his history, as well as in the hands of the expert. Such beliefs stultify development of personal responsibility, self-esteem, and purposeful effort.

Further, to the extent that additional professionals and informed Important Others react to the person in terms of these secret "truths," such beliefs become actualized. That is, we are our relationships, and at least in part we become others' conceptualizations of us, the dumb one, the crazy one, the guilty one.

Finally, secrecy from the client limits the professional's own growth. It perpetuates his belief in the validity of his privileged perspective. In the absence of the client's challenge to his technical formulations, he is less likely to question, and thus to alter, his interpretations or the operative paradigm.

Historical Reasons for Not Sharing

The practice of maintaining secrecy from the client seems to be grounded in the natural science foundations of the mental health professions. Psychiatry is rooted in medicine as well as in historically mechanistic psychoanalysis. Similarly, when psychology and sociology adopted the methods of classical physics, man and world were assumed to be independent substances each following the laws of physical nature. Insofar as man and world impinge upon and react to each other, these relations have been understood in cause-effect terms, thus constituting the content of scientific (i.e., scientific, physicalistic) explanation. The natural scientific method, of course, has been that of external, objective observation and measurement.

Despite numerous divergences from the above vision of naturalistic science, the prevailing attitude has been that it must be the trained outsider, rather than the experiencing person, who knows what is "really real." Although the client's experience or understandings are helpful in explaining his behavior, they are assumed by mainstream scientists to be only epiphenomena, shadows of natural science processes.

From this perspective (as well as from the history of medical practices), it follows logically that the professional, knowing more than the client, must assume major responsibility for him. While the client rarely is kept totally in the dark, the complete technical formulations are not shared with him, since he does not have the specialized training necessary to understand them. Also, since it has been thought that the client cannot alter the "traits" and "dynamics" which have been identified, it has seemed wiser not to risk frightening or discouraging him by the starkness of the "facts," "latent homosexual tendencies," for example. Besides, the layman does not understand such formulations in the ways that professionals do. In addition, of course, there are individual, personal reasons for not sharing professional opinions with the client: the effort and time required, possible loss of role status, risk of being proven wrong, the chance of a lawsuit.

This hesitancy to share with the client data about him has seemed reasonable within a natural (physicalistic) science paradigm. However, the appropriateness of a strict natural science approach to human phenomena is currently under question from many directions. The Rosenthal studies, theories of interpersonal relations, existential theories, the client-centered therapy movement, humanistic psychology, popular demand for relevance and results, and individual and civil rights movements, for example, all question this paradigm. Illustrative of today's contradictory mixture of both scientific and human science approaches is the American Psychological Association's (1970) policy statement on psychological assessment. In the spirit of most professional codes of ethics, this document humanistically affirms the individual's right to decide not to be tested; but it also states that he should be *informed* as to who will have access to any test data. Furthermore, "informed consent" to be tested has been taken as consent to the release of (secret) "results," which are assumed to be natural science facts (see Fischer, 1970a).

The following principles and practices are proposed in the interest of maintaining the rigor of science while still allowing for man's character as something more than an object of nature.

Principles

1. The suggested paradigm utilizes a *radical structural approach* to human phenomena. Specifically, explanation of behavior can be constituted by a description of its interrelated components. When all the components are present, the phenomenon exists; no one component is more basic or causal. For example, it might be said that a client is anxious when he is uncertain of his ability to do something that he feels he absolutely must do if he is to continue to be himself (W. F. Fischer, 1970). Within a structural approach, such constructs as "overweening superego," "inadequate defense mechanisms" are not needed.
2. This structural approach is radical in that it emphasizes a *relational unity between person and world*. Man behaves in accordance with the world as he experiences it; he cannot humanly respond to a world except as he coconstitutes it. In other words, it is inappropriate to assume an objective stimulus as a cause of impetus of behavior. The unit of study is man-in-his-world rather than man-affecting-world or world-affecting-man. Hence, a given behavior is better understood by addressing the person's experience, perspectives, and ways of moving through his world, in addition to outside observation.
3. *Truth, then, is perspectival.* That is, all understandings are coconstituted by man and events. Different views are available from varying stances, locations, perspectives. To explain a person's behavior, in other words, one must include descriptions of where he stands as well as what he sees. Further, the views of organized science, psychiatry, religion, society, and so on, are not necessarily more truthful, valid, or "really real" than those of the experiencing individual. In short, if the professional's files are to be faithful to the structure of a client's behavior, and thereby be of most use to the client and his helpers, they should not contain causal, jargony reductions. The *client* can be reached most readily through understandings of his own world, rather than through pre-existing theoretical formulations. There is, then, no need for secrecy from the client. Indeed, in some ways he is the best judge of the report's accuracy.
4. Finally, *well-being* ("mental health") can be conceived *as latitude*, a range of possibilities for the individual and society. In line with the notion of perspectivity, behaviors or experiences cannot be prejudged as pathological. The full context must be considered especially the person's world in relation to those of society. Thus, the question is not one of internal disruption, but rather of the various possibilities that are opened and precluded by particular ways of being in given contexts. From this perspective, clients and professionals are faced with individual responsibility for values and goals.

Practices and Effects[2]

The above principles suggest that mental health professionals do not have to follow natural science principles and methods, but can, instead, implement a human (structural) science which emphasizes the client's lived world and his ways of traveling in it. With this sort of data, secrecy from the client is bypassed; there are no purely external formulations from which he should be shielded. The following practices are among those which thus far have proven effective in implementing the human science principles. They have been used and developed by a wide range of professionals: psychiatric aides, classroom and special education teachers, clinical psychologists, psychiatric nurses, social workers, and community mental health workers.

1. *Common ground* is the optimal setting for exploring a client's lived world. Specifically, the client must be a coassessor helping himself and the professional to delineate his perspectives as well as to identify the circumstances in which he behaves in particular ways. Rather than dialoging interview or test responses with his already existing theoretical constructs, the professional attempts to comprehend the client in the latter's own context of everyday objects, people, and events. They stick with the person's own language, for example, "firm" rather than "resistive." "screwed up" rather than "neurotic," or "hibernating" as opposed to "withdrawing." Further, they try out in joint imagination various concrete recommendations until they arrive at ones that seem feasible to both of them. In this way, not only do the participants arrive at maximally useful, human science information, they also bypass any problems of invading privacy. That is, when they look together, from common ground, at the same phenomenon, they are in a relation of shared privacy. It is the difference between telling me that I am a hostile person, as opposed to acknowledging my being impatient and irritable when I perceive bureaucrats as unnecessarily impeding a good cause.

2. *Contextual methods*, then, are applied to "locating" specific experiences and behaviors ("experiaction," in von Eckartsberg's [1969] more precise term). There is no need for reductive or broad "personality pictures." The context of a behavior includes the person's (as well as outsiders') grasp of the situation and his available means of moving through it, in addition to the consequences of the behavior. The person's experience of a situation is, of course, influenced by physiological, neurological, physical, cultural and historical components which are also part of the context in that they too participate in the person's experience.

Assessment and therapeutic efforts must locate the *When-Not context* of a problematic behavior; this is the starting place for expansion to greater latitude. The When/When-Not contexts are the data of a structural approach to behavior. Happily, they do not confuse, mislead, fix or objectify the client who hears them. Indeed he has helped to formulate them with the professional. Even when the professional has come to tentative interpretations via theory, test data, case history, or other external sources, they are transformed into the client's lived life via discussion or observation with him or his Involved Others. For example, "You know, you've asked me for a lot of guidance about just how you're supposed to do these designs. Can you tell me about other times when you check things out carefully before you begin? – And about times that you don't, too?" In addition, contextual methods frequently involve observation, therapy, or education not in the professional's office, but in the client's own territories of work, play, and rest.

3. "Results," then, are recorded in their most usable form: *contextualized events* rather than pure abstractions and traits. That is, intervention must begin in the client's everyday life, and that is just the kind of information that is recorded where records are necessary. Since "results" are interpersonal, rather than "objective" impressions, the client may add disagreements or clarification to his records. Similarly the report should specify the context of the interpersonal relations through which the recorded understandings arose. Readers can then judge for themselves whether the client might come off differently with another person. They can also come to their own understanding of the client through the

contextual samples, which always speak beyond the formulation of which they were an intended example. In like manner, giving priority to the client's lived life over professional jargon renders the helping professions truly interdisciplinary. Finally, since the client is knowledgeable about the "results," he may specify which persons may have access to them. His consent may be truly "informed."

To Conclude

Human science data are already located in the client's everyday life data. They are *not* interpretations, constructions, or abstract explanations; they do not require processing before feedback can be given to the client. Contextualized lived relations and life events require no secrecy from the client, while at the same time they are the most efficacious starting place for expanding "experiaction." A human science paradigm provides concrete means of actually moving beyond the scientific and medical models, which we have presumably rejected, but to which we have clung for want of a viable alternative. It cannot be denied that this proposed human science requires systematic, empirical accumulation of structural/contextual patterns. It does not intend to remain completely naive in the face of each new client even while stressing the latter's particular embodiment of universal man/world relationships. It is also undeniable that less talkative clients require innovative methods of approximating their perspectives and experience.

In the meantime, the structural/contextual paradigm is consonant with many major developments related to a changing philosophy of science: interaction theory (Carson, 1969), situatedness of S-R patterns (Mischel, 1968), social learning and behavior modification (Ullman & Krasner, 1965; Lazarus, 1971), Bertalanffy's (1968) general systems theory, and Giorgi's (1970) phenomenological human science psychology. However, the proposed paradigm goes beyond all but the latter approach to include specifically man's experiential bond with his world. Hence, the human science approach is even more consonant with the recent influential views of social reality and psychopathology as coconstituted by man (Berger & Luchmann, 1966; Braginsky, Braginsky, & Ring, 1969; Laing, 1964, 1967; Szasz, 1970). Further, these evolutions in theory and practice are accompanied by societal movements such as the Federal Fair Credit Act, which assures citizen access to credit bureau files. Similarly, the U.S. Supreme Court *Gault* decision seems to give accused juveniles the right to their psychological evaluations. The Superior Court of Maine's *Bates* case decision apparently gives college applicants access to their letters of recommendation. A Russell Sage Foundation (1970) conference has recommended guidelines to assure students and parents a right to potentially detrimental material.

In summary, the proposed structural/contextual paradigm may offer a way of systematically and scientifically actualizing the emerging Zeitgeist of respecting perspectivity as well as expecting personal accountability, from citizen and professional.

Notes

1 Copyright 1972 by the American Psychological Association. Reproduced with permission. The official citation that should be used in referencing this material is: Fischer, C. T. (1972). Paradigm changes which allow sharing of results. *Professional Psychology*, 3(4), 364–369.

2 A more detailed account of contextual methods may be found in Fischer (1973). Also, Fischer (1970b) presents an account of how effective contextual assessment necessarily is attended by expansion of well-being. Contextual assessment is already "therapeutic."

References

American Psychological Association (1970). Psychological assessment and public policy. *American Psychologist, 25*, 264–266.

Berger, P. L., & Luchmann, T. (1966). *The social construction of reality*. N.Y.: Doubleday.

Bertalanffy, L. V. (1968). *General systems theory*. N.Y.: George Braziller.

Braginsky, B. M., Braginsky, D. D., & Ring, K. (1969). *Methods of madness: The mental hospital as last resort*. N.Y.: Holt, Rinehart & Winston.

Carson, R. C. (1969). *Interaction concepts of personality*. Chicago: Aldine.

Fischer, C. T. (1970a). Consent to release of what? *Professional Psychology, 1*, 424.

Fischer, C. T. (1970b). The testee as co-evaluator. *Journal of Counseling Psychology, 17*, 70–76.

Fischer, C. T. (1971) Toward the structure of privacy: Implications for psychological assessment. In A. Giorgi, W. F. Fischer, & R. von Eckartsberg (Eds.). *Duquesne studies in phenomenological psychology* (pp. 149–163). Pittsburgh: Duquesne University Press.

Fischer, C. T. (1973). Contextual approach to assessment. *Journal of Community Mental Health, 9*, 38–45.

Fischer, W. F. (1970). *Theories of anxiety*. N.Y.: Harper & Row.

Giorgi, A. (1970). *Psychology as a human science*. N.Y.: Harper & Row.

Laing, R. D. (1967). *The politics of experience*. N.Y.: Pantheon.

Laing, R. D., & Esteron, A. (1964). *Sanity, madness and the family: Families of schizophrenics*. N.Y.: Basic Books.

Lazarus, A. (1971). *Behavior therapy and beyond*. N.Y.: McGraw-Hill.

Mischel, W. (1968). *Personality and assessment*. N.Y.: Wiley.

Russell Sage Foundation (1970). *Guidelines for the collection, maintenance, and dissemination of pupil records*. Russell Sage Foundation, Hartford.

Szasz, T. S. (1970). *The manufacture of madness*. N.Y.: Harper & Row.

Ullmann, L. P., & Krasner, L. (1965). *Case studies in behavior modification*. N.Y.: Holt, Rinehart & Winston.

Von Eckartsberg, R. (1969). *On experiaction ecology*. Unpublished manuscript, Duquesne University.

CHAPTER 3

INTELLIGENCE CONTRA IQ

A Human Science Critique and Alternative to the Natural Science Approach to Man[1]

With the transformation of intelligence into IQ as a concrete reference point, this article indicates the general social impact of psychology practiced as a natural science. A metascience examination of the latter's approach to man reveals the interrelations of its assumptions, methods, and content, while thus suggesting the need for a specifically human science. This alternative's assumptions, methods, and content are specified as being rooted in a rigorous existential-phenomenological philosophy. The human science approach is proffered as one comprehensive enough to account for man's possibilities as well as his necessary restrictions. A human science understanding of intelligence is presented, along with remarks about its practical implementation.

This paper first briefly overviews the prevailing psychological paradigm, that of psychology conceived as a pre-Heisenberg natural science. Specifically, the interrelations of its assumptions, methods, and content are pointed out. Then some of its general negative social consequences are summarized, followed by specific mention of its consequences for conceptions of intelligence. The assumptions, methods, and content of a specifically human science paradigm are then presented. This section is followed by a human science discussion of the meaning of intelligence. The paper closes with a few remarks about implementation of a human science approach to intelligence.

Critique of the Natural Science Approach to Human Phenomena

Mid-nineteenth century found European intellectuals celebrating man's increasing participation in his own destiny. They were certain not only that the natural world was orderly, but that as partially an object of nature, man too was orderly. Above all, his relationship to nature could be discovered, comprehended, and utilized by man. In England, the Lockean tradition of philosophical empiricism nurtured efforts to discover the laws underlying phenomena as widespread as the influence of events on mental associations to genetic influence on ear shape. Efforts to evaluate the effectiveness of experimentation in agriculture yielded statistical procedures for all empirical fields. In France, Descartes' tradition of mind-body split and interaction, enhanced by the Lockean *tabula rasa* notions, supported efforts to liberate man by providing appropriate environments for the children of the Revolution, for Pinel's insane, Itard's feral child, and Binet's public school children. In Germany, these thrusts were located primarily in the work of such physicists and physiologists as Fechner and Helmholtz, who sought to apply existing methods of natural science to the presumed interactions between the mental and the physical. The ensuing psychophysical methods, which sought to discover universal laws, evolved into *the* method for psychology, determining its content in the process.

In retrospect, we now can see that the initial threefold interest in man as a participant in his destiny, as a seeker of greater freedom, and as a unique phenomenon traveling through nature, was subverted by the accompanying interest in the natural world. In effect, psychology became a natural science, and man became strictly an object of nature. Psychology assumed that its business was to uncover the universal laws operating out in nature, independent of man. Hence, it also assumed that its work was independent of values and of philosophy. Psychology's "philosophy of science" was automatically equated with nineteenth-century logical empiricism and positivism. Now, however, a broader philosophy of science, known through studies of metascience, is examining the assumptions underlying varying approaches to human phenomena – from the natural scientific to the social/humanistic (e.g., Radnitzky, 1970; Graumann, 1970). These and related analyses (Giorgi, 1970) demonstrate the interdependence of approach, method, and content.

The assumptions of the pre-Heisenberg natural science approach are that reality is separate from and independent of observation, and that man too is an object of nature. Reality is ordered in a mathematical, logical (Aristotelian) manner, amenable to classification. All events are explained ultimately in terms of physical causation – absolute determinism, although the (quantitative) characteristics of the (isolatable) variables do interact. These interactions are describable via mathematical equations. In short, the natural science approach to man is that of scientistism – the assumption that all science must be modeled after the pre-Heisenberg physical sciences. In addition to these standard, explicit assertions from the early field of natural science, there are two usually unacknowledged guiding interests or concerns (Habermas, 1966) – those of attaining certainty and of controlling or directing the process of nature.

The methods of natural science are, then, objective observation, quantitative measurement, analysis into parts and interactions, and controlled experimentation. The latter takes the form of establishing particular conditions and measuring the success of the experimental operations. The resulting data are presumed to represent absolutely determined reactions to identical repetitions of procedure. Further, these data are regarded not as constituted through a prior organization of our experience, in terms of instrumental action and function, but as "givens" – isolatable, immutable, unequivocal facts about an external reality. Through this paradigm experimentation necessarily hypostatizes its observations. Finally, in its search for certainty about universal order, natural scientific psychology transforms the person's individualness into a statistical location on a predetermined dimension. Thus, the content of the field of "individual differences" is in actuality tables of mass data indexed in terms of standard deviations, correlation coefficients, etc. They address neither the individual nor difference *per se*.

The general limitation of applying this natural science to man is that it fails to account for the scientist's co-constitution of his science. More specifically, scientistic psychology can study man only in the third person; it cannot address the (first person) experimenter himself. Put still differently, it cannot account for the possibility of the experimenter manipulating nature. Indeed, natural science can account only for the realm of the necessary. It has no way to approach the realm of the possible, let alone that interface between necessity and possibility, between man's subjectness and subjectedness, which is the subject matter of a human scientific psychology. These limitations bear heavy social consequences.

Social Consequences of Imposing Scientistic Order on Human Phenomena

In General

The view that scientists merely uncover unequivocal, immutable facts leaves its believers resigned to adapt to the laws of nature. This view minimizes efforts to alter existing situations. Thus, the scientistic approach to man tends to serve the *status quo*, as often as not thereby also perpetuating unwitting as well as motivated oppression. The obvious example here is the conclusion that blacks should be channeled into jobs requiring only rote memory skills since standardized tests have shown blacks to be inferior in abstract thinking.

The above example also illustrates another consequence of the scientistic approach: Its conclusions are assumed to be somehow purely scientific – untainted by moral, philosophical, political, economic, or other involvement or implication. Scientific findings have been beyond social reproach since facts in themselves are said to be value-free. Similarly, the manner and circumstances in which appearances are apprehended as facts go unquestioned; no effort is made to examine human participation in what it *takes* as "given."

In like manner, whatever is not amenable to the scientist's existing methods of measurement is regarded as not real. If it is not directly observable or quantifiable through its products, it isn't. Disputation is limited to existing scientistic variables. Where science has not "worked," the solution is sought in still more of the same sort of data. The natural science psychologist is locked into one system; other persons, views, and phenomena are locked out.

Since it is assumed that only science uncovers valid reality, scientists have become an elite group, with power over the destiny of those who march to different drums. Applications for government grants, manuscripts, doctoral examinations must all be presented in accordance with the scientistic paradigm. Further, this paradigm requires terminology so far removed from the everyday life from which it was derived, that only the elite can speak their technologized language. Hence, most "factual" research reports are mystifying to the public. Indeed, the subject of a psychological or educational evaluation frequently is not allowed access to his own records, on the grounds that he wouldn't understand them anyway. Besides, it is said, he might not be able to cope with the ultimate truth to which his life has been reduced. Thus, the person is doubly subjected to being treated as the product of forces and traits beyond his comprehension as well as to secrecy from him among the powerful elite. Initiative and self-responsibility thus are systematically undermined.

This undermining of initiative is also a consequence of the scientistic penchant for categorizing persons into presumably distinct classes, according to "given" traits. Here a dual assumption is operative: (a) A person either has or doesn't have the trait or "enough" of it; (b) "it" must be stimulated from outside to become operative, hence necessitating placement by quantity of "it" into various categories of environment. Further, not only does this categorizing thus fulfill its own prediction of level of achievement, it also fosters a divisive society. People frequently see themselves in terms of "us" and "them," groups with immutable, "given," differences. Change is seen in terms of reaction to force. The only conception of dialectics is of the antithetical sort; external categorization of "givens" does not lend itself to a sense of mutuality of person and world (or other person). Scientistic psychology thus impedes true community. We have no psychology of dialectical process, of growth through mutual evolution, of social possibility. We have instead a psychology of determinism and control, which in effect subverts hope, initiative, and dialogue.

In Regard to Intelligence

Psychology has no established literature on intelligence. That nineteenth-century laboratory interest in psychophysical relations evolved into an elaborate quantitative methodology that *produced* psychology's content. Scientistic psychology has failed to take human phenomena in their own right first, and then attempt to develop methods appropriate to them. Our current scientific literature, then, is about IQ, not intelligence. IQ is an artifact of the psychometric movement. It is also intimately related to Western public school criteria of educational success, which were explicitly built into the first intelligence test at the turn of the century by Binet. Specifically, IQ-test items are aimed at exposure to (a) predetermined and single perspective truth, (b) memorization of facts-as-facts, and (c) application of presented facts to logical problem-solving. In actuality, IQ-tests test for level of school achievement; but IQ is then regarded as what underlies that achievement. IQ is seen as the core of intelligent being, as necessary for, and determinative of, success. This circular reduction not only keeps the low scorer down, it is also oppressive to society in general. Specifically, it gives scientific recognition and approval to only one kind of intelligence: the one-truth/analytic perspective. Competence in other approaches equally necessary for the survival of high-quality society are not adequately recognized, rewarded, or promoted. Examples: respect for truth as perspectival, aesthetic comprehension, sense of community, capacity for awe, interpersonal sensitivity, initiative and self-responsibility, atunement to transition, joyful participation, etc. In short, the reduction of intelligence to IQ imposes limited and limiting values on all those who are subject to professional influence, whether as students, job applicants, or patients.

Even where controversies about intelligence arise, they have been argued primarily within the IQ paradigm. The *current* question of racial inferiority could be posed only within a system of hypostacized, isolated, measured, presumably interacting, traits. Only where man is wrenched apart into such quasi-natural forces (Habermas, 1966) could intelligence be said to consist of "80%" genetic factors. Similarly, questions of IQ constancy as well as of general versus specific factors of IQ could arise only where the research conditions are restrictively controlled, where items are preselected along a limited dimension, and where achievement is staticized. Efforts to correct the abuses of the psychometric tradition must aim at its foundations, not its content. For example, blacks will not improve their situation by continuing to demand black norms and testers for standardized IQ-tests. They are condemned to being judged as deficient as a group by virtue of being different, until efforts are made to study difference qualitatively.

Finally, the reduction of intelligence to IQ has discouraged efforts to attend to the individual person. The school child, for example, is programmed and evaluated primarily against an actuarial "average" person of his own age. The criterion of both academic potential and success is "how much," rather than "what/when/how." Further, the focus on "how much" limits attention to the past – as already given potential or as already scored achievement. The individual's active participation, his *moving toward* accomplishment, goes unattended. Likewise, except as objectified stimulus variables, the person's situation as he lives it is lost. Thus, we lose the opportunity to study the relations between person and surrounding institutions in specific, and in general the relation between necessity and possibility, between what must be accepted and what man can hope to alter.

Even such a cursory critique as the above can serve to liberate us from the automatic practice and consequences of applying natural science assumptions and methods to human phenomena. But critique is not adequate; an alternative approach must be attempted.

A Human Science Approach

In General

Giorgi (970) has introduced the title "psychology as a human science" to indicate an explicit alternative to the traditional practice of natural science psychology. This alternative approach attempts to accept man in his own right, as more than an object of nature, and *then* to develop research methods that are specifically appropriate to him. This human science approach is, then, an existential-phenomenological psychology. It is concerned with existential man – who behaves in accordance with his participative experience of situations. The unit of study is the relational unity of person and world, man-in-his-world, rather than man affecting world or world affecting man. When we look to our everyday lives, we find that man is always intentional – not just in the sense of being purposive, but also in Brentano's sense of always intending *something*, of always being in tune with a perceived world. While person and world are certainly distinguishable, in this sense they are not separable. Similarly, for man there can be no world except that as known by man; he co-constitutes his own observations. There are no facts except those apprehended by man in his own way. Natural science is a construction derived from this lived world. (See Sartre, 1956, 1963, as primary references to existential themes, or Strasser, 1963, as a secondary source.)

It is the method of psychology as a human science that is phenomenological. Here this term does not refer to introspectionism nor to mere acknowledgement of the importance of individual experience. The phenomenology referred to at present is in the philosophical tradition of Husserl, (1931) and Heidegger (1962); see Zaner (1970) or Gelven (1970) as secondary sources.

In the psychological endeavor, however, there is no attempt to attain a presuppositionless position nor to pursue Husserl's transcendental reduction. And while human science psychology is indebted to the ontological work of phenomenology, its own effort is directed toward describing universal structures of embodied existence. The works of Merleau-Ponty (e.g. 1963, 1968) have been seminal for this project.

More specifically, the human science method is directed toward apprehending phenomena *as they appear* prior to theoretical interpretation. The method, then, is a dialectical one – an effort to understand and to appreciate the already-there lived perceptions on the part of self and others, through dialogue between researcher and researched. In this dialogue there are mutual implications and influences between the method and its subject as well as within the dynamic past-present-future. The goal is to describe the phenomenon not with instrumental or other final precision, but so that it becomes transparent – recognizable through its varied manifestations in various contexts. Just such definition of the phenomenon should precede any of the more traditional research in which the phenomenon is regarded as a factor, or even as a variable. Research procedures include review of the literature, and reflection on one's own experiences, as well as on instances one encounters in everyday life. Then a more formal and easily sharable procedure can be the collection of recorded reports from research subjects. The common phenomenal characteristics can be drawn out and presented in an integrated form as the phenomenal structure – the phenomenon as immediately experienced. Upon further reflection, the fuller, fundamental structure can become apparent. The latter effort involves explicitation of the situational and existential preconditions of the phenomenal structure. Always, these descriptions try to be faithful to lived experience, and to avoid reductive interpretation.

An example of a phenomenological structural analysis (of the experience of anger): "Anger is the prereflective experience of being made unable by an other who prevents us, and it is the counteraction of this sense of inability by an affective transformation of the other and of the relationship with the other. The body is experienced as bursting forth, and expresses itself, publicly or privately as each person's prereflective restrictions allow, in expansive, explosive, nontypical behavior" [Stevick, 1971, p. 144; see analyses of anxiety, W. F. Fischer (1971); privacy, C. T. Fischer (1971); and learning, P. F. Colzizzi (1971) in the same volume.]

The above existential-phenomenological psychology *is* scientific. Specifically, its rigor consists in the insistence that its analyses account for every encountered instance of the phenomenon; there are no statistical probability levels. The effort toward transparency continues as further nuances or variations stand out. In addition, the transparency must be evident to all viewers addressing the lived world. It is rigorous also in that it attempts to specify its own assumptions and perspectives, including the active engagement of the researcher. Finally, this human psychology is scientific in that it accounts for phenomena in a sharable, demonstrable, repeatable manner. It does so not by reducing the phenomenon to a different order or by pointing to causes, but by describing *what* the phenomenon is, including the conditions necessary for its occurrence.

Physiological, neurological, etc., conditions are also part of the fuller structure, although so far most phenomenological studies have simply assumed them without investigating how their variations participate in varied phenomenal structures. The core *content* of human science, then, is structural analyses of phenomena as humanly experienced. These structures consist of the mutually implicatory dimensions and preconditions necessary and sufficient to the phenomenon. Similarly, human changes from one state to another are understood as restructurations, as dialectical transformations, rather than as linear reactions.

Note that this human science does not posit an absolute freedom. It simply acknowledges that the meanings of the situations in which man finds himself are co-constituted by him. He participates in the significance to him of restrictions to his forward movement, thus escaping complete determination. Study of this co-constitution and forward thrust, which are admittedly limited by their own structure and situatedness, encourages liberation of hope and action (the "possible") from those conditions which are only *man*ufactured necessity.

In Regard to Intelligence

Except for the scientized version, "intelligence" has referred to the variable ways a person is in effective touch with his world. Specifically, "intelligence" is akin to the layman's sense of "personality;" both terms point to a person's multiform styles and modes of openness through which he deals with typical, varied, and new phenomena. "Intelligence," however, points to these approaches more specifically in terms of their effectiveness. While one can make general statements about typical approaches and degrees of accomplishment, in actuality intelligent behavior always occurs in a concrete situation. The productive approach is always to something in particular and always within a specific context. Further, any judgment of effectiveness presupposes valued ends – effectiveness in accomplishing what, toward what further goal? Assumptions about man's nature are always implicit in these values. In short, intelligence is not *something* which one *has*, but is instead an interpersonal judgment about the power of the way one does something.

The above human science conception can serve to de-reify intelligence and to expand it beyond the one-truth/analytic value that is embodied in IQ tests. But as yet there are no phenomenological research analyses of various universal ways of moving effectively. To date, most empirical/reflective analyses have focused on states of being rather than on movement. Analyses of effective approaches, however, would certainly attempt to apprehend their structural unity. That is, they would try to describe their distinguishable dimensions without conceiving of them as separate categories.

For example, I refer to behavior, or experiaction (von Eckartsberg, 1971) as "moving." As a means of staying in touch with the latter's complex structure, we can acknowledge the simultaneity of both the "how" of one's moving, and the "territory" through which he moves. The "how" and the "territory" are, of course, mutually implicatory, as are their components. This "how" the moving occurs could be abstracted roughly as consisting of *bond* (e.g., openness, being at, guardedness; want, ought, must; can, uncertain, can't), *embodiment* (e.g., sweating, breathing easily) of *mode* (e.g., imagining, reflecting, willing, touching), and *style* (strategies, pathways, sequences). "Territory" consists of the lived places, objects, persons, and events that one moves through, toward, for whom, from about, and from the face of. Many further distinctions could be made, of course, such as territory as taken for granted, as goal, as obstacle, etc. This general conception is not intended as a grid to be imposed on behavior, but rather as a reminder that human being is not completely object-like. Human being also implies a relational unity with its world. Note, for example, that any given moment of moving could be mapped out in terms of how the person gets through what. However, even the described moving would be understood as being from the perspective of the engaged observer. This mapping describes what the behavior is. No further explanation would be called for. There would be no need to hypothesize affect and intellect as separate and interacting. And effective approaches would not be limited to a purely cognitive realm.

Even when phenomenological analyses of effective moving become available, however, evaluation of individual intelligence would have to be conducted individually. After all, it is the concrete form of the universal structure that must be described if the individual is to be understood and served in his own right. An excerpt from such an individual assessment:

> *When Irene is familiar with some of the features of a new task, she confidently settles on an overall plan which begins with the familiar points. Then she flits about within the plan, venturing into the new until it too is familiar. For example, when antiquing a desk, she boldly applied paint to some of the broad surfaces, then tentatively dabbed at a drawer knob, went back to complete the top surface, then experimented with the decorative front, and so on to completion. But when confronted with a less familiar task, Irene sits back somewhat apprehensively and awaits assistance, as when she was being taught to produce alpha waves. Or, when nevertheless sure of her ultimate success, she maps out a detailed sequence of steps and self-hints, as when she determinedly wrote out lengthy notes prior to embarking on her first overseas trip. Within all these variations, Irene ensures that details are completed in such a way that they serve the final product, whether it be an attractive desk, an alpha wave, or an efficient and enjoyable journey. It is when left in unfamiliar, uncertain territory, without supervision, that Irene is least effective.*

This partial excerpt can illustrate that all ways of moving get one somewhere, and that inquiry must be made about which further possibilities are both opened and closed by a particular approach. This is the point at which effectiveness is judged, and at which values must be questioned. Moreover, dealing with such concrete events, rather than with test scores, allows concomitant investigation of both inhibitory and facilitative aspects of the person's environment. In addition, intelligence is not wrested from comportment as though it were an independent, determinative, entity. As well as bypassing totalizations or reductions, description of actual behaviors also diminishes esoterica and professional elitism. For example, with this sort of data, there is no need for keeping evaluations secret from the assessee. Finally, description of "moving" is a reminder that any situation includes both given contingencies and the person's own relation to them. The latter can be a passageway to at least some change, initiated either by self or by other.

Implementation of a Human Science Approach to Intelligence

The practice of psychology as a human science has been proposed here as a corrective to the negative consequences of the natural science approach to man. No doubt, this human science shall prove to have its own limitations; but at least these should occur within a system that recognizes greater potential in man than has natural science psychology. In the meantime, the age of technology and mass media has awakened the populace's sense of multiperspectives, relativity, and of dimensions versus dichotomies, while at the same time exposing the subjective, perspectival, and altogether fallible character of modern expertise and professionalism. We are ready for a science that can take into account man's more-than-object nature.

However, crisis and readiness are not enough. Nor does the availability of an alternative theory and research methodology provide an adequate addition.

Consonant language and practices for use in daily life must be provided. And while the theory may be as complex and as guiding as that of established psychology, if it is to be a proper corrective its referents and validity criteria always must be life events as they appear in everyday existence. In addition, bridges must be built between the practices and data of the earlier approach and those of the newer one. For example, I have published a definition of IQ-intelligence with which theorists of varying persuasions can agree (Fischer, 1969). It offers clarification of many standard IQ controversies, in addition to opening the way to the sort of conception of intelligence suggested here. Then, in other sources [e.g., 1973] I have presented concrete procedures for clinical and educational assessment, accompanied by actual examples. It is through the work of practitioners that theories have their effects; it will be the introduction of such human science practices that shall occasion dialectical change for both forms of science.

Note

1 Reprinted with permission from Karger Publishers, Basel, Switzerland. The official citation that should be used in referencing this material is: Fischer, C. T. (1973). Intelligence contra IQ: A human-science critique and alternative to the natural science approach to man. *Human Development*, *16*, 8–20.

References

Fischer, C. T. (1969). Intelligence defined as effectiveness of approaches. *Journal of Consulting and Clinical Psychology*, *33*, 668–674.

Fischer, C. T. (1974). Exit IQ: Enter the child. In G. Williams & S. Gordon (Eds.), *Clinical child psychology: Current practices and future perspectives* (pp. 333–350). N.Y.: Behavioral Publications.

Gelven, M. (1970). *A commentary on Heidegger's "Being and time."* N.Y.: Harper & Row.

Giorgi, A. (1970). *Psychology as a human science: A phenomenologically based approach.* N.Y.: Harper & Row.

Graumann, C. F. (1970). Conflicting and convergent trends in psychological theory. *Journal of Phenomenological Psychology*, *1*, 51–61.

Habermas, J. (1966). Knowledge and interest. *Inquiry: An Interdisciplinary Journal of Philosophy*, *9*, 285–300.

Heidegger, M. (1962). *Being and time*. N.Y.: Harper & Row.

Husserl, E. (1931). *Ideas: General introduction to pure phenomenology*. N.Y: Macmillan.

Husserl, E. (1970). *The crisis of European sciences and transcendental philosophy.* Evanston: Northwestern University Press.

Merlau-Ponty, M. (1963). *The structure of behavior*. Boston: Beacon Press.

Merlau-Ponty, M. (1968). *The visible and the invisible*. Evanston: Northwestern University Press.

Radnitzky, G. (1970). *Contemporary schools of metascience*. Stockholm: Scandinavian University Books.

Sartre, J. P. (1956). *Being and nothingness*. N.Y.: Philosophical Library.

Sartre, J. P. (1963). *Search for a method*. N.Y.: Knopf.

Stevick, E. L. (1971). An empirical investigation of the experience of anger. In A. Giorgi, W.F. Fischer, & R. von Eckartsberg (Eds.), *Duquesne studies in phenomenological psychology* (pp. 132–148). Pittsburgh: Duquesne University Press.

Strasser, S. (1963). *Phenomenology and the human sciences*. Pittsburgh: Duquesne University Press.

CHAPTER 4

UNDERCUTTING THE SCIENTIST-PROFESSIONAL DICHOTOMY

The Reflective Psychologist[1]

The Predicament: Residual Technocracy

Since the 1949 Boulder Conference on Training in Clinical Psychology, the prevailing assumption has been that the clinician should be trained as a scientist-professional. That is, the would-be clinician first is schooled by the University in scientific principles, standards, and research procedures. This schooling is his or her primary foundation for additional University clinical courses and for field training in professional service. However, from the beginning this training model has been accompanied by antagonism between academicians and practitioners. Professors have decried clinicians' straying form scientific rigor, both in use of subjective procedures and in their refusal to act in accordance with the statistically demonstrated superiority of computer-type prediction over the individual clinician's own judgment. Likewise behavior modification over psychotherapy. In turn applied psychologists have protested the sterility and nonadaptability of laboratory techniques for clinical work, including evaluation of its effectiveness. The relationship between scientist and professional more often than not has been dichotomous rather than cohesive.

More recent forms of the split between the science and the clinical practice of psychology include the establishment of professional schools of psychology, the community mental health movement's employment of AAs, BAs, MEds, etc., to do what in the past only PhDs did, and the 1973 Vail Conference's advocacy of a professional-professional model of training. Such developments arise from dissatisfaction with *both* interest groups: University training in science clearly has been inadequate in teaching psychologists how to function clinically; and clinicians' own efforts to utilize tests and trait theory as well as the psychodynamic literature are under popular in addition to in-house attack for being too pat, fixed, mechanistic, reductive, and thereby restrictive.

Along with the community mental health movement's growth, dissatisfaction with the slowness and inefficiency of old methods also has grown and contributed to the newest form of the scientist-professional antinomy. On one hand, instant group therapies and self-help workshops flourish and promise grand scale results with less expensive staff. On the other hand, science would seem to have found its way into the applied clinical realm via behavior modification practices, which promise efficient results in schools, mental hospitals, prisons, clinics, and privated offices. The dangers of both sets of effort have been clearly delineated as each "hand" points accusingly at the other. Specifically, instant therapies all too often are applied indiscriminately to all populations by undertrained persons, without adequate concern for external contingencies or long-range consequences. And behavior modification too often is applied as social control, failing to acknowledge the complexity and personhood of its subjects.

From my perspective, in all these developments the implicit obstacle to an integrative, smoothly functioning scientist-professional model is that of *residual technocracy.* Its background is this: in the founding years, modeling our field after the (nineteenth century) physical sciences did allow us to establish psychology as an empirical discipline. That tradition does continue to serve as a guard against unsystematic observation and loose conclusions. However, as our discipline has matured, and we have grown in sophistication, we rightfully have come to refer derisively to a strictly physicalistic orientation as being "scientistic." Science, physical and social, in its larger sense now acknowledges the constitutive role of the observer in the formation of data, the empty or misleading clarity of mathematical precision in regard to human processes, and the more than passive or reactive character of human activity (e.g., Bakan, Giorgi, Habermas, Heisenberg, Oppenheimer, Polanyi, Popper, Radnitzky, Toulmin).

Our predicament is that while we have rejected scientism, we have not yet formulated an adequate science of humans with which to comprehensively revise it. In the meantime, faced with nonstop challenges, we fall back on our Western *objectifying* attitude of problem-solving – an attitude that had underlay and now survives scientism. Through it, psychologists focus on method or technique, letting the resultant data bear the responsibility for evaluating truth and for making decisions. In other words, despite sophisticated theoretical disclaimers, in practice our (derived) data frequently are regarded as more real than the original behavior that occurred in everyday life. No wonder the psychologist as scientist has so often been irrelevant to clinical practice. But the clinicians have fared no better by trying to tack-on humaneness or experiential variables to their own fundamentally objectifying paradigms. More radical clinical reactions against technocracy, such as reliance on personal intuition or humanistic tenets alone, have presented their own polar dangers.

The Reflective Psychologist

What seems to be needed by scientist and clinician alike is a conception of psychology that recognizes the inevitability of technocracy but places it in the service of working with life events in their own right, all the while acknowledging the psychologist's conceptual and personal involvement. Whether researcher, theoretician, consultant, or clinician, the ideal practitioner of this psychology could be called the "reflective psychologist." The basic sense of "reflective" that runs through this presentation is that of the Latin, *reflectere*, meaning to bend back toward the point of departure. The following three-fold approach of the reflective psychologist is applicable to both researching the individual client and cross-individual phenomena.

More specifically, (1) the reflective psychologist acknowledges that his/her *point of departure* into measurement, professional literature, deduction, classification, or whatever, was or ought to have been *publicly observable events.* (And by "public,"

I mean the common notion of the public at large, not the specialized sense of consensus via replicable measurement.) For example, the reflective psychologist will ascertain the behavioral and situational referents of "hostility" and regard these rather than the construct as the referral focus.

(2) The reflective psychologist's *point of departure is also his/her point of return* – the ultimate destination served by theory, experimentation, classification, rumination, and other intermediary activity. Scores, recordings, abstract laws, reductions, categories, formulae, and other such aids to comprehension are not primary data but rather are derived conceptions, tools, whose business is unfinished until the psychologist can, in part through them, redescribe the original event more articulately than before but still in terms of publicly observable events. Nevertheless, even though the reflective psychologist returns from the realm of *derived conceptions and data*, what he offers is necessarily a *conceptually informed description of those publicly observable events*. An example: Timothy's throwing sand at other children, smearing feces on the slide, stealing candy, and urinating on the toilet lid may be explored fruitfully through such diverse notions as anal aggressive fixation, socialization quotient, an existential a priori of power, and/or of reinforcement history. But the point of return would be a situated understanding such as: "From the perspective of formal observers, Timothy *can* be viewed as striking out physically against what *may* seem to him like unjust obstacles or determinedly uncaring presences. But to those caught up with Timothy, his actions seem unprovoked and malicious. Such persons often respond punitively, only to find themselves singled out for later attacks from Timothy." (Such description should be accompanied by concrete, situated examples.) This return from derived conceptions and data to the realm of daily life facilitates individualized direct intervention while concomitantly encouraging the psychologist to specify the pertinent social perspectives and values. But it also sustains psychology's empirical orientation, minimizing the sort of slippage in which our conceptual devices take on greater reality and explanatory status than the structure of the visible events.

(3) Finally, as already suggested in the above example, our psychologist is reflective in circumspectly acknowledging the participation of the observer's and the subject's *biographical presences* to whatever is publicly visible. Each perceiver views through a moment in history and culture, through a particular conceptual and methodological access, and through personal history, values, interests, and goals. The reflective psychologist tries to take his/her own and others' biographical presences into account, even though reconciled to the impossibility of doing so completely, precisely, or conclusively. Objectivity for the reflective psychologist does not lie in the exclusion of personal perspective, but in taking it into account as systematically as possible.

Some disclaimers: In proferring the "reflective psychologist" as an approach to undergird our training model, I am *not* accusing psychologists of having been unthinking. I am instead trying to strengthen a particular way of thinking: the "bending back" that is inherent in an awareness of our inevitable participation in what we perceive, and in respect for the daily event as primary data. Nor do I wish the term "reflective" to imply a turning and staying inward; the reflective psychologist "bends back" only to re-address the public world. Nor do I believe that these ideas are new. Theoreticians and experienced clinicians frequently have reminded us of the dangers of being procedure and test-oriented, of the covering function of statistics, and of being forgetful of psychology's history as well as of our underlying assumptions. Likewise, the earlier-mentioned philosophers of science repeatedly have urged us to remember that there is no knowable reality independent of our "biographical presences." Finally, I do not regard the reflective psychologist as distinct from the scientist-professional. Rather, the former is a name for an attitude that could truly unite researchers, theoreticians, consultants, and clinicians as each shares the common point of departure and return – the everyday-life event. Divisiveness could be attenuated further if practitioners in each area of emphasis acknowledged the specific perspectivity and relativity of their efforts.

In short, the notion of the reflective psychologist is intended as a unifying reminder that publicly observable events should be the scientist's and professional's point of return as well as of departure no matter what the particular realm of intermediate expertise, and that both initial and refined understandings of events are always constituted in part by historical, cultural, methodological, and personal perspectives. In these ways, the work of the scientist grows in clinical applicability while the practicing clinician's work becomes more rigorous through his/her specification of personal and conceptual involvement. The "reflective psychologist" approach is a guiding principle toward responsible science/service and way from residual technocracy.

Implications for Clinical Child Psychology

This guiding principle affords a unifying touchpoint for the following representative thrusts already underway in clinical psychology in general and in clinical child psychology in particular.

Reliance on life events as primary data immediately facilitates implementation of the recommendations of the Hobbs (1973) report (of the Project on Classification of Exceptional Children; italics indicate a Hobbs' theme). *Assessment necessarily is individualized* to a greater extent when the child's actual actions are addressed rather than his/her location on Gaussian distributions. Similarly, *jargon and labeling are minimized as* they remain in their place as intermediate data subordinate to initial observations and to *intervention-oriented* refined understandings of life events. *Files can then be opened to* children and parents. Psychological *testing is restricted* to efforts to observe a particular child's areas and means of accomplishment; concerns with test-identified *deficits are de-emphasized* in the interest of *extending actual achievement.* The reflective psychologist's recognition of the importance of each person's access ("biographical presence") to publicly observable events supports an *ecological approach*, a mindfulness of the participation of family, school, community, society. This recognition likewise aids in finding ways to *help the child to help him/herself*, and to *include the child's involved others directly in educational/therapeutic efforts.* Moreover, such efforts now would be more likely to occur *within the child's own setting.*

As suggested above, the reflective psychologist approach also is relevant to psychology's worries about how to cope with the Buckley Amendment's opening of public school files to parents. Rather than continuing the search for ways to subvert the law (such as establishing double files or curtailing assessment), reflective psychologists already prefer to record primary data – life events, with which the parents probably are familiar or which at least they can understand without translation. But contrary to early implementation policies of some school districts, which sanction recording only of events without comment, the reflective psychologist advocates that the publicly observable events be accompanied by the name of the observer and a description of the events' context and significance from his/her perspective. Assorted test scores are noted only as additional samples of achievement, ones with broader bases of comparison but of no greater validity than classroom accomplishment. Personality indices have no place in the records unless explicitly presented as aids to the professional's exploration of specified incidents. "Reflective" records are individualized, usable, nonobjectifying, accountable documents of professional effort and of student growth; there is no need for secrecy.

Reflective psychology's dual emphasis on life events, as publicly observable data that can be known only from personal perspectives, also affords partial guidance through clinical child psychology's training dilemmas:

1. Perhaps the student in a reflective psychology program would find a lessening of the gap between developmental psychology's research tradition and the service orientation of clinical child psychology. On the broader scene, perhaps such students later could develop a resolution to the "Statistical versus clinical prediction" controversy. The common dimension here is that even in research the subject as individual, with his/her qualitative differences, would not be lost sight of.
2. At any rate, it would seem that University training should include greater and systematic exposure to actual children of varying ages and in diverse settings. These are the focal data base, the touchpoints for reflection through theory and research. If this shift were to come to pass, graduates would be less likely to defensively regard any particular theory as "the" truth. And they would be more likely to explore the ever-expanding variety of techniques that evolve after their University training; but they would do so reflectively, not looking for "the" way.
3. If basic training were to center on situated life events, rather than leaping first into theory and methods, the recently proposed lattice system of horizontal as well as vertical movement of human services professionals might be more feasible. Certainly cross-disciplinary communication among child-workers would be facilitated by shared behavioral/situational referents and by freedom from jargon.
4. The reflective psychologist model supports job-description in terms of demonstrated effectiveness in bringing about particular kinds of change rather than in terms of technical knowledge, academic degree, or time-in-grade. This eventuality, however, would provide an even stronger case for the doctorate to reflect an integrative familiarly with diverse "kinds of change," as well as thorough training in avoidance of technocratic practices, or, put more positively, in assisting the various child-workers to reflect into the ongoing developments of theory and research.
5. The reflective psychologist as behavior modifier would continue to contribute his/her insistence on empirical rigor, detailed observation, and close ties with research studies. But he/she also would try to individualize a child's program in terms of that child's sense of things. Likewise in terms of the child's involved others. Moreover, some management practices are more consistent with the theoretical stance of the reflective behavior modifier than with the older, strict behaviorism. Note also that his contemporary behavior modifier can openly reflect into psychodynamic or other personality literature in order to individualize his/her modification efforts to a particular client.

6. Re-instatement of coursework in individual assessment is called for by the reflective psychologist model. But the emphasis now would be on the child, that child's situation, and on identifying avenues for growth and enrichment. Scores and the like would be used as secondary data. This assessment would not fall into the old pathology orientation, but it would be prepared to reflect into our knowledge of such patterns rather than ignoring them as has been the recent trend. Assessment would not be as distinct from therapeutic endeavors as it has been; reflective assessment returns to life events with practical, concrete, individual suggestions for change. Moreover, the assessment process itself is acknowledged as being interventional, by virtue of the child's "biographical presence" to the professional's activities as well as by the latter's intention to invite the child's active involvement in influencing his/her own life. In this sense, it seems that the question of whether the clinical child psychologist necessarily is a child-advocate would be answered in the affirmative.
7. Both assessment and research training could open the way to development of qualitative methods. This training would emphasize disciplined respect for perspectivity, situatedness, complexity, and ambiguity. It might make attempts to describe behavior not only as a completed act but in terms of the actor's ways of experiactionally moving through his/her milieu, shaping and being shaped by it.
8. Finally, all of the above developments just might help to regain funding for clinical child psychology programs and internships. At least we could do a more convincing job of showing legislators that our work, while sophisticated in theory and research, is *not* self-serving (elitist, technique-oriented, separatist in regard to other child disciplines), and *is* directly useful to children and their involved others.

In conclusion, it seems to me that whatever our eventual differential definition of clinical child psychology, it would benefit us to frame it within the general guidelines of the reflective psychologist model. My intention has been for the above sample to evoke others' related versions of what I hope is not seen as particularly new or controversial but as a come-of-age rallying point for guiding our speciality past technocracy and toward responsible, integrated, science and service.

Note

1 Copyright 1976 by the American Psychological Association Division 12. Reproduced with permission. The official citation that should be used in referencing this material is: Fischer, C. T., (1976). Undercutting the scientist-professional dichotomy: The reflective psychologist. *The Clinical Psychologist*, *29*, 5–7.

Reference

Hobbs, N. (1973). The project on classification of exceptional children. *Journal of Abnormal Child Psychology*, *1*(1), 121–124.

CHAPTER 5

HISTORICAL RELATIONS OF PSYCHOLOGY AS AN OBJECT-SCIENCE AND A SUBJECT-SCIENCE

Toward Psychology as a Human-science[1]

Textbooks and other teaching of psychology's history oversimplify to the point of presenting it as the evolution of an exclusively object-science – despite general familiarity with integral extrascientistic practices and assumptions. Representative examples are presented, along with an overview of object-psychology's cultural/practical routes to dominance. The purpose of highlighting these facets of psychology's development is to call for psychology to take explicit account of humans' subjecthood as well as objectness, on the way rereading our history toward an integrated science.

It is in terms of the currently prevailing paradigm that textbooks typically define not only their subject matter but its historical evolution. As Kuhn (1962) has illustrated for the case of science in general, so the history of psychology has been presented predominantly as a linear development – a systematic, univocal uncovering of nature-as-truth. Although more psychologists now acknowledge the human, political, social character of science [e.g., Giorgi (1970), Habermas (1971), Mitroff (1974), Riegel (1975)], pursuits of human phenomena as uniquely human generally have been omitted from mainstream textbooks. Where they have been reported, it usually has been as extraneous ventures or as missteps that have since been, or are in the process of being, corrected. Similarly, despite varied explicit disclaimers by leading scientific philosophers and theorists, such as Heisenberg (1966), Polanyi (1964), Popper (1957), and Toulmin (1960), our mainstream psychology textbooks continue to imply that the goals and criteria of our science are clearly noncontroversial, that there is only one general way of being scientific – that of the natural sciences.

The present paper is written from an alternative perspective, one that not only takes into account man's object character but also explicitly addresses his subjecthood. Here, acknowledgment of subjecthood is for the purpose of accurate science rather than for any later humane or humanistic application. Such an approach conceives of psychology as a human-science. This is not an opposite of object-science, but rather a more comprehensive and adequate science of humans. This contemporary psychology as a human-science has developed strong philosophical underpinnings as well as impressive individual reflections, but admittedly has only begun to produce systematic empirical content [e.g., Giorgi, Fischer, & von Eckartsberg (1971), Giorgi, Fischer, & Murray (1975)].

Standing within this approach, one can look back through psychology's evolution to find that the contemporary undercurrent interest in comprehending man's subject character has flowed all through psychology's history. Moreover, that undercurrent has been present within the written works of proclaimed natural scientists and it has flowed in operative form through ostensibly natural scientific practices. In point of fact, it is not the case that the long dominant object-psychology is only now giving rise to a counter-movement, nor is it so much the other case [suggested by recent authors such as Miller & Buckhout (1973)] that psychology is still preparadigmatic. Rather, "third force" psychology, notwithstanding its relatively recent naming by Maslow (1966), has been present throughout psychology's formal (and presumably natural scientific) existence. In this sense we have been sustaining a mixed if not muddled paradigm.

I will identify four forms of the historical coexistence of object- and subject-psychologies in the next section of this paper. Then I will sketch the extrascientific character of psychology's evolution, followed by an outline of some of the historical routes taken by object-psychology to its position of dominance. Finally, I will scan the current scene in hope of finding incipient shifts in direction of which we might take advantage. My guiding intention is to underscore that all history is man-made and remade, and that we can make psychology, and remake its past, advisedly and comprehensively. Specifically, the following pages are a call for psychology to take explicit account of humans' subjecthood as well as objectness, on the way rereading our history toward an integrated science. The historical material presented in these pages is well-known by many if not most psychologists. Likewise the forms and themes are unsurprising. Nevertheless, our leading textbooks and journals continue to ignore their implications for a truly human psychology – one that explicitly respects the inevitably and uniquely human constituents of its science. So, although aware of the alogical progress of our "discipline," I speak into changing times, hopeful that the particular organization of this paper will serve to gestalt some of the issues confronting those psychologists who are already looking for an authentically human psychology.

Forms of Coexistence

Even prior to the nineteenth-century advent of an acknowledged discipline of psychology, the dilemma of how to account for man's two-fold character of being both active subject and passive object had been a central theme for psychology's progenitors, the philosophers of knowledge and of science. As always, we could begin at least with Aristotle, and find in his distinction between form and matter the forerunner of multiple variations on this persistent theme. It is probably best known as the mind-body split, but depending on the particular guiding interest at the moment, this dualism has also appeared in such pairs as spirit-material, freedom-determinism, holism-atomism, dynamics-mechanics, process-product, meaning-fact, subjectivity-objectivity, and consciousness-behavior. The subject-object paradox is so basic that many historians and systematists of psychology have organized their presentations of schools and theorists in terms of attempted resolutions of this tension.

Acknowledgment of the subject character of humanness has coexisted with the historically prevailing emphasis on objectness in at least four major forms of tension and convergence. Three of these forms have been present implicitly; the one explicit form is that of opposition between schools.

Disagreement Between Schools

The 1800s were a time when educated people were celebrating simultaneously man's ability to manipulate nature to his own ends (e.g., the Industrial Revolution) and his greater freedom from Church domination. He set about exploring man's inner nature and its relation to physical nature. Thus, physicians, physicists, and anatomists on one hand, and philosophers on the other, began researching and publishing in a field that was known for a while both as psychophysiology and as philosophical psychology. In Germany, which was the center of these new developments, there had evolved earlier a distinction between two equally respected modes of knowing: *verstehen* referred to the kind of scholarly understanding involved in the study of such areas as art and history; *erklaren* referred to the kind of knowing that comes through the analytic and manipulative sciences. However, the term for "science" ("*wissenschaft*") applied to both areas of knowledge; both were regarded as science but of different contents. *Geisteswissenschaft* is the science that focuses on spirit, mind, or consciousness, and *naturwissenschaft* is what we know today as natural science, such as physics and biology. Although it is today generally regarded as of esoteric historical interest, the nineteenth-century beginnings of a new discipline were shaped by lively disagreements between these two traditions as they converged in their interest in psychology.

Specifically, our textbooks cite 1879, the year Wundt established his experimental laboratory, as the formal beginning of scientific psychology. Today's students readily recognize the names of Wundt's physicist and physiologist mentors and colleagues such as Helmholtz, Fechner, Müller, and Weber, in addition to those of his graduates, such as Titchener and Cattell, who championed his laboratory work in this country. Our students are only passingly if at all exposed to a simultaneous and enduring, albeit now minority, version of psychology, whose authors are written off in this country as extraneous philosophers.

Nevertheless, it was also in the Germany of this exact period that certain academicians insisted that although psychology could be an empirical science, it did not have to limit itself to the methods of the physical sciences. Brentano [1838–1917; see Rancurello (1968)] stressed the active quality of consciousness, and criticized Wundt's *objective* descriptions of the contents of consciousness as too restricted to account for the fullness of the process involved. Dilthey [1833–1911; see Hodges (1944)] explicitly distinguished "human sciences" from "natural sciences" in regard to psychology. Similar to Kant (1966) before him, Dilthey sought to describe the basic ground of logical method itself, ground appropriate to both life philosophy and natural scientific philosophy. But it was Husserl (1962) who developed most systematically the idea that since all science deals with experience (not only the scientist's experience of dial readings, but the life experience that allows the posing of questions), the description should be of the experienced phenomenon, with every effort made to hold assumptions and hypotheses in abeyance. This aged critique has resurfaced in the works of such contemporary psychologists as Bakan (1968), Giorgi (1969), Lyons (1963), and van Kaam (1966).

It was also in the Germany of the 1920s that Kurt Lewin directed dissertations that in modified form later would become the foundations of American social psychology. His researchers explored the perceptions and affects of individual subjects, discussing with them their experiences of being confronted with various experimental conditions (e.g., obstacles to finishing tasks). Laboratory reports were in the form of commentaried case studies. The individual research participant was regarded as critical for careful formulation of lawfulness (Lyons, 1963).

But for about eighty years, arguments by the earlier proponents of a subject-inclusive science served primarily to sharpen the object-scientists' line of attack on nature. The former did not lose their arguments; rather, American audiences were not interested in what they regarded as outright philosophy. The earlier Lewinian concern for individual descriptive data rather than group statistical data likewise was not so much confronted as it was eschewed as time-consuming and tolerant of ambiguity. American psychologists adopted a scientistic stance without awareness of the viability of theoretical alternatives. When practitioners discovered that this technological approach was inadequate, they attempted to simply add "humaneness" to its application.

At this point practitioners far outnumber the more scientistic psychologists who continue to dominate American journals and university professorships. Many of these practitioners reflect and promote popular concern about our technocracy's destructive impact, and they turn increasingly to the writings of such minority members of establishment psychology as Allport (1955), Koch (1959), McLeod (1964), and Sanford (1965), who for twenty years have called for a recentering of psychology, for the development of a science around man rather than for him to fit the methods and conceptions already instituted by physical science. The current confrontation with such scientistic psychology is jointly maintained by the clinically oriented humanistic movement and by the research and theoretical efforts of philosophically oriented authors. But to repeat, this contemporary call for psychology to accept a subject-inclusive corrective is a refrain as old as psychology itself.

Inconsistencies Within One Author's Work

The remaining three forms of coexistence of object- and subject-psychologies, unlike the above explicit opposition between approaches, are all implicit. These forms can be represented through brief examples. James's works provide historically influential examples of coexistence within the same author's work. Within the same volume (James, 1890) in separate discussions he defined "empirical" in both natural scientific, positivistic terms and in terms of personal experience or consciousness. Similarly, when accused by scientistic psychologists of dealing with nonobject phenomena, James often side-stepped the dilemma by agreeing that at that moment he was speaking as a philosopher rather than as a psychologist. Allport (1943) devoted a paper to the internal paradoxes of James's work. Skinner's work (Skinner, 1971) provides contemporary examples: he expounds a system of absolute determinism while *arguing* for man to *evaluate* his current condition and to *plan* a better community. Similar inconsistencies, of course, can be found within schools as a whole. In a sense, these are only apparent inconsistencies; indeed, a human-science approach acknowledges both thrusts. The point here is that the authors have not explicitly acknowledged and then systematically integrated the more-than-object aspects of their work.

Thematic/Operative Inconsistencies

Another type of inconsistency is that between what an author or school explicitly expounds as its theory and what it actually does in practice. Titchener's (1929) posthumously published *Systematic Psychology: Prolegomena* explicitly thematized psychology as a natural science of observable events, but his chapter on the practice of psychology is a highly experiential account of how one guides himself through research. Wolpe (1958) serves as an example of contemporary thematizing of the deterministic nature of change, one accomplished through behavior therapy or modification. But transcripts of his, and other professionals', initial interviews reveal that, in practice, they are solicitous, respectful of the clients' values, and generally accepting of the clients' experiences of hierarchy locations as well as of the clients' own goals for therapy. Again, the point here is not that psychologists have been naive in their practice; indeed, the practice typically is more sophisticated/integrated than the theory. Rather, the implication is that explicitation of the operative (here, especially subject) dimensions of science would mitigate simplistic reading and learning by newcomers. Moreover, such (explicitation) would discourage psychologists' workaday slippage into reductive research and formulations.

Historical Reevaluations

With shifts in the prevailing paradigm, earlier figures and their works are reevaluated, often in ways diametrical to initial criticisms and even to each other. For example, Freud was severely criticized by his positivist contemporaries for introducing into science such anathema as mysticism, subjectivism, and social relations, not to mention human sexuality. Today Freud is variously criticized for having condemned women to live out a biological role, for being overly mechanistic, for underplaying interpersonal relations, and simultaneously for not being rigorously operational in his definitions. The development of such criticism has been nonlinear and nonunivocal, being as much a part of shifting political social consciousness as of logic and nature. The same can be said of Freud's own varying characterizations of his work.

Wundt is a second example. He prided himself even in his assistantship days as being an original critic of positivism, but he was criticized by Husserlian colleagues for not going far enough toward holding naturalistic assumptions in abeyance. Moreover, despite Wundt's publication of *Logic* – a forerunner of his empirical metaphysics – in 1880, one scant year after the famous 1879, he remains today acclaimed as the father of our still positivistic, antimetaphysical, experimental psychology. If Wundt's affinity to Husserlian phenomenological method, his metaphysics, and his *Folk Psychology* rejection of laboratory experimentalism (as inadequate for study of human higher processes) ever became widely recognized, he could properly be acclaimed as a progenitor of empirical phenomenological psychology – one form of psychology as a human science.

Binet can serve as a final example of historical shifts in emphasis on our human twofold character of being subject and object. He also serves as an example of differences between nations in their evaluation of historical figures. Specifically, our country reveres Binet as a pragmatic inventor of the intelligence test; today we variously quote his warnings against becoming test-bound, and remind students that his work was, of course, statistically primitive. Rarely does anyone mention that Binet was initially recognized by Americans for his humane involvement as a leader in a social-action-oriented Mental Retardation Association. Nor is there ready contemporary access to those writings that reflect his interest in intelligence as being what I would call "goal-directed consciousness."[2] Despite his self-identification as an empirical theorist, and as one who placed quantification as secondary to other description, Binet's research sophistication is acknowledged in France, where he carries the titles of father of psychometrics and of experimental psychology. In short, values and goals coexist with, and become a shifting context through which, "facts" are selected and reunderstood. But rarely do our textbooks alert readers to this metascientific – subject-directed – context.

The "Extrascientific" Journey of "Scientific" Psychology

Thus far, we have recalled briefly that subject-oriented psychology has always been with us explicitly as theory and implicitly in the last three forms of coexistence with object-psychology. The subjecthood of psychologists themselves is evident in the extrascientific routes by which they have brought our presumably natural science to prominence. Objectivist psychologists have addressed only method and content, but, for example, they have not asked how it is possible for putative things (psychologists) to ask questions and to create science.

The following subsection presents a sample of usually unexamined, uniquely human, alogical, and apositivistic aspects of naturalistic psychology's journey to its present success. In general, these interrelated themes involve political-economic values – particularly those of technocracy, along with unplanned circumstances, in-group favoritism, product-packaging, and a loose fit between practice and preachment. These themes are extrascientific only from an objectivistic perspective; they are presented here as variations of the necessarily human construction of science, which we ought to take into explicit account if we are to "make psychology advisedly" into a more comprehensive, truly disciplined science.

Historical Routes to Dominance

1. Historically, the rise of scientific psychology has taken place as part of a larger political-economic system. Tenacious clinging to positivistic practices despite radical transformations in formal philosophy of science can be understood in part as a living out of our materialistic, technological values. Think of the emphasis on instruments, statistical data, prediction, control, production, and funding.[3] Scientific psychology has been part of and has furthered general societal values through which research interests are guided by, for example, grants for preselected topics, promotion possibilities, and publish-or-perish policies. For that matter, individual motivation for entering or changing fields of scientific endeavor often has been economic. Recall, for example, Freud's leaving laboratory neurophysiology for general medical practice so that he could earn money to marry. This, of course, was a happenstantial beginning of psychoanalysis.

2. Methodological changes often have initiated or redirected fields of inquiry rather than being formed deliberately to suit the latter's research needs. For example, when Freud found that he could induce hypnosis in some of his patients, he tried to produce deep concentration by reclining the patient and applying mild pressure to the temples. He soon gave up this "pressure technique," but the patients' residual recumbent associating became the fulcrum of psychoanalytic technique, data, and theory. Havens (1973) has documented other changes that occurred in both prepsychoanalytic and Freudian theories of psychopathology as a result of ascientific, happenstantial shifts in method. Skinner's (1959) description of his invention of the cumulative polygraph is an example of the serendipitous character of many procedural breakthroughs. Indeed, that paper as a whole is an explicit account of extrascientific aspects of the development of method and procedure, which scientists of lesser stature do not admit [see Mitroff (1974) for private admissions by leading physicists; see Perrott (1974) for unwitting admissions by doctoral students]. But the main point here is that new worlds are opened much more powerfully by shifts in activity and in language than by deduction and argumentation. Contemporary examples are the rapid mass adoptions of behavior modification and "human potential" ideologies primarily via readily available new techniques and accompanying jargon.

3. A related theme, then, is that historically those conceptions that provide their audience with fairly mechanical, manipulable constructs and "how to do it" instructions have risen to dominance. Think of the contrast between Cattell's early laboratory manuals (DuBois, 1970) and James's (1899) contemporaneous lectures. Today's psychologists are more familiar with the structure of the former than the latter. Variations of this theme are that the dominant endeavors have been those that provided immediate, tangible results as well as highly visible procedures and outcomes that appear to cope with a clear-cut natural order. Another variation is that this precision has often exceeded non-technological understanding. An example at once historical and contemporary is the heavy production of intelligence tests in the 1920s and 1930s, when today we still have not agreed on what intelligence is, aside from complex progeny of Boring's (1923) definition of intelligence as "what intelligence tests test."

4. Historically, those thinkers who have respected and tried to describe the ambiguity of human existence have been written off as having lost their way [e.g., Wertheimer (1970) on Wundt's later philosophy and folk psychology] or as not really being psychologists. How many contemporary psychologists have read James? How many have even heard of Merleau-Ponty (1963)? Others are acknowledged as well-meaning but then dismissed as soft-headed or inadequately empirical; Rogers and Maslow are current examples. Earlier figures rarely made the history books. Those who have not been written off have suffered drastic leveling and simplification of their thought. Where can one readily find English versions of Wundt's discussions of consciousness? Or of Binet's? Mainstream psychologists and consumers generally have preferred and promoted systems that appear at least potentially capable of explaining all phenomena in a few basic causal axioms, even while complex corollaries and data matrices have been appreciated as evidence of scholarly and scientific achievement. A supporting backdrop of esoteric language also has helped. Watson's victory over American "New Psychology" is the most obvious example, especially when joined with related learning theories. Note that this preference for simple causal formulations thus far has prevailed despite

the insistence by experimental psychology's theorists that explanation is limited to complex patterns of relationships.

5. It also seems that to become dominant a psychological paradigm requires that a few major figures serve as reference points. These may be "great men" like Freud, purifiers like Skinner, importers and interpreters like Beck or May, systematists like Boring, and so on. There must also be lesser popularizers, charismatic spokesmen, teachers, data-producers, disciple-gatherers, and organization-founders. Dominance is assisted by development of key phrases that help professionals and lay persons alike to distinguish the differences among theories and methods (e.g., "talking treatment," "New Psychology," "client-centered," "behaviorism," "medical model," "third force"). Publication of brief surveys and equally brief definitive stances, both with clear titles, are helpful so long as there is also a backdrop of esoterica.

6. A closing theme for this abbreviated listing is that of the controlling power of established academicians and the leadership of psychology organizations. This control is maintained despite the numerical prevalence of our pragmatic practitioners, including uncritically additive eclectics and the paradoxical "humanistic behaviorists." The established group advises governments on awarding of research grants, determines university curricula, passes on the scientific sufficiency of all graduate students regardless of the latters' career and theoretical interests, selects or rejects articles for publication, advises commercial publishers which manuscripts are reputable, and so on. Even with recent open, important, and relatively rapid adjustments in this picture, it still remains the prevailing situation.

The above presentation of all these extrascientific routes to dominance, as well as the forms of coexistence, are of course oversimplified. In actuality, they don't lie straight but instead meander, intermingle, and for that matter wax and wane.

Shift in Destination

Generally, a replacement of generations has been necessary before a paradigm shifts significantly. These are, however, unprecedented times. Change in the structure of disciplines, like that of our daily lives, has speeded up drastically. Eighty percent of extant PhDs in psychology were granted in the past ten years; more than 2,700 psychology PhDs were awarded in the United States in each of the last three years (1974–1977). In short, explosions in education, publication, and popularization have weakened the authority of the old guard. Recent arrivals are looking for new fields in which they might themselves become founding experts. Moreover, as the ranks of clinical practitioners, counselors, and community consultants swell, we find that coping with actual life events minimizes theoretical differences. Contact with humans as humans humanizes. Or, familiarity breeds understanding. For example, clinical behavior modification now has expanded to include self-control programs that are developed collaboratively with the client. In addition, by now the separate schools of psychology are highly enough developed that it becomes increasingly evident that each is valid, although definitely perspectival.

Perhaps the technological culture that nourished positivistic psychology in this country has also brought us into confrontation with an ultimate Kuhnian anomaly. The accomplishments of dedicated objectivism stifle and threaten to destroy what only in this circumstance are we now learning to revere as uniquely human. It *is* the case that psychology is evolving through concerns with a causal past (psychophysical, psychoanalytic, and behavioristic determinism), then with the present (Gestalt interest in life space, Esalen-type focus on immediate experience, third force concern with situated meaning), and now with building for the future (social activism of APA, preventative mental health programming, the search for an integrative paradigm). The startling increase during the past five to ten years in textbooks on the history of psychology can be understood as an effort to reunderstand our destination. History itself is a creation in the present looking to the past as it strains toward a future.

Conclusion

The future of psychology toward which this paper has been directed is one that takes explicit account of the full humanness of its subjects *and* its practitioners. I have reviewed the fact that recognition of their more-than-object character has been present since the inception of formal psychology. I have outlined this actual but implicit coexistence with object-psychology in the forms of inconsistencies within individual authors' works, unthematized practices, and temporal and cultural changes in evaluation. I overviewed what we can now more accurately term the "extrascientistic" progress of scientific psychology. All of this reviewing has been in the interest of encouraging an informed, purposive convergence (vs. coexistence) of subject-inclusive psychology with object-psychology into an explicitly human-science psychology.

This paper has offered historical support for recommendations such as Epting's (1973), that while traditional psychology must loosen up to make room for personhood, a science of persons must pursue greater rigor. Within that effort, subject-inclusive psychology must also directly engage traditional psychology's approach, method, and data. We all should work to make an integrative human-science vision more visible and possible to implement to others. Our courses and textbooks in "History and Systems" in particular ought to resist reductive and dichotomous simplifications of psychology. Particularly because our shaping of history also shapes our future, we ought to specify what we know implicitly about the manufacture of science. We should encourage presentation of these efforts to lay persons as well as to students and a diverse range of professionals. Human-science researchers should produce usable results. Those who wish to provide a subject-psychology corrective should work toward developing articulate scholars, practitioners, administrators, teachers, spokesman, and researchers, and at placing them in influential positions. In short, each thematized historical route to dominance holds a message for those who would direct psychology toward becoming a human-science.

However, we need not merely accommodate to apparent contingencies. We should also work toward revising certain materialistic and technocratic societal values and toward encouraging both popular and professional acknowledgment of the complexity and inevitable ambiguity of human existence. It is toward this end that we ought to introduce our students to hermeneutic (dialogal) reading of original cross-disciplinary texts, as recommended by Romanyshyn (1974) and Sardello (1975). Let us direct our efforts toward this comprehensive project in such a way that future readings of the *history* that we are *proposing* will, despite the inevitable repetitions and variations of themes identified in this paper, judge that at least we worked advisedly and consistently toward the goal of an integrated science of and by humans.

Notes

1 Copyright 1977 by John Wiley & Sons. Reproduced with permission. The official citation that should be used in referencing this material is: Fischer, C. T. (1977). Historical relations of psychology as an object-science and subject-science: Toward psychology as a human-science. *Journal of the History of the Behavioral Sciences, 13*, 369–378.
2 See Introduction to Robert H. Pollack and Margaret J. Brenner, (Eds.) (1969). *The experimental psychology of Alfred Binet: Selected papers.* New York: Springer.
3 See Steiner Kvale (1973). "The Techological Paradigm of Psychological Research," *Journal of Phenomenological Psychology, 3*, 143–159, and Gerard Radnitsky (1970). *Contemporary schools of metascience.* Göteborg: Scandinavian University Books.

References

Allport, G. W. (1943). The productive paradoxes of William James. *Psychological Review, 50*, 95–120.
Allport, G. W. (1955). *Becoming*. New Haven: Yale University Press.
Bakan, D. (1968). *On method: Toward a reconstruction of psychological investigation.* San Francisco: Jossey-Bass.
Boring, E. G. (1923). Intelligence as the tests test it. *The New Republic, 34*, 35–36.
DeRivera, J. (1976). *Field theory as human-science: Contributions of Lewin's Berlin group.* N.Y.: Gardner Press.
DuBois, P. H. (1970). *A history of psychological testing.* Boston: Allyn & Bacon.
Epting, F. R. (1973, September). *The possibility of a science of persons.* Paper presented at the meeting of the American Psychological Association, Montreal, Canada.
Giorgi, A. (1969). Psychology: A human science. *Social Research, 36*, 412–432.
Giorgi, A. (1970). *Psychology as a human science: A phenomenologically based approach.* N.Y.: Harper & Row.
Giorgi, A. Fischer, C. T., & Murray, E. D. (Eds.). (1975). *Duquesne studies in phenomenological psychology* (Vol. 2, pp. 82–103). Pittsburgh: Duquesne University Press.
Giorgi, A., Fischer, W. F., & von Eckartsberg, R. (Eds.). (1971). *Duquesne studies in phenomenological psychology* (Vol. 1). Pittsburgh: Duquesne University Press.
Habermas, J. (1971). *Knowledge and human interests.* (J.J. Shapiro, Trans.). Boston: Beacon Press. (Original work published 1968.)
Havens, L. L. (1973). *Approaches to the mind: Movement of the psychiatric schools from sects toward science.* Boston: Little, Brown.
Heisenberg, W. (1966). *Philosophic problems of nuclear science.* Greenwich: Fawcett.
Hodges, H. A. (1944). *Wilhelm Dilthey: An introduction.* London: Paul, Trench, Truber.
Husserl, E. (1962). *Ideas: General introduction to pure phenomenology.* (W.H.B. Gibson, Trans.). N.Y.: Collier Books. (Original work published 1913.)
James, W. (1890). *Principles of psychology.* N.Y.: Holt.
James, W. (1899). *Talks to teachers on psychology and to students on some of life's ideals.* N.Y.: Holt.
Kant, I. (1966). *Critique of pure reason.* (F. M. Muller, Trans.). N.Y.: Doubleday. (Original work published 1781.)
Koch, S. (1959). Epilogue: Some trends of study I. In Koch, S. (Ed.), *Psychology: A study of science: Vol. 3. Formulations of the person and the social context* (Vol. 3, pp. 729–788). N.Y.: McGraw-Hill.
Kuhn, T. S. (1962). *The structure of scientific revolutions.* Chicago: University of Chicago Press.
Lyons, J. (1963). *Psychology and the measure of man.* Glencoe: Free Press.
Maslow, A. (1966). *The psychology of science: A reconnaissance.* N.Y.: Harper and Row.

McLeod, R. (1964). Phenomenology: A challenge to experimental psychology. In Wann, T.W. (Ed.), *Behaviorism and phenomenology*. Chicago: University of Chicago Press.

Merleau-Ponty, M. (1963). *The structure of behavior*. (A. L. Fisher, Trans.). Boston: Beacon Press, 1963. (Original work published 1942.)

Miller, G. A., & Buckhout, R. (1973). *Psychology: The science of mental life* (2nd ed.). New York: Harper and Row.

Mitroff, I. I. (1974). *The subjective side of science: Philosophical inquiry into the psychology of the Apollo moon scientists*. Amsterdam: Elsevier.

Mitroff, I. I. (1974). *The subjective side of science*. N.Y.: American Elsevier.

Perrott, L. A. (1974). *Research on research: A human science investigation (Doctoral dissertation)*. Pittsburgh: Duquesne University Press.

Polanyi, M. (1964). *The study of man*. Chicago: University of Chicago Press.

Pollack, R. H. & Brenner, M. J. (1969). (Eds.). *The experimental psychology of Alfred Binet: Selected papers*. N.Y.: Springer.

Popper, K. R. (1957). *The poverty of historicism*. London: Routledge & Kegan Paul.

Radnitsky, G. (1970). *Contemporary schools of meta-science*. Goteborg: Scandinavian University Books.

Rancurello, A. C. (1968). *A study of Franz Brentano*. N.Y.: Academic Press.

Riegel, K. F. (Ed.). (1975). *The development of dialectical operations*. Basel: Karger.

Romanyshyn, R. D. (1974, September). *Phenomenology and the attitude of history*. Paper presented at the annual meeting of the American Psychological Association, New Orleans, LA.

Sanford, N. (1965). Will Americans study human problems? *American Psychologist, 20*, 192–202.

Sardello, R. J. (1975). Hermeneutical reading: An approach to the classic texts of psychology. In Giorgi, A., Fischer, C. T., & Murray, E. L. (Eds.). *Duquesne Studies in Phenomenological Psychology* (Vol 2: pp. 273–280). Pittsburgh: Duquesne University Press.

Skinner, B. F. (1959). A case history in scientific method. In Koch, S. (Ed.). *Psychology: A study of science* (Vol. 2, pp. 359–379). N.Y.: McGraw-Hill.

Skinner, B. F. (1971). *Beyond freedom and dignity*. N.Y.: Knopf.

Skinner, B. F. (1974). *About behaviorism*. N.Y.: Knopf.

Steinar Kvale, S. (1973). The technological paradigm of psychological research. *Journal of Phenomenological Psychology, 3*, 143–159.

Titchener, E. B. (1929). *Systematic psychology: Prolegomena*. N.Y.: Macmillan.

Toulmin, S. (1960). *The philosophy of science: An introduction*. N.Y: Harper and Row.

van Kaam, A. (1966). *Existential foundations of psychology*. Pittsburgh: Duquesne University Press.

Wertheimer, M. (1970). *A brief history of psychology*. N.Y.: Holt, Rinehart, and Winston.

Wolpe, J. (1958). *Psychotherapy by reciprocal inhibition*. Stanford: Stanford University Press.

Wolpe, J. *Behavior therapy*. American Academy of Psychotherapists Tape Library 26. Available from the American Academy of Psychotherapists, 1450 Western Ave., Suite, 101, Albany, NY, 12203.

CHAPTER 6

DILEMMAS IN STANDARDIZED TESTING[1]

Today, the phrase *ethical dilemmas in standardized testing* appears straightforward but dull. Less than ten years ago it would indeed have been dynamic because of its apparent contradiction: The primary ethics of testing *were* standardized construction of tests, standardized administration, standardized interpretation, standard report writing, and closed filing. Ethical issues had to do with deviating from these procedures, intentionally or unintentionally.

Of course, the goal of standardized testing has been to obtain measures of the child that could be compared against those of his age group. A standardized test, whether for use with groups or individuals, has been scientifically constructed and demonstrated to be reliable and valid under specified circumstances. Graphs and tables indicate the range of scores that were obtained. Testers are trained to judge whether these norms are appropriate for new test takers and to keep abreast of emerging research. They also are trained to administer the tests according to the manual's explicit instructions, so that each test taker has been exposed to the same testing circumstances, and the resulting scores can be interpreted in the standardized way. Historically, the testing movement rightfully has taken pride in its scientific character: No matter which test administrator gave and scored a test, the measured result would be as similar as possible for a given child (this is the definition of *objective test*).

Today, it is just this allegiance to standardized procedures that raises ethical questions. Ethics are the formal, well-established standards that a profession follows in order to protect and promote the welfare of its clients and society. Dilemmas arise when a client's welfare seems to bring established standards into conflict. Such conflict is most likely when scientific knowledge and/or social consciousness evolve beyond a profession's established ethics. The Karen Quinlan case is an example: Medicine now can keep bodies alive even when all other human capacities are gone. Today's doctors must decide individually whether it is best to uphold their pledge to maintain life.

Partially because of changes in the philosophy of science, partially because of humanistic psychology's teachings, but mostly because of protests by minority groups, users of psychological, developmental, and educational tests find themselves in conflict about whether clients' welfare is best served by standardized testing. In particular, we are increasingly aware that tests are subject to discriminatory use, that rather than being value-free, they inevitably reflect cultural and scientific values, that we have given test technology's reality more credence than directly observable behaviors, and that we have transformed children's lives into a few cognitive and usually unsituated "variables." In short, we have given location on the bell-shaped curve priority over individualized understanding and helping.

I have found that today's ethical dilemmas in standardized testing can be grouped, overlappingly, as struggles of new consciousness against continued respect for earlier versions of "objectivity," "professionalism," and "efficiency." For this chapter I have selected three dilemmas representative of each cluster from instances presented to me by graduate students in field settings and by practicing professionals. After presenting each cluster, I will explore the implicit historical assumptions that no longer need be part of objectivity, professionalism, and efficiency but that still seem to be at the heart of conflicting concerns for clients' welfare. I also will describe my own resolutions and continuing concerns.

Let us consider the dilemma of objectivity first.

> *Often, even as I gain clinical skill, I find that standardized administration of tests gets in the way of working effectively with personal material. To obtain objective scores and to ensure that a child's energy is concentrated upon responding to the test items before she becomes fatigued, I am supposed to proceed systematically according to the manual, but I'm just sure that sometimes the scores aren't as helpful to the youngster as my immediate response might have been. For example, just yesterday during a Wechsler test, a fifth-grader began to elaborate upon the fact that the bigger boys pick fights with him; but I felt that I had to move him along to the next Wechsler comprehension item. When I brought it up later, he wouldn't talk about the fights. I had lost a chance to explore part of the referral issue – "Mark's social wariness." On the other hand, it was also important to get as valid an IQ as possible, and I wasn't sure that this would be possible if he became emotionally involved in the fight discussion. I just don't know where my greater responsibility to the child lies, so I usually take the conservative course of sticking to the standardized procedures. Yet I'm not certain if that's the right thing to do.*
>
> *My supervisor says our job is to provide accurate measures on the children and to indicate to which established categories they belong, since other people who work with the children and also locate services and funding for them best understand their needs in terms of categories. He says that it's up to the childcare workers to use that information responsibly. But sometimes I think that for the child's sake it would be worth the risk of overstepping professional boundaries, to add my comments about possible misinterpretations or about ways to best use our measures for a particular child. He says that would just be my subjective opinion, which has no place in objective records. I see his point, but somehow it still seems like a "cop-out" from an opportunity to be more helpful to the child.*
>
> *Well, I personally think it's unethical to objectify a client through overly rigorous standardized assessment. You can't see the kid as an individual if you treat him like all the others. And standardized results can't say anything about his uniqueness; they just say how many standard deviations he is from an average. But I'm in a bind here, because I also don't think it's ethical just to go in and make decisions based only on my own impressions without test scores as supportive data. And I guess for the scores to be useful they have to be valid, which, according to the manual, means derived in a standardized manner. There must be a middle road, but I don't see it.*

It seems to me that the issue in all three cases is whether the professional can be *objective and involved* at the same time. The answer is yes, and the dilemma dissolves when we reexamine the meaning of *objectivity*. In general, objectivity assures that observations are not merely subjective, that referents and procedures can be readily agreed upon and shared by different people. That is what standardization provides for tests. In a still broader sense, objectivity is the assurance that many perspectives on empirical touchpoints have been taken into account and have converged in a consensus. What we sometimes forget is that the test score is only a summary of (age-based) right–wrong judgments of specific behaviors. True, the score is an averaging across *many* behaviors, and contrasted to natural observation, it is more difficult to imagine the testing environment as it might have been experienced by the child. But this distanced, general, and abstract quality should not be mistaken for a sign of a reality more basic or valid than firsthand observation of the effectiveness of particular behaviors. Averages are no more than generalizations, and they do not generalize beyond the specific kind of circumstance in which the data occurred. This is true for the individual child as well as for group norms. Test scores represent a sample of a particular set of problem solvings. In the case of the traditional intelligence tests, for example, that set of problems was put together by middle-class academic whites in a capitalistic society. The tests value efficient production, one-truth answers, and Aristotelian logic. In short, tests do provide us with objectivity via their standardization, but that objectivity is inescapably a limited one: Tests necessarily call for particular values and only selected, decontextualized aspects of the test taker.

The assessor is obliged to provide not only publicly available – that is, potentially objective – grounds for his testing conclusions but also correctives to the limited perspective of the standardized test. That may require assessment of areas not found on the test. Sometimes the assessor intervenes during testing to explore how the child is missing certain items or to investigate the circumstances in which the child performs more happily or effectively. Often the assessor must assist score users to understand the limits of the particular scores and the necessary place of additional information. In short, assessment is more than testing; the assessor must be more than a servant of technology. The assessor must be *involved*.

So in the above dilemmas, I would amend technological objectivity with broader involvement. In Mark's case, I would talk with him about those bigger boys when he introduces that problem for two reasons. First, the ultimate purpose of applied testing is constructive intervention – helping the child toward fulfillment. Why not begin that process during testing by tailoring the assessment and helping him to be a part of it? Second, for most purposes, an estimate based on additional items or other subtests will place the child in the same range as the precise IQ, and ranges or percentile bands are more reliable than a specific number anyway.

As for including unsolicited assistance in interpreting scores: I am all for it. We are partially responsible for the uses and abuses of our assessments. Score consumers should be helped to use scores in a less absolute way. Accompanying information on the circumstances of testing, information on limitations of the test for particular uses, and additional observations on the child help the recipient make more reflective use of scores.

Standardized findings can be set apart from personal or speculative observations by labeling the latter as such – for example, "Assessor's Comments." In these ways we can provide other workers with data they request but in ways we believe best benefit the client.

By now, the third case seems artificial; we do not very often have to choose between strictly standardized procedures and personal impressions. Neither is adequate by itself. Each is a way station, not a final destination. Both objectivity and the client are best served where different perspectives (for example; the tests' and the clinician's) are specified and integrated by the assessor.

However, I personally feel that any impressions should be documented so that they, too, become available for examination. For example, concrete behaviors, interchanges, or the assessor's responses could be described. This kind of involvement also moves toward individualizing the assessment, which, in turn, goes a long way toward encouraging the child's helpers to see new possibilities. Otherwise, score receivers tend to see "individual differences" as sameness and scores as ceilings or limits rather than present locations or starting places. This is especially true where classification by score replaces team conferences. The same danger occurs when the report is written in third-person, objectifying terms as though there were no historical context for the tests in general and no specific situation for this particular assessment.

The second dilemma is one of professionalism.

> *The medical doctor in charge of our unit in the hospital routinely makes out a referral for "*WISC *IQ and* WRAT*" (Wechsler Intelligence Scale for Children and Wide Range Achievement Test). He seems to think that numbers in the child's record fulfill his obligation to be sure every child has been assessed. My problem with this is that, as an assessor, I know that this referral is often inappropriate; other tests are often more useful for a particular child. But our director of psychological services says that our obligation is to provide the doctor with what he needs for his own purposes. At first, I tried to give the tests the doctor wanted and then add whatever else I felt was helpful for the particular child. But there just isn't time to do both. Besides, with most of our children, attention span and interest preclude extensive testing at any one time. Anyway, in my opinion the scores themselves aren't all that helpful for treatment planning; they usually don't add to what the ward staff already knows from interacting with the youngster. And yet, the ward staff seems to feel that the assessor's basic contribution into the multidisciplinary team is test results. They feel more secure about their own judgments if they jibe with my scores.*
>
> *I don't know what to think about something that happened last week. It's still bothering me. I was supposed to do a "standard battery" on a five-year-old orphan whose foster parents of six months had brought her back to our agency complaining that she just didn't "fit in" and that they'd rather have a lively boy instead of this quiet girl. In order to give us time to investigate the situation, my boss had promised the foster parents that he would not yet tell Marie why she was being tested; she was told instead that she was being brought in for a "doctor's check-up." But respecting confidentiality in regard to the foster parents meant that I had to be devious with Marie, and I think she knew something was wrong and probably felt that she was defective, I wish I could have been honest with her to help her cope with what was going on.*
>
> *How would you answer this? Some parents came in and wanted to see their son's counseling file. I explained that this file included the psychiatric consultant's notes as well as the school psychologist's results and that the Buckley Amendment did not apply. They argued that the writer's profession should not*

> *limit parents' access to documents that were influencing their son's welfare. So I also explained that laypersons would be confused or misled by the language, scores, and concepts written by and for professionals. I also felt that it would be damaging to both the youngster and the parents to see some of the labels and psychologisms in the record. I know I had both law and ethical standards behind me, but then why do I feel uneasy and defensive every time parents question me about access to the counseling files?*

The major assumption in the previous instances is that professionalism requires uncritical adherence to intra- and interprofessional traditions. It is true that traditions embody a certain working wisdom and that client welfare requires cooperative relations among professionals as well as a judicious approach in innovation. But it seems to me that the above examples involve protectionistic rather than responsible professionalism. In each case the clinician has neglected to examine the grounds for established practices and to clarify his understandings of the meaning of tests. The responsible professional places the client's welfare first, with personal confidence in his procedures – confidence that comes, in part, from reflection on the historical situations out of which particular practices evolved.

So, in the above examples, as part of my *professionalism* I would *take the initiative* in the following ways. I would assume the position that it is the psychologist who carries primary responsibility for the selection and use of tests developed by his profession, and I would, in fact, begin to use whatever developmental/educational tests I thought would best serve the child. But also I would have to take further initiative – namely, addressing the situations of the other workers. I would have to take into account their need to feel as competent and comfortable with the new measures as they were with the old ones. Therefore, I might continue to provide WRAT and WISC estimates at first, while gradually familiarizing the staff with additional measures. Through my ways of speaking about tests and through my valuing of direct behavioral observations, I would help the staff to deabsolutize scores. I would help them develop their own senses of how scores are peoplemade aids or tools rather than states of nature or final results. We become servants of the tools rather than the other way when they cover over more of the individual child than they reveal.

The example of foster child Marie illustrates how easily we can forget about the individual child and about our personal responsibility when we think in terms of professional roles. The assessor in this case has created an unnecessary bind; one does not have to pit allegiances against each other. Instead, I would matter-of-factly explore with Marie her concerns about being brought in, and I would help her to face the possibilities of the foster parents' wondering whether they were a good fit for each other. I would explain that I am not a doctor (physician), that I am not looking for things that are wrong, but that I want to get to know her to see if that might help her foster parents to do the right things. In short, I would take an honest middle ground. Later, I would explore with my boss whether our office might formulate a policy of not confronting youngsters prematurely but also of letting guardians know that neither they nor we should deceive their children.

About the problem of closed files: I do think we are obliged to abide by laws and formal policies. But I do not believe that psychiatric or psychological records should be exempt from disclosure, and I have worked within the system for change. In the meantime, I would advise the parents in this case of their options. For example, they could request that an independent practitioner evaluate the files and advise them about whether anything should be challenged or studied for additional assessment. Of course, I am assuming that the school staff has already discussed the general relevance of the file for the student's progress with the parents. Parents should also be advised about the status of any relevant court cases and of the existence of interest groups.

It may well be that the historically ethical practice of closed files with their stark scores and labelings not only impedes maximal child welfare but sometimes is detrimental. If so, unself-critical ethics are morally wrong. For example, the recording of scores without notations about the assessor, about the daily correlates of test performance, the ways the child went about answering the questions, and other situational data falsely leads the reader to believe that the score is independent of these essential constituents. The reader may then assume that scores are limits of capacity rather than starting places. Moreover, even when records are available to parents and children, they often cannot question scores. If they could see reports of specific behaviors, they would be able to put into context what the assessor said. Similarly, the assessor's growth and development is restricted when such challenges and dialogue do not occur.

The responsible professional examines the rationale for closed files and works to change protectionism from within the system. For example, I stamp my reports "Contents have been, and may be, shared with the subject." I can do this because my reports contain no jargon (unless parenthetically explained), no opinions that have not already been shared with the client, and no scores that have not been translated into classroom or everyday behaviors. In other words, I recognize that jargon, conceptions, and scores are tools that I have to use but that my results should consist of concrete suggestions for working with a particular child in his particular situation. Reporting on tools and conceptual efforts is to report unfinished business. If the school or agency has no intention of finishing – that is, of finding out what actual behaviors, experiences, and interventions the tests might point to for a particular child – the records then should be kept only for research, with the children's names removed, or for occasions when genuinely individualized assessment is undertaken.

Finally, I talk to assorted staffs and to school boards, lecture to my students, and write chapters like this one about alternatives to closed files. In this process I not only influence others but I develop and adapt my own ideas, learning from others' efforts. I believe that some such interchange is necessary for genuine professionalism. In sum, the responsible professional person questions traditional ethics and looks for constructive means of meeting the underlying intention of protection of client welfare.

So far, we have not looked directly at instances in which one worker believes another is misusing tests. There are a number of examples. The inexperienced special education teacher interprets House–Tree–Person (HTP) drawings literally from a manual ("dark lines equal hostility"). The pediatrician, not trained in a test's standardization, does not take into account that parts of the test were developed at different times with somewhat different implications; perhaps, too, he gives credit on the test for the first emergence of a behavior, before it is clearly developed, falsely raising scores and expectations. The nurse administering the Denver Developmental Screening Schedule does not evaluate whether the parent is answering according to what she thought should have been the case or to what actually was the case. The school psychologist interprets statistically insignificant scale differences as primary evidence of learning disability. An audiologist's technician administering the Peabody Picture Vocabulary Test falsely concludes that a deaf child is retarded when, in fact, the technician had not seen to it that the youngster was attending to the visual instructions. Incidents like these are all too frequent.

It is our moral and ethical obligation to go directly to such colleagues and share our experience with these complex instruments. Sometimes it is helpful to refer them to textbooks on psychological testing or to specialized works such as Palmer's *The Psychological Assessment of Children* (1970) and Sattler's *Assessment of Children's Intelligence* (1974). If necessary, we must then go to that person's supervisor or (eventually) even to her association's ethics or peer review committee. Professionals are responsible not only for their personal competence but for that of their profession at large (see your own association's code of ethics on this matter). They must also be concerned with the competence of members of other professions if the child's welfare is in question. Yes, one must be tactful and helpful rather than negative. I notice that as I become older and look older – and presumably more mature – my interventions are better received! And yes, in each case, one must balance the welfare of the present client(s) against that of future clients. For example, the former may require a good working relation between you and the problematic professional. Nevertheless, future children can often be helped by working through the dilemma involving the present child. The goals usually are not so mutually exclusive as to justify taking no action.

Now let us consider the dilemma of efficiency.

> *I know that assessing twenty pupils a week does necessitate one- or two-page, often test-oriented, reports. I've learned much more about each youngster than I have time to write up. And I know that the brevity of the reports makes the findings seem so absolute that they may be misleading. It's demoralizing to all of us, knowing that there is usually so much more we should check into and report. But I don't see any other way. These kids have to be processed, and the county is not about to pay for more assessors.*
>
> *We run a standardized screening program for developmental disabilities. It's really quite sophisticated, and we've been able to identify and help many disabled youngsters. Since we have this technology available, I think we are morally obliged to use and even to extend it. But many of the teachers and many of the ethnic families strongly oppose the whole program, protesting that our tests are racially biased, that labels and developmental classes hold their children back. Granted, there are always a few false positives, but the numerous correct identifications seem to justify the program. Moreover, even the so-called false positives could use some help, or they would not have scored so poorly on the tests, even if they do perform better in other situations. My dilemma seems to be that although I can make a strong case for the program as a whole, I do feel somehow responsible for the youngsters who perhaps would be better served by some other kind of specialized screening or norms.*
>
> *We're required by state law to keep records of each student's potential and present achievement. Standardized tests are considered to be the fairest way to compare children, so no one can complain about teacher bias. But I often feel that our records are too test-oriented. They're good for tracking progress or pointing out possible motivation problems, but I wonder if the lawmakers*

> *realized that our careful records don't help teachers or parents to develop more effective programs for the individual child. It seems to me that the students would be better served if we sacrificed group testing and just concentrated on developing constructive individual programs for children identified by their teachers as not keeping up or moving as well as they could in the classroom. But our director says that this wouldn't be efficient and wouldn't meet the state law.*

Efficient recording of mass data seems to be winning out over *service to individual children* in all three of these examples. Other ways of saying this are that records have become more important than education or intervention and that scientific form or appearance is more important than practical function. How could we have taken such a position? The historical reason is that in our earlier positivist, operationalist understanding of science, we thought of scores as more objective and even more real than actual experience and behavior. But now we find ourselves in dilemmas because we also are beginning to recognize that scores are derived data secondary to behavior and experience. We are realizing that assessment is more than testing, that it requires person-to-person evaluation of the child's perspectives, situations, and options, as well as abstracted end products (scores) from contrived tests. Moreover, service requires going beyond assessment of the present to individualize suggestions for the child's future.

Therefore, my resolution to these dilemmas is to look for ways to deal more directly with the lives of children, reminding myself and others that scores and categories are unfinished beginnings rather than satisfactory assessment or record keeping. True, we still have to be as efficient as possible, especially for monetary reasons.

For example, we might use scaling devices into which we could enter brief phrases describing behavioral instances that illustrate or contradict a child's score equivalent on the scale. I can envision a couple of sheets of paper with a full range of scales including such neglected areas as comportment outside the institutional or clinic setting and, perhaps, self-responsibility. Where life examples had not been filled in for various acceptable and unacceptable reasons, the reader of these records would see that he had, indeed, only a partial record. This contrasts sharply with the more typical assumption that a few test scores tell the basic story.

A national project on the *Issues in the Classification of Children* (Hobbs, 1975b) led to Public Law 94–142 regarding handicapped children's special needs. Schools now are being required to write out an individualized program for each child with such special needs. Thus, a child's record would go beyond traditional diagnostic categories to include, for example, that he requires dental work, extra reading assistance for a year, and a big brother. Reconceptualizing overall classification schemes so that they preserve the individuality and specialness of each child remains a challenge for children's services professionals.

Many assessors are already developing ways both to render evaluations more relevant and to bring in more personnel by serving as consultants to the critical adults in children's lives. Brief interviews with parents and teachers, for example, can provide concrete life instances of test performance as well as the opportunity for mutual development of specific suggestions for these persons. Perhaps we could extend Brown's (1975) procedure of bringing parents into the assessment setting to participate in administering tests. We might train groups of parents to participate in the assessment process at home. Behavior modifiers are doing this now in a specialized way. Besides being time saving and relevant, such procedures go a long way toward returning responsibility and initiative to parents and children. Again, I believe that we are obliged to present fellow workers, the public, and our legislatures with piloted alternative practices and conceptions, with specific suggestions for implementing them. Granted, the changes suggested above require greater skill and reflection than does score-oriented testing but no more than should be expected of a professional. Nor have I encountered any competent students or professionals who have been unable to develop such practices, albeit usually with considerable *initial* time-consuming struggle with the problems of working efficiently while still respecting the individuality and complexity of the child.

Before concluding this section I shall single out for comment the dilemma concerning screening. Despite a historical sense of how we have gotten ourselves into our current binds, I am repeatedly amazed at how blind we have been to the manufactured nature of our tests and to the restrictive, destructive effects of behaving as though these tests were handed down to us by a Grand Scientist who constructed them to be appropriate for all humans at all times. In particular, I am amazed at the continuation of testing programs that have been clearly demonstrated as inappropriate for certain minorities. At the very least, professionals are responsible, as individuals and as associations, for keeping up with research and issues and for refusing to carry out testing programs that both science and ethics present as deleterious to the child. After all, courts and legislatures traditionally have respected the authority of professionals when the latter have presented a unified opinion.

I have often found that as long as I presented useful data and suggestions, even as an individual, many situations have not required scores and sometimes not even categories. When all efforts to change another worker's overreliance on scores to the detriment of the child have failed, I have found that personal, direct proposals to take the problem to our area's peer standards review committee have sent the offender to our assorted standards publications for clarification. In the process he discovers that technological efficiency is not adequate to assure professional and ethical comportment, and change ensues. However, I should acknowledge that my interventions have been effective partially because of my reputation as a person familiar with developments in research and standards and involved in my professional association's governance.

If this sounds a bit abstract, let me remind the reader that Mercer (1973, 1975) showed how California Chicano children have been shunted into relatively unstimulating classes for the retarded on the basis of IQs, even though most of these same children were found to be functioning at nonretarded levels when evaluated in their communities. Also, until recently, deaf children were expected to be intellectually below average. Today, they are not, and the total dynamics of their language disabilities are more fully understood and handled. Other handicapped children continue to be misassessed. For example, boys with Duchenne muscular dystrophy are frequently diagnosed as retarded when, in fact, they may be reflecting a limited learning environment or reacting to the emotional components of the disease. Even when the dystrophy diagnosis has been made, the psychological assessment too often neglects to explore the related dynamics. Perhaps, as we look beyond scores to the complexities of the overall life situation, we may discover that the historical supposition that Duchenne dystrophy boys can be expected to be intellectually deficient has been in error. At least we should not assume reduced mental functioning to be a component of the dystrophy before we discover the etiology of the disease itself.

There are two points in these examples: (1) Test conditions are necessarily artificial and may have little bearing on the profundity of a child's resources or on his effectiveness in his everyday life. (2) The American Association on Mental Deficiency (AAMD) and many state standards formally require that adaptive social and emotional accomplishment be included in determination of retardation. We know this, but often practice as though we do not, despite well-publicized articles such as Bersoff's (1973) presenting rationale and procedures for psychosituational assessment. Through our IQ-oriented technology, we have created and perpetuated many cases of retardation. To function as mere technicians is not only unethical; it is destructive.

In sum, although I may have to work within restrictive policies or laws for a while, I insist upon deabsolutizing scores by such practices as adding clarifying life events to the record or even exchanging scores for life events alone. Meanwhile, I work with colleagues to develop systemwide alternatives that meet the spirit of regulations and thus allow the latter to be changed. Efficiency and scientific form are not worthwhile in themselves; we are better off without them if they are not in the service of children's individual welfare and growth.

Procedures that work against the best interest of the child as an individual are unethical. Standardized testing can work against the child; it becomes unethical when scores are taken as more real than daily behaviors and experience and when these are presented as though they were independent of dimensions such as cultural values, historical context of test construction, the specialized, contrived nature of testing, the personality of the tester, and the child's sense of the situation. The danger is that scores will be seen as underlying causes rather than as being extracted aspects of the child's complex, total existence and that they will thus be taken as levels of capacity rather than as sampled areas for investigation or encouragement.

The dilemmas presented in this chapter showed workers caught between older traditions and emerging changes in our understandings of science and social responsibility. Ethical resolutions are ones that acknowledge new developments and that strive to develop practical procedures based on those developments.

My own resolutions involved acknowledging the inevitable human involvement in testing and encouraging innovative intervention in the interest of service to the individual. All of these resolutions in one way or another rejected subservience of the assessor to tests and sought to promote recognition of the child's life events as the primary data and concern.

Case Presentation for Problem Solving

For years, the teachers, counselors, and school psychologists of the Dobson School system had been distressed that students could continue even as far as high school before finally being identified as developmentally disabled. It was not just that these youngsters had been deprived of special instruction that could have helped them to benefit much more from their school years; perhaps more disturbing was that family, teachers, and peers had assumed that these youngsters were simply stupid or, more often, that they were lazy or otherwise perversely motivated not to learn. Worse, these students often wondered if such assumptions might be true. They developed assorted defenses that were not particularly adaptive either to school or later life: They became class clowns. They disdained academics. They associated with dropouts and delinquents.

Although the problem diminished somewhat after inservice training was provided by the community mental health consultation and education service, it persisted. So the Dobson Schools leaped at an opportunity for preschool screening even though the federal funds covered only the hiring of one school psychologist who was to screen kindergartners and follow up questionable cases with further evaluation himself.

John Ockar was hired as the screener. He constructed a behavioral check list for preschool teachers and aides, emphasizing attention span, ability to follow directions, motor skills, counting and color naming, and peer relations. He mailed these out to the teachers with instructions to collect a human drawing from each child, and to feel free to add comments or to call him for clarification.

Five-and-a-half-year-old Joanna Pace was selected for follow-up. The teacher explained to Mrs. Pace that Mr. Ockar had noted remarks about Joanna's fast tempo and roughhouse ways and, in combination with her self-drawing, which included a furry puppy – indicating needs for warmth and security – he had felt that perhaps Joanna would not be ready for first grade. Both the teacher and the Paces were a bit dubious but agreed that the best thing was to give permission for the follow-up testing.

About a month later, Mrs. Pace asked Joanna if she had yet taken the tests from Mr. Ockar. Joanna said she didn't think so, although a man had taken her to another room "to play some games." But he did not really play and even slapped her hand away from his box of toys. She had become frightened and was glad to get back to her room. Mrs. Pace then obtained Mr. Ockar's number from the teacher and left messages for him to call. Two weeks later, the secretary called with an apology from Mr. Ockar, whose testing schedule of twenty children per week had not yet allowed parent conferences. The next day Mrs. Pace called back to request a change in her scheduled meeting, which had turned out to conflict with a dental appointment. In turn, Mr. Ockar's secretary later requested a second change since he would be on the other side of the county that day. While waiting for a return call of suggested times that would meet her schedule, Mrs. Pace complained of the situation during her psychotherapy session. Her psychiatrist suggested that, as a mental health professional, he could request a copy of the report, which he could then interpret for her. After his review of the report, the psychiatrist pronounced it incompetent and recommended that the Paces make arrangements for a private evaluation. He sent the report to Dr. Irene Taylor, a psychologist. The report:

> *Tests*: Bender-Gestalt, House–Tree–Person, Rorschach, Wide Range Achievement Test. *Intelligence Test:* Stanford-Binet, Form L-M.
>
> *Results: Binet: CA: 5–11, MA: 5–5, IQ: 91. The building principal should make this report available for the information of other concerned school personnel. Special care should be taken in orally interpreting report information*

> *to parents. Under no circumstances should the report be given or read to the parents. Mental ability may be explained in general terms (above or below average, etc.) but no specific MA or IQ should be given.*
>
> *Joanna is currently in kindergarten and scholastic progress has been slow. Reaction time to directions is slow. The child appears to be unhappy and expressionless. This evaluation is part of preschool readiness testing to determine feasibility for entrance into first grade.*
>
> *The Stanford-Binet Intelligence Scale, Form L-M was administered to Joanna at this time. She passed all items at year level 4–6 and failed all items at year level 7–0. This gave her a mental age of 5–5 at this time. This certainly appears to be sufficient mental capability for entrance into first grade.*
>
> *On the Wide Range Achievement Test Joanna had extreme difficulty in identifying letters of the alphabet. It is also noted that Joanna had extreme difficulty in speech with certain sounds. She had difficulty responding verbally to the examiner, and she looked somewhat anemic. I noticed that she bites her fingernails. Her reproductions on the Bender-Gestalt for young children appeared extremely poor. This would tend to support visual discrimination problems at this time. It was also noticed that on several occasions Joanna had a nervous twitch of the eyes.*
>
> *Joanna is an extremely large child and repeat of kindergarten would not appear to be in the interest of this child socially. Although she obtained a mental age of 5–5 and is eligible for entrance to first grade, it is felt that she will continue to have learning problems in first grade. Nonetheless, I am recommending entrance to first grade.*
>
> *A parent interview was required in this case so as to assess background information, both socially and medically. Parents could not come in at this time for an interview. Some resistance on the parents' part was encountered here.*
>
> *John W. Ockar, M. Ed.*
> *Clinical Psychologist*

In October, Dr. Taylor met with Joanna for two-and-a-half hours, during which she repeated the Bender, drawings, and WRAT, and substituted the Wechsler scales for the Stanford-Binet. Joanna scored well within the average range on the WISC and on the reading and spelling portions of the WRAT. She was below first grade level on arithmetic. Her WISC scores and Bender-Gestalt figures vacillated; for example, the former varied between four- and eight-year-old levels. She appeared neither anemic nor large. The referral section of the four-page (single spaced) report included the following: "However, Dr. Meyer [psychiatrist] felt that the report's brevity rendered its predominantly negative and finalistic tone misleading to those who might have had prior hopes of helping Joanna to develop fully. Hence, at Dr. Meyer's suggestion, Mrs. Pace requested that I attempt a fuller psychological evaluation – hopefully one that might provide some understanding of the ways in which Joanna functions rather than primarily reporting her levels of achievement. Presumably, such an understanding would go beyond the prior prediction that 'she will continue to have learning problems in the first grade,' to suggest a basis from which parents and teachers might better aid Joanna's development."

The report went on to describe the ways in which Joanna had gone about working on the tests. An excerpt from "Conclusions":

> *"Thus, although she scores predominantly in the average range on the intelligence and achievement tests, it appears that there is indeed cause for concern about Joanna's future progress in school. Specifically, her current ways of handling new demands drastically curtail learning. She seems to vacillate between two extremes of an activity-passivity continuum: when passive, she withdraws from the new task, refusing to try herself out; when active, she turns her attention away from the problem and involves herself instead with familiar things. Neither course is conducive to learning, especially learning of school-type concepts and reasoning. Joanna's difficulty with arithmetic may be an example." The concluding paragraph began: "Although this report has thus far focused primarily on the youngster's difficulties, it is obvious that they are the reverse side of otherwise promising gumption, assertiveness and sensitivity to others."*

Concrete suggestions for working with Joanna followed.

Both Mr. and Mrs. Pace met with Dr. Taylor, each reading a copy of the report, which included illustrations of the assessment activities but on which IQs had been blocked out. They requested that copies be sent to Dr. Meyer and to Joanna's past and present schools. Six months later, a telephone follow-up indicated that Joanna was in her class' accelerated reading group, keeping up in arithmetic, and being a bit of a *Peanuts* Lucy with her peers but otherwise doing well socially.

In the meantime Dr. Taylor had enquired informally of colleagues in one of the local university's school psychology programs whether they knew of John Ockar (they did not) and whether school psychologists could refer to themselves as "clinical psychologists" (at that time they could if they wished). She debated going to the director of school psychology in the public schools to discuss Ockar's report which she saw as incompetent and destructive. Eventually, she decided just to hope that through her report personnel in the two schools would be alerted to future incidents and would manage to inform the right people about this one. She was fearful that, as a newcomer to town and as a clinical rather than a school psychologist, any personal action at this point could be resented and might jeopardize her later professional relations. In later years, she felt that her judgment had been correct but her decision wrong.

Some questions that could be asked in this case presentation are: (1) How would you have handled Mr. Ockar's responsibilities for screening and follow-up? (2) What are your reactions to Mr. Ockar's report? (3) What do you think of the excerpts from Dr. Taylor's report? (4) If you were Dr. Taylor, would you have contacted Mr. Ockar? Would you have contacted the kindergarten teacher or the principal? If so, what would be your reasoning in each case? (5) Would you have given the parents the IQs in the conference if you were Dr. Taylor? (6) What is your evaluation of Dr. Taylor's handling of the issue of the competency of Mr. Ockar? What are the various factors you would take into consideration?

Note

1 Copyright 1978 by Judith Mearig. Reproduced with permission from Sandra Mills. The official citation that should be used in referencing this material is: Fischer, C. T. (1978). Dilemmas in standardized testing. In J. Mearig (Ed.). *Working for Children: Ethical issues beyond professional guidelines* (pp. 115–134). San Francisco: Jossey-Bass.

References

Bersoff, D. N. (1973). Silk purses into sows' ears: The decline of psychological testing and a suggestion for its redemption. *American Psychologist*, *28*, 892–899.

Brown, L. K. (1975). Family dialectics in a clinical context. *Human Development*, *18*, 223–238.

Hobbs, N. (Ed.) (1975). *The future of children: Recommendations of the project on classification of exceptional children.* San Francisco: Jossey-Bass.

Mercer, J. R. (1973). *Labeling the mentally retarded child.* Berkeley: University of California Press.

Mercer, J. R. (1975). Psychological assessment and the rights of children. In N. Hobbs (Ed.) *Issues in the classification of exceptional children* (Vol. 1.) San Francisco: Jossey-Bass.

Palmer, J. O. (1970). *The psychological assessment of children.* New York: Wiley.

Sattler, J. (1974). *Assessment of children's intelligence and special abilities.* Boston: Allyn & Bacon.

CHAPTER 7

INDIVIDUALIZED ASSESSMENT AND PHENOMENOLOGICAL PSYCHOLOGY[1]

How might we go about retaining the particularity of a client as we assess him or her in terms of standard deviations, diagnostic categories, and environmental contingencies? How might we make assessment directly relevant to treatment, placement, and the client's personal interests? Perhaps we could do this by setting as our goal an understanding of and intervention with the client in terms of his or her own life. But then how shall we do this in a systematic and valid way?

Increasingly, clinicians are involving clients more directly in assessment and planning, and they are developing more person-specific or at least more behavioural recommendations. Recent revisions in the "individual differences" field explicitly address the particularity and agency of the person, albeit at an academic level (see Korchin, 1976; Sundberg, 1977; Tyler, 1978). Too often, however, applied efforts have been haphazard, inconsistent, or incomplete. And no wonder: clinicians are left on their own to integrate whatever still makes sense in our psychoanalytic heritage with the practical successes of objective personality and abilities assessment, and more recently with behavioral approaches. In clinical practice, efforts to assess what it is like to be a particular client and to respect that person's self-responsibility, for the most part have been loosely tied to humanistic and commonsense attitudes.

This article presents rudiments of a philosophy of science that can ground individualized assessment. Specifically, some major themes of phenomenological philosophy as they are relevant to psychology's foundations are introduced, albeit briefly and in invitational rather than expository form. Then established individualized practices (see Fischer, 1969, 1970, 1973a, 1973b, 1974, 1976a, 1978a, 1978b, & 1978c) are reviewed with allusions to the theoretical themes. Phenomenological psychology as such is not necessary for all practices of individualized assessment, but it has in fact been the route by which these relatively thoroughgoing innovations were developed. Some such notions about the nature of knowledge and of human functioning do seem necessary if we are to be empirical, systematic, and helpful to the client as an individual.

Phenomenological Psychology

European phenomenology was conceived by its major contemporary authors, Husserl (1962/1913) and Heidegger (1962/1926) as a critical discipline – a study of foundations underlying all philosophy and science. In particular they held all knowledge to be contingent – inextricably dependent upon the method of study and mode of understanding. Truth, then, is intersubjective – the interface of multiple, indeed infinite, presences to an event. Hence it is deemed crucial that descriptions of an event include information about the observer's mode of presence. The observer also attempts to acknowledge and put aside his prior understandings so that the event may be seen as much as possible free of assumptions and conceptions. Phenomenology is the study of ("ology") such appearances (phenomena). Phenomena may then be reflected upon in terms of assorted systems and disciplines. However, at that point we are well aware, for example, that although we can mathematize events, they are not primordially quantitative.

Note that in North America this is not what usually is meant by phenomenology. Perhaps our lay version should be called "phenomenalism" – an interest in a person's experience in its own right. *Philosophical* phenomenology is interested in specific appearances only insofar as invariant aspects of consciousness in general can be identified. Such description of consciousness is seen as necessary for understanding how scholars and scientists participate in the development of knowledge. Phenomenological *psychology* is not so much interested in a philosophy of consciousness as it is in a comprehension of experience as it is lived – existentially/behaviorally/reflectively.

Faithful descriptions of particular kinds of experiences (e.g., being anxious) can be researched for their common structure. Such research findings can be most helpful to the assessor or therapist who compares them with his own "direct" impressions of a client. These descriptions, both research and clinical, are radically empirical in that they come as close as possible to presenting direct experience of an event (rather than indirect measures or conceptual abstractions), and in that the observer's interest in and approach to the event are specified, again as much as possible. Readers of such descriptions thus are provided with relatively full access to what happened. (See Giorgi, Fischer, & von Eckartsberg, 1971; Giorgi, Fischer, & Murray, 1975, for examples of research and clinical applications.)

Phenomenological psychology's descriptions and analyses in one way or another rediscover the inevitability of what has been called situated intentionality. "Intentionality" here does imply the everyday sense of purposiveness; we do live any circumstance partly in terms of its implications for our future. However, intentionality also refers to the (differentiable but) unitary character of the person "and" his world as he lives it. That is, consciousness, whether figuratively bodily or cognitive, "intends," "has in mind," is directed toward, a meaningful world rather than merely being impinged upon by external (or mediated) stimuli. Intentionality is another way of referring to the intrinsic mutuality of the seer/seen.

"Situated" (in "situated intentionality") is a qualifier referring to our finitude, our always experiencing "and" behaving in accordance with our situation – our very particular biological/interpersonal/biographical/cultural circumstances. Contrary to popular misconceptions, the existential implication here is that freedom *is* constrained by the way a person lives his or her situation as well as by physical contingencies.

For the purposes of this article, situated intentionality serves as individualized assessment's general point of departure from customary practices. We will see in the assessment section below that this also implies a hermeneutic, dialectical, and structural approach. For now I want to indicate that phenomenological psychology's approach is structural in several of the usual meanings. Whether as individuals, researchers, or clinicians, when we put aside for the moment our theories and categories, whatever we experience is already patterned, unified, whole. No one of its differentiable aspects is more primary; all are essential to that particular phenomenon, and all imply the whole. Any change is also a change of the structure. However, this approach is more radically structural than, for example, Piaget's structuralism or general systems theory in that here a phenomenon already includes the person's lived relation to his world. Here, there is no separate world requiring processing or reaction by the structure.

The individualized assessment practices reviewed below do not appear in the writings of phenomenological theoreticians; they are one application of philosophical foundations. This writer's conceptions and practices have been influenced most by, but do not necessarily adhere to, the writings of Merleau-Ponty (e.g., 1962, 1968, 1975). One could come to a similar place via other process or co-constitution philosophies (e.g., those of Cassirer, Langer, Polonyi, Toulmin, Whitehead), but as it happens it is human–science psychology (i.e., as broader than natural science, and as founded in phenomenology; see Giorgi, 1970) that thus far has been developed most radically in both theory and practice. ("Co-constitute" refers to that mutual participation of seer/seen. It may also refer to the multi-perspectival make-up of truth. It is generally meant to connote process as well as outcome, a synergetic dialectic rather than linearity, interaction, or synthesis of opposites.)

Individualized Assessment

The following practices are not merely conjectural. They have been developed, carried-out, and taught for about ten years. They have proven viable for a wide range of student assessors, colleagues, clients, and settings. I will present the practices roughly in their clinical order, with their overlapping principles being repeated in various forms. First I *contextualize the referral.* That is, I do not act as though there were a universal referent for the referral abstractions (e.g., "test for IQ," "evaluate suicide potential," "determine extent of organic dysfunction"). Instead I go directly to the referring person (whether another professional or the self-referred client) and inquire about the decisions facing him/her, the concrete events that led to that dilemma, and the particular meanings to him/her of the referral categories. During this discussion we often discover that the dilemma is an artifact of objectivistic thinking (e.g., "is the client *really* a this *or* that?"). To de-reify such conceptions, we explore the contexts in which a troublesome behavior both has and has not occurred, and we try to get in touch with the context as seen by the client and the involved others – including professionals. Thus "testing for IQ" would become an investigation of the client's experience of situations in which he or she has been relatively effective and ineffective, of the involved others' perceptions of these situations, and of the assessor's sense of how the client approaches and moves through these occasions. In this way, we take into account that even the referral focus is already co-constituted by the professionals and the client, always in the context of personal, social, and scientific values.

The client is an *informed participant* right from the beginning. I do not try to present a standardized "blank slate" or "stimulus condition" through which the client presumably will inadvertently reveal his or her true self. Rather, after asking for a clarification of the events and circumstances that led up to the referral, I share what I know of the referring person's concerns and rationale, as well as what I see as the implications of our upcoming assessment. As this joint exploration continues, I not only acknowledge but also utilize the client's inevitable meaning-giving to our situation, and I become more keenly aware of my own (also inevitable) participation in the assessment outcome. Each of us becomes better attuned to our responsibility for our own choices, however limited they are.

Throughout the assessment process, it is *life events that are primary data.* In contrast to traditional practice, test scores are secondary, derived data. Test scores, categories, and diagnoses are abstractions from particular actions, and these abstractions already are grounded in assumptions about the orderliness of human affairs. Thus to test for IQ typically has been to look for the degree of underlying ability that accounts for current achievement and allows us to predict future accomplishment. I would say that when we test for IQ in that way we have forgotten that Binet originally selected items for his test in order to sample particular achievements that were requisite to further academic development. From my perspective, the client's accomplishment with an intelligence test is an instance of his/her coping with academically oriented tasks; this particular achievement does not underlie other instances.

True, to make use of primary data, the assessor does interpret, but does so *hermeneutically*, *"reading behavior"* for what relevance it might have for clinical concerns. (Hermeneutics is the study of interpretive reading, usually the Bible or other classical texts. It is a study that is aware of how its questions foreshadow its discoveries. It asks not "the real" meaning of a text, but rather, what is that reality with which both the earlier author and we are in touch? How can that author's work from an earlier time throw light on today's efforts to comprehend an age-old phenomenon?) The assessor reads in a way that general understandings are modified while "listening" actively to this particular client's situation – the meanings, projects, and limitations through which the now-focal behaviour evolved. During this reading the assessor is attuned to more than what is literally present; through my own biography I am in touch with variations of the client's experienced demands, invitations, hopes, obstacles, and so on. Concretely, the "suicidal" client's slouch and downcast gaze speak into not only my past experiences with such persons but also into times in my own life when I have approximated such postures. Since all knowledge occurs through biographical presence, rather than try to "control out" such personal meanings, I try to make explicit use of them – both for understanding and for engaging the client.

My difference from mainstream approaches here is that I do not make a firm separation of this so-called clinical art from scientific psychology. As I see it, to be effective, a particular personal access ("art") must be recognized as such and be critically examined to determine with what it is in touch (e.g., is the client resigned, indifferent, depressed, or despairing?). Part of this examination is a reflection into formal, consensual (scientific) knowledge; even my personal history through which I am present to clients includes my training in theory, conceptions, research findings, controversies. "Objective" tests, data, criteria, and conclusions are consensual but also unavoidably grounded in historicity, situatedness, perspectivity, etc. Being explicit about this man-made character of science helps me from lapsing uncritically back into the "natural attitude" – in which we view events as being "out there," independent of our perception. More specifically, being circumspect about the origins of science helps me to avoid slipping into anonymous opinion, absolute statements, unsituated conclusions, and deference to presumably immutable laws of nature. Thus, even after consulting an MMPI profile, a Rorschach summary sheet, and assorted norms, I do not come up with a yes-no conclusion or even a statistical probability of suicide. Instead, I go on to specify what I know of the personal and environmental circumstances in which the client could commit suicide, I describe in what ways those circumstances already exist, and I suggest changes that could move the client out of suicidal circumstances. This assessment process, although utilizing diverse research and theory, ends with primary data (slumped posture, present home situation, etc.). These data have been refined and understood through reflection on biographical touchpoints and on formal literature, but this interpretation was not a transformation into a different level of reality; there was no reduction to either psychologisms or to natural forces.

Other aspects of phenomenologically informed assessment are its *collaborative and interventional* thrusts. When possible, the client works with the psychologist ("co-labors") to differentiate the "whens" and "when-nots" of experiaction. (The term "experiaction" [from von Eckartsberg (1971)] expresses the originary unity of experience "and" action. Although these aspects of a whole are differentiable, they are not separate prior to reflection.) For example, a brain-damaged patient acknowledges that he feels "safe" while drawing the Bender designs down the extreme edge of the paper – just like following the order provided by this morning routine at home. We discover that it is when he envisions being someplace that he used to get to automatically, but now does not see a concrete, serial route to, that he becomes profoundly unrealistic and/or distressed. Note that these differentiations include not only the physical environment but also the ways the client experiences "and" shapes the world while moving through it in unique ways. Admittedly the psychologist cannot actually experience the client's world; to some degree one is always left to imagine what it must be like. Moreover, often the client cannot reflect or verbalize effectively (for our purposes). Nevertheless, to whatever extent possible, the client should help in this exploration.

One reason for this emphasis on collaboration is that experience (the world as it is lived) is not merely the product of ecobiological processes; it participates in, and is essential to, the complete structure of being human. In particular, intervention into the client's lived world can be transformative of the entire structure (physical/biological/intentional). Indeed, the client's collaborative participation in the assessment already is a movement toward greater confidence and self-direction, albeit within physical/biological constraints. In other words, even standardized assessment solicits a particular involvement on the client's part, and in that way influences the latter's conduct and sense of self. Phenomenologically grounded assessment acknowledges this inevitable involvement and uses it constructively. Thus the brain-damaged patient and I practiced with the WAIS Block Designs until he began to recognize the feeling of leaping unrealistically toward finishing; at those times we then practiced looking back to a concrete starting place. This exploration, therefore, is not only an assessment of present status but also of viable alternatives.

The earlier example of the brain-damaged patient's Bender-Gestalt illustrates another theme of phenomenological assessment: *test activity serves as a lived metaphor* for structurally similar past events. In a sense, the patient's sticking to the paper's margin "is" his following a laid-out morning routine. Living out the assessment task renders taken-for-granted everyday events available for sharing and for examination of their common constituents and context. But the assessor does not look for "underlying" traits or for interactions among perception, affect, and behavior. To the contrary, the terms "structure" and "metaphor" are meant to evoke a sense of indivisible wholeness, in which any change is a transformation of the distinguishable constituents as well as of the whole; there is no "element" or "variable" that is more essential or primary than the others. The relation of the two terms of the metaphor is not one of logic or of actual identity; rather, the metaphor "Bender behavior 'is' morning routine" jars one out of such analytic modes into one in which the unitariness of perception "and" meaning/affect is experienced immediately. This comprehension is certainly less clear-cut and efficient than that of traditional partitive analysis, but it is true to life as lived – that realm in which the client can recognize the landmarks and changes in terrain that call for shifts in his course. What's more, this recognition does not have to rely on specifiable insight or cognitive articulation; it can be effective as a lived recognition.

Another way of saying this is that *comportment through tests provides access to process*. Here, "process" refers to the evolution of a physically visible outcome ("end product"). This process is a dialectical one in which the person shapes "and" is shaped by the world while moving through it. I refer to this sedimented yet creative response to the world's solicitation/repulsion as "style" – the particular way in which an individual, in a particular situation, is at once shaping/shaped. In the assessment situation, we observe together how the client moves through "and" differentiates the terrain which I present. The tracks across the Bender page are a record of the outcome. But I also have access to the history, orientation, projects, solicitations, etc. out of which the visible behavior and tracks take shape if I watch the client moving through the task, myself anticipating intimations of the person's lived world. More concretely: while watching the brain-damaged patient carefully follow the instructions inherent in the order of the page's edge, as well as those inherent in my successive presentation of stimulus cards, I had a sense of his world being one without a planned future; it was a world limited to the present. Then while he was working on the Blocks, I became attuned to an impatient, then anxiously uncertain quality to his movements, which eventually became a flipping of the blocks at random with the patient grandly saying that he could "make them easy." I could now see what I might describe as a living toward what still feels at first like a familiar, reasonable, taken-for-granted future, but one that then unaccountably resists reasonable effort, and becomes a future gamely but desperately related to through an old role ("I can make them easy") even as the future begins to loom now as catastrophic.

Note that the above "lived world" and "style," akin in many ways to what is called the "life of the unconscious" by the psychodynamic tradition, are both available and critical for helping the client to help himself or herself to traverse the terrain in a modified way. If we can momentarily bypass the scientistic tradition of seeing the person and environment as separate and as interacting in a chronological chain of finished events, then we can literally see with a different vision. This nonobjectifying vision is an opening into an orderly realm, but one in which the particular viewer's and subject's perspectives and involvement are integral.

This leads to the next theme of phenomenologically grounded assessment, that of its *descriptions being representational*. Specifically, in my assessment report, I describe the client by representing samples of physically visible incidents accompanied by a description of my own access to the incidents. "My own access" is my particular biographical presence, interest, approaches, etc. For example, I might say, "When I sat back and stared at Edward, somewhat in the manner of a stern teacher, his posture stiffened in what I took as defensive defiance." This description is one of "contextualized primary data," and is intended, among other things, to attune the reader to the previously invisible – the style of the client's evolving course. A practical implication is that all the client's involved others have access to the same primary data and style, and thus can deal directly with the client and with one another in terms of life events rather than in terms of abstractions and objectifications. The client can also read this sort of report and meaningfully offer comments on it.

Note also that when data are actual events as seen from a particular (specified) perspective, readers quickly can determine their degree of confidence in the report by how well they recognize it as another profile of the client as they have seen this person (or will later). Inter-subjective recognition is a strong form of empirical validity.

A disclaimer: although the assessor's description is an outcome of one's own shaping/shaped relation with the client, and is thus perspectival, none of this is to be taken as license for undisciplined subjectivity. To be valid, the description must be capable of holding up as a perspectival variation of what can be seen by any others who sincerely observe the client's comportment. Indeed, readers familiar with the client should discover what they already knew prereflectively.

A second disclaimer: The competent clinician, no matter how sophisticated about phenomenology, is conversant with natural-science clinical research, practices, and conceptions. Such a practicing clinician is a human-science psychologist, that is, one whose philosophical and research approach is phenomenological, but who fully recognizes the essential participation of environment and neurophysiology in human affairs. Thus one sees worth to classifying persons, for example, as "OBS," "process schizophrenic," or "major affective disorder," provided that such diagnosis does not substitute for individualized, collaboratively interventional assessment.

A final theme: throughout: this presentation, I have regarded *structural description as explanatory*. That is, rather than search for underlying personality variables or environmental contingencies to explain a given state of affairs, I describe what I can of that state of affairs' holistic whatness, including its process of coming about. Whatever history is operative is in the present (even though looking into the past can help us to have a feel for that present). Similarly, the role of the neurochemical/physiological order is that of participation in the present structural whole, rather than simply that of cause or even of mediation. Human processes cannot be reduced to the physiological order; medical specialists, for example, know the seriousness of doing surgery on the heart of the man whose wife has just died in contrast to the heart of the man who is planning his daughter's wedding. Nevertheless, I quickly acknowledge that to the extent that a client's functioning is constricted to the physiological order, to that same extent the assessor's efforts to be psychologically collaborative and interventional are limited.

The difference that makes a difference between reductive and structural explanation is that the latter remains open to "the possible," while the former restricts itself to "the necessary" – the irrevocably determined. By remaining open to the influential participation of intentionality, we do sacrifice the apparent neatness of the natural sciences; however, we gain not only in attunement to specifically human possibility, but in comprehensiveness, in depth, and in respect for the ambiguity within order.

Concluding Comments

It is true that many mainstream psychologists do carry out some of the above practices even while not making them thematic. Phenomenological psychology as such is not essential for these procedures. But without the support of its explicit grounding and its insistence on what I have called primary data, clinicians have been seen as loosely subjective or as merely conducting the art side of psychology. And from my point of view they have not been consistent or properly reflective in their practice. In contrast, a thoroughgoing phenomenologically grounded human-science approach can provide a truly effective integration of (a) the practitioner's sensitivity to the client as individual and as intentional, with (b) the scientist's concern for empirical criteria, consensual judgment, and explication of lawfulness. This integration similarly can be a meeting ground for behavioral and psychodynamic psychologies. It also suggests a transcendence of the scientist-professional divisiveness of our clinical training model (see Fischer, 1976b). In short, it seems to me that phenomenological psychology offers a critical touchpoint for further development of human-science individualized practices and theory.

Note

1 Originally published as: Fischer, C. T. (1979). Individualized assessment and phenomenological psychology. *Journal of Personality Assessment*, *43*, 115–122.

References

Fischer, C. T. (1969). Intelligence defined as effectiveness of approaches. *Journal of Consulting and Clinical Psychology*, *33*, 668–674.

Fischer, C. T. (1970). The testee as co-evaluator. *Journal of Counseling Psychology*, *17*, 70–76.

Fischer, C. T. (1973a.) Contextual approach to assessment. *Community Mental Health Journal*, *9*, 38–45.

Fischer, C. T. (1973b). Intelligence contra IQ: A human-science critique and alternative to the natural science approach to man. *Human Development*, *16*, 8–20. (Also in R. F. Riegel (Ed.), *Intelligence: Alternative views of a paradigm*. Basel, Switzerland: S. Karger, 1974.)

Fischer, C. T. (1974). Exit IQ: Enter the child. In G. Williams & S. Gordon (Eds.), *Clinical child psychology: Current practices and future perspectives* (pp. 333–348). New York: Behavioral Publications.

Fischer, C. T. (1976a). Psychological assessment of Lawrence Holderin. In N. Tallent, *Psychological report writing*. New York: Prentice-Hall.

Fischer, C. T. (1976b). Undercutting the scientist-professional dichotomy: The reflective psychologist. *The Clinical Psychologist*, *29*, 5–7.

Fischer, C. T. (1978a). Collaborative psychological assessment. In C. T. Fischer & S. L. Brodsky (Eds.), *Client participation in human services: The Prometheus principle* (pp. 41–61). New Brunswick, N. J.: Transaction.

Fischer, C. T. (1978b). Dilemmas in standardized testing. In J. Mearig (Ed.), *Working for children: Ethical issues beyond professional guidelines* (pp. 115–134). San Francisco: Jossey-Bass.

Fischer, C. T. (1978c). Personality and assessment. In R. Valle & M. King (Eds.), *Existential-phenomenological alternatives for psychology* (pp. 203–231). New York: Oxford University Press.

Giorgi, A. (1970). *Psychology as a human science: A phenomenologicaly-based approach*. New York: Harper & Row.

Giorgi, A., Fischer, W. F. & von Eckartsberg, R. (1971). (Eds.). *Duquesne studies in phenomenological psychology* (Vol. 1). Pittsburgh: Duquesne University Press.

Giorgi, A., Fischer, C. T. & Murray. E. L. (1975). (Eds.). *Duquesne studies in phenomenological psychology* (Vol. 2). Pittsburgh: Duquesne University Press.

Heidegger, M. (1962). *Being and time*. New York: Harper & Row. (Originally published 1926.)

Husserl, E. (1962). *Ideas: General introduction to pure phenomenology*. London: Collier. (Originally published 1913.)

Korchin, S. J. (1976). *Modern clinical psychology: Principles of intervention in the clinic and community*. New York: Basic Books.

Merleau-Ponty, M. (1962). *Phenomenology of perception*. New York: Humanities Press.

Merleau-Ponty, M. (1968). *The visible and the invisible*. Evanston: Northwestern University Press.

Merleau-Ponty, M. (1973). *The prose of the world*. Evanston: Northwestern University Press.

Sundberg, N. D. (1977). *Assessment of persons*. Englewood Cliffs, N. J.: Prentice-Hall.

Tyler, L. E. (1978). *Individuality: Human possibilities and personal choice in the psychological development of men and women*. San Francisco: Jossey-Bass.

Von Eckartsberg, R. (1971). On experiential methodology. In A. Giorgi, W. F. Fischer & R. von Eckartsberg (Eds.), *Duquesne studies in phenomenological psychology* (Vol. 1) (pp. 66–79). Pittsburgh: Duquesne University Press.

CHAPTER 8

INTIMACY IN ASSESSMENT[1]

The personal and interpersonal character of most therapies has long been acknowledged. It is understood that in one manner or another the therapist participates in the ways clients change their lives. Intimacy, albeit of a specialized sort, is assumed, and its positive and problematic aspects are addressed in professional training and literature. In contrast, psychological assessment has been more closely grounded in the tradition of laboratory science, the goal being to obtain objective knowledge about a subject's characteristics. Standardization – of materials, instructions, scoring, and interpretation – is meant to control potential variance in findings that would be due either to assessor characteristics or to transactions between assessor and subject. Professional training in assessment therefore emphasizes standardized procedures. For example, rapport is addressed not as an interpersonal relationship, but as a condition that results in optimal test output. Although test findings may be regarded as presenting a penetrating, and in this sense intimate, portrait, intimacy as a relationship is not often associated with assessment.

There are, of course, many exceptions to this laboratory tradition of assessment. But either they are aligned in spirit with the laboratory model or they are not formalized nor sanctioned as alternatives. For example, there are studies reporting that self-disclosure on an interviewer's part results in increased disclosures from clients. But the framework remains one of manipulating stimuli in order to affect client output; the relationship between persons remains within the laboratory model. Another example is the widespread use of projective techniques, which are frequently castigated as insufficiently objective. Nevertheless, even if sometimes not meeting rigorous standards, these techniques too have been administered to elicit responses that are to be interpreted unilaterally in accordance with the assessor's statistical, clinical, and theoretical norms. True, some clinicians have extended the use of projectives across several sessions, using them as counseling devices or as part of the initiation of therapy. But publications about these practices are infrequent, and the practices are not regarded as belonging to the realm of assessment. A final apparent exception to the laboratory model of assessment is the increase during the 1970s of articles on "sharing results" with the client. Several factors have coalesced to support this trend: government-mandated access to records, the post-1960s anti-elitism, the influence of humanistic psychology, the decline of the medical model of mental illness, and the emerging dominance of behavioral approaches. Nevertheless this sharing occurs after assessment, not as part of it. The findings were obtained within the laboratory framework. The sharing is either in the form of an explanation of the assessor's findings or, again, as the beginning of counseling or therapy. (See Dana, 1981, for an overview of the literature on these innovations, and for his own method of post-testing but prereport discussion with clients.)

What the laboratory tradition of assessment offers is an opportunity to compare individuals with one another on operationally defined criteria. That is indeed a positive feature of assessment, but it seems to me that assessment can also address individuals idiographically – as individuals – and that these persons can participate directly in the assessment process. That is, they can assist in the discovery and clarification of their previously unthematic goals and fears, their ways of getting to and away from them, the physiognomies of different critical situations, some personally viable alternative routes to goals, and landmarks that can guide them along the way. Such exploration can occur not just through the use of scores, but through joint observation of how the client approaches and copes with test items. Together, client and assessor pursue more effective, personally tailored ways in which the person could achieve his or her goals. This pursuit may involve, for example, practicing ways to pause in order to reflect prior to responding, or perhaps experimenting with ways of not apologizing for answers. Inevitably, who the person sees him- or herself as being comes into play, not just through discovery of habitual patterns of responding but through the search for alternatives that are experienced as personally viable. This individualized assessment is indeed still assessment and not therapy, although it points clearly to the work to be done, and it includes the client as a co-assessor of the specifics of what can and should be done. Collaborative, individualized assessment is obviously more intimate than the laboratory tradition of assessment.

Half of this chapter describes such an individualized approach to assessment. Although a terribly simplified overview, it is presented as a substantial segment of the chapter, both because most readers are not familiar with a formal approach to individualized assessment, and because it is within such a context that "intimacy in assessment" is most likely to occur. It is in the other half of this chapter that intimacy is addressed, but only after descriptions of two other relationships that occur within assessment. These are rapport and privacy. This long route to "intimacy in assessment" seems appropriate, if not necessary, since our laboratory tradition has not equipped us with analyses of the relational nature of the assessor-assessee enterprise. It has instead tried to control it out of relevance. In contrast, an assessment approach that values the perspectival, situational character of fact and truth must look into the nature of the relationships that occur within assessment. It is in terms of these relationships that a client's assessment behaviors arise and should be understood. But we should do more than be mindful of assessment relationships case by case. For example, my own studies of rapport, privacy, and intimacy have resulted in understandings that are contrary to common popular and professional assumptions. Specifically it will be seen later in this chapter that rapport is not a unilaterally manipulated variable, nor is it a complete harmony of pursuit; privacy is neither a guardedness nor a monadal state, and intimacy does not necessarily involve a divulgement nor even a relationship between two lives. It further turns out that within the assessment situation, rapport is necessary for shared privacy, which is necessary for witnessed intimacy.

Collaborative, Individualized Assessment

The purpose of individualized assessment is to tailor assessment procedures, reports, and suggestions to the particular client for the sake of greater client participation, and hence for greater specificity and effectiveness. Many assessors have individualized their practices to some degree, but in the absence of formal guidelines for going beyond standardized procedures, these efforts typically have not been consistent nor thorough. The following guiding principles are intended to encourage development of theory and practices that support extension of traditional assessment into individualized service. These guidelines have been variously described in previous publications (Fischer, 1970, 1973a, 1974, 1976). Their grounding in the European phenomenological philosophy of science, and in Duquesne University's human-science psychology, may be found in Fischer (1973b, 1979, 1980a). Recent concrete examples of practices appear in Fischer (1978a,b). A book-length treatment, including sample reports, is in press. Before overviewing the principles and practices of individualized assessment, however, I should clarify that of course not all assessment requires individualizing. In many instances where individual guidance or intervention are not called for, normative and categorical data are sufficient and appropriate.

The last section of this chapter will present analyses of the above three relational phenomena (rapport, privacy, and intimacy). First, this section will describe an approach to assessment that has turned out to be more personal than has traditional assessment. It is within this revised approach that the significance of the relational phenomena stands out.

Life Events as Primary Data

For individualized assessment, actual life events are the primary data. Test scores are secondary data, derived from test comportment. They, along with constructs and diagnostic categories, are tools, aids to thinking about the client's life. Scores and categories are not the goals or results of individualized assessment. When presumably full assessment reports conclude with secondary data, such as an IQ or a diagnosis of major depression, they are reporting unfinished business. In contrast, for individualized assessment, life events are the point of return as well as the point of departure into testing. The results of individualized assessment are collaboratively developed reunderstandings of those life events, reunderstandings that open the way for the client to move through his or her life in a positively modified way. The testing events serve as immediate referents for client-assessor discussions and exploratory interventions.

Actual comportment is the focus for these discussions and explorations because our comportment is who we are. One's comportment is one's past as it is taken up on the way to one's future. Etiology is not clear in the present alone, but perceptual/affective/cognitive/actional dynamics as they are currently lived are evident in (as) comportment. For example, I conducted a "management appraisal" with Matt Rinald, an entry-level manager who appeared not to be fulfilling his earlier promise as a bright, dedicated candidate for quick promotions. Toward the end of our session, I understood better my first images of 28-year-old, six-foot Matt: He sat across from me, impeccably dressed in a three-piece, well-tailored suit, striped blue and brown tie chosen to blend with both his rust-colored hair and the muted rusts and browns of his suit. His flashing blue-green eyes and decisive hand gestures led me to imagine that when we turned to tests, he would maintain his comfortably alert posture while working energetically and confidently. He had brought a neatly folded list of questions for me to address after our session. As he held the typed list up and then returned it to his suit pocket, I wondered why I didn't feel a bit intimidated, how instead I found his questions about my role and credentials to be sociably pleasant as well as frank. By the end of our time together, we knew that these simple impressions were both an access to and instances of Matt's deepest sense of himself and of his difficulties with his corporation. How that was true is touched upon in the remaining guiding principles.

Tests as Instances of Everyday Challenges

Individually administered testing creates simplified situations like many of those that confront the client elsewhere. Testing does *not* reveal *underlying* traits, tendencies, dynamics, capacities, and so forth; rather, it allows a person's responses to challenges to be witnessed. For example, an intelligence test provides instances of effective problem-solving, not evidence of capacity to solve. Moreover, testing allows both client and assessor to recognize how the client perceives and approaches situations, and how that person works his or her way through them, being affected even while effecting the outcome.

Matt and I had noted that his Bender-Gestalt copies looked surprisingly imprecise and sloppy, even though he had done them quickly and with an air of assuredness. But he had also briefly apologized for asking so many preliminary questions. When I hazarded a guess, Matt ruefully acknowledged that his Bender reproductions had suffered from his efforts to please me by not taking too much time. Following quiet reverie, he then suggested several other instances that he now thought might be similar examples of undermining his work in efforts to please superiors. Later I pointed to Matt's last designs, where distortions had resulted from his shifting lines to avoid coming too close to the figures that had already been drawn. After I asked Matt when else he had "made room" for already established persons by changing his own plans, he exclaimed that now he could see what his immediate superior had meant by "overly accommodating" and "unorganized." Previously these characterizations had puzzled him since he had seen nothing wrong with wanting to please, and he knew that he always started out with a plan in mind.

Thus viewing tests as life situations encourages observation of process, not just of products. That process is also more than a sequence of observable acts. It is the person's cognitive/affective/physical/aware/unaware progress towards goals that are at once sought, habitual, and accidental. Looking together with the assessor at a mundane instance of that progress allows the client to be a co-assessor, to explore differences and similarities with other instances, to delineate differential contexts and outcomes, and to consider alternative comportment. An important aspect of the use of tests for these purposes is that the client not only observes, but experiences his or her *movement* into a problematic outcome. With practice through other instances presented during the assessment, the client begins to learn when to shift course toward more positive outcomes.

To repeat the main theme of this subsection, a test as simple as the Bender can lead to critical change precisely because it is such a simple instance of many challenges. The client can recognize, dwell with, and thematize new ways of comprehending old patterns of life. Matt was amazed as he voiced our discovery: "If you look at it this way, it's my eagerness to please that winds up disappointing people's expectations about my competence. – I think my wife understood something of this even before we were married."

Assessment as Collaborative

As indicated in the above example, when the goal is to clarify the way a client is living his or her life, that person is a key resource. Client and assessor work together (co-labor) to clarify the referral problem, to explore related instances, and to develop and tailor genuinely feasible options for the client. The assessor is the expert on conducting the assessment, on the use of tests, on psychopathology, and on behavior change. But it is the client who knows best what it is like to be him- or herself, what other happenings have been similar to those that occur during the assessment, and which options presented by the assessor seem personally viable.

Collaboration requires repeated give-and-take clarification of one another's perspectives. The above interchanges between Matt and myself were arrived at much more circuitously than I have indicated. I had to ask him to explain how the organizational chart of his company's production division differed from that of the sales division. I had to explain that by "sociable" I didn't mean superficially friendly. He said I was wrong about my guess that he double-checks his paperwork, that instead his carefully checking completed block designs against the cards was more like what he does in unfamiliar situations. Through these explorations, a certain camaraderie of common cause between otherwise differing persons grows throughout the session, despite any enduring disagreements and unspoken impressions.

In short, in conjunction with circumstances, we all co-author our lives; as professionals we can assist our clients to do so with the benefit of a collaboratively developed comprehension of how that authoring has worked both for and against them to date, and of variations that might work better in the future. Of course this collaboration is most possible with well-integrated, resourceful persons, and most limited with restricted persons. Nevertheless, it is true in all cases that to the extent that a person participates in evaluating him- or herself and engages in realistic efforts to develop his or her future, the individual is that much more free and responsible than before. The more restricted the person, the greater is the burden on the assessor to find ways to comprehend that person's experience and to step into it in ways that allow him or her to work as collaboratively as is possible with the referral issue.

There is no need for secrecy from clients, since the primary data are clients' life events, and since assessment findings are revised understandings of those events accompanied by tailored recommendations. There is no call for the professional to share all the conceptions and hypotheses that led to reunderstandings and conclusions, but if the latter are not explainable in terms of what they come down to in the client's life, then the professional's work is still unfinished. To the degree that clients can communicate and read, they can discuss the assessor's plans for any written report, and they can read and append a commentary to the report.

Assessment as Interventional

Any external interruption of a person's course influences that course in one way or another. In this sense, any assessment is already an intervention. Traditionally, assessment has been regarded as a unilateral enterprise, in which testers do things to elicit scorable and interpretable responses from testees. Insofar as testees experience themselves as doing things that are meaningful to experts but not to themselves, that is, as explainable only by the experts, then the intrusion of an assessment is a destructive one. That intrusion has said to clients that, unbeknownst to them, mysterious variables have been operative, causing or influencing their actions. Transforming assessments into collaborative enterprises not only bypasses this likelihood, but clarifies and reaffirms clients' agency – their active participation in their own lives.

But individualized assessments are calculated to do more than avoid negative influence. When assessments are intended to be of service in working with or guiding a client, then exploring the workability of alternative courses and interventions ought to be part of the assessment. Such tailored exploration is much more helpful than merely saying what sort of person this is, and then extrapolating in an abstract manner to general recommendations. Therefore, individualized assessments frequently intervene into the assessor's own otherwise standardized administration format, to explore observed comportment and to try out alternative variations.

For example, in Matt's case, we found upon discussion that his making room for others worked well and was appreciated in most social contexts. Furthermore, when on home territory, both literally and figuratively, he generally had held to his own position if he felt that was important for the outcome. For instance, he rarely had accepted guests' suggestions for altering his gourmet recipes, about which he was confident from years of experience. Similarly, at work he had been insistent about subordinates' means of record-keeping, with which he had also had years of experience. But later in the assessment, during Digit Span on the Wechsler Scale, he stopped midway in repeating digits-backwards to say that he wasn't sure if he was going to be correct; with that, he forgot the remaining digits. Upon reflection, he recognized a familiar pattern: Just the day before, he had become so concerned that he might not be making himself clear during a conference discussion that he interrupted himself to ask his boss if he were being clear – only to lose his place in his line of argument. Later he had realized that his colleagues had understood him, and that his line of argument would have been clearly valid to all he had simply stuck to it. We then agreed to repeat digits-backwards, so Matt could try to hold his own this time. During this practice we discovered that he began losing his place when he looked to "a person in charge" for guidance or reassurance. So we practiced with other subtests until Matt could identify "a queazy feeling and wanting to glance around" as indications that he should resist an upcoming inclination to look for an authority, and that he should instead continue his course, knowing he could review it later if he still wished.

Of course other themes were also pursued, and were related to his past and future. When we finished the session, Matt not only understood how he had been getting into trouble, but how *he* could do something in particular about it. As he left the session, he remarked that he hadn't learned anything that he didn't already know, but that now he knew these themes in ways that allowed him to take stock of his life differently. "And I feel more familiar with myself, and as though my choices will not endanger who I've been, even though they may alter my direction."

Description as Re-Presentational

The language of individualized assessment sessions and of reports is descriptive. Any scores, categories, or professional jargon are presented in terms of concrete happenings. That is, the client is represented in the report by re-presenting the assessment events that have best clarified the referral issues. The description addresses, as illustrated above, the context in which the understandings were developed, including the assessor's and client's involvements in developing these understandings. The assessor refers to him- or herself in first-person. Most description is adverbial and in past tense, that is, it describes how the client went about doing something, rather than saying that the client is such-and-such a kind of person. For example, the report said that (under specified circumstances) Matt had "looked 'to a person in charge' for guidance or reassurance." It did *not* say that "the client is a passive-dependent person," or even that he "looks" to superiors for guidance and reassurance.

Structure as Explanatory

When we deal with individuals as individuals in clinical settings, we would do well to regard our unit of study as the "person living his or her world." We should address an event in terms of how the involved parties participated in it affectively/cognitively/behaviorally, and so forth. If we refrain from breaking our subject matter into perceiver and perceived, into subject and object, into actor and acted upon, and so on, no external or underlying causes need be posited. The event is already accounted for adequately for purposes of effective anticipation and influence. In short, structure – specification of the instantaneous coherence of the constituents of an event as it was lived – is both necessary and sufficient for accounting for a psychological event as a psychological event.

Surely past events were necessary for the evolution of the present, and knowing more about them is usually helpful. But they are operative only in their evolved form, which also is the only access for intervention. Likewise, biology, physical environment, and so on, also are operative in terms of how they are taken up by the person. Yes, these realms can be dealt with in their own terms, and often should be (e.g., diagnosis of a brain tumor, or prescription of a diet). But if we are to assist people in understanding and redirecting their lives, then we must also address the "person living his or her world." Indeed, looking at a psychological event as a structural whole allows access to understanding and influence through any available constituent – each of which implicates the others.

From this structural point of view, maximal clarity and rigor require specification of context and perspectives – as they occur for the participants, here assessor and client. There is no "real" truth, but only perspectival variations as they appear to individuals; things are known only in relation to perceivers in their various presences to things. Hence, clients participate actively in individualized assessment, exploring the idiosyncratic approaches through which they know and affect the world. Even in cases where the client's future development is not the point of the assessment, that collaboration is critical if the assessor is to comprehend that person's individual manner of seeing, shaping, and being shaped by the world.

Clarifications

Before addressing some of the presences through which assessment takes place, I want to quickly respond to anticipated comments about individualized assessment.

Yes, the general spirit of this approach can be utilized even with severely restricted persons. Yes, it does take more time than standard assessment and reporting procedures, but not more total work hours than are required for effective individual planning and intervention. Yes, the assessor does have to be knowledgeable about tests, norms, personality patterns and development, psychopathology, and so on. Yes, objective test data, developmental history, neurological findings, and so forth, are integrated into this approach. No, clients' perceptions are not more basic than are their physical, neurological, environmental, and other circumstances; these all come into play in how clients live their worlds, and these worlds can be altered through all these realms. No, this approach is not original. It has been presented here because philosophers rather than psychologists have been the ones to address the principles, and because clinicians have not written about nor embodied the practices in a systematic, consistent manner. No, not all evaluations require an individualized approach. Yes, behavioralists, more than psychometrists, find this approach consonant with their own. Differences from most assessors' practices have to do with individualized assessment's emphasis on the dialectical shaped/shaping of comportment, on process, and on lived world.

Rapport, Privacy, and Intimacy

We all act in accordance with our experience, which includes the concerns and intentions through which we perceive. When assessors address themselves to an individual as an individual (rather than describing that person in terms of classifications), then it becomes particularly important to identify the kinds of presence through which the client has perceived and coped with assessment tasks. For example, there is no "the meaning" to Matt's Bender. One must know that Matt saw the assessor as someone to please, and the designs as a task the assessor wanted him to complete quickly. One must also know that on other occasions Matt has constituted situations and outcomes differently as well as similarly. Likewise, it is important to know something of the kinds of presence through which the assessor perceived and responded to the client. This is one reason why references to the assessor in reports should be made in first person.

The remainder of this chapter describes three kinds of presence of particular relevance to an assessment situation, specifically, rapport, privacy, and intimacy. These three were not chosen in advance by some sort of logic. Rather, I was confronted by each in turn as I tried to conceptualize for myself and for my students the character of individualized assessment, and its points of departure from the more traditional approach to assessment. In retrospect, I suppose these three in particular arose as issues to be dealt with because all of them were general societal concerns surrounding psychological assessment. They occurred quickly to persons who were wondering how an assessment enterprise could be so personal and yet remain nonintrusive, objective, and professional.

Each of these three topics turned out to be a kind of presence, a relationship. Rapport was found to be a mutual relationship between assessor and client; privacy is a presence on the part of the client to assessment events; and intimacy is the client's relation to the meaning of central aspects of his or her life as revealed in the assessment events. As mentioned before, it turns out that intimacy, when it occurs, is in the context of privacy, for which rapport is a precondition. Other relations pertinent to collaborative, individualized assessment, but which I have not studied, include for example, trust, hope, defense, closure. Just as the laboratory approach is insufficient for individualized assessment, so too it is not appropriate for studying the relationships that occur within this version of assessment. Hence, the method of study adopted was one developed at Duquesne University explicitly to address descriptively the structure of the way things appear to experiencing persons. Brief reviews of this empirical phenomenological research method may be found in Fischer and Wertz (1979), W. Fischer (1974), and Giorgi, (1975 a,b). Suffice it to say here that the method involves acquiring descriptions from individuals of an actual experience of the phenomenon under study, and then analyzing these for commonalities. The unit of study is the person-world relationship, and the object is not to reduce phenomena to underlying variables but to describe holistically whatever occurred across instances.

The following descriptions were developed in the above manner. The studies were rigorous in that the findings pertained to every case, but extensive follow-up studies have not been undertaken, neither qualitative nor quantitative. Nor have all the described experiences that I studied taken place within the context of an assessment. Nevertheless, even the differences from popular and professional assumptions about the three relations will resonate with the reader's own experience.

Rapport

First I analyzed protocols from students, in which they had described instances in their daily lives where rapport had been present. "A good working relationship" turned out to be an appropriate shorthand term for the resulting structure. Then I began keeping notes on those of my collaborative assessment sessions in which both the client and I had felt that indeed an optimum working relationship had existed. Many of the usual activities traditionally associated with rapport sometimes did show up, but none of them was essential. These included introductory social chatting, overtly seeing to the client's physical comfort, making statements intended to indicate the assessor's concern or understanding, and efforts to motivate the client to cooperate or to do well.

The upshot is that *rapport in a collaborative assessment context is a mutual respect for the power and limits of the other person's perspectives, as these pertain to a shared project.* Forthright discussion, at least on the assessor's part, has led to an implicit or explicit acknowledgment of what each other's purposes in regard to the assessment are. Each senses that "where the other is coming from" is both that person's access to understanding and to communication, and a limitation to understanding and to communication. Each recognizes that whether or not one agrees with or values the other's perspective, a productive session for either requires that perspectives be taken into account. This rapport is not established prior to assessment, but instead gradually builds during the work of exploring and making sense together of the referral issues. Nor is this working relationship established once and for all. It ebbs with the inevitable onesided reminders of the other's judgmental assumptions, and flows again with mutual acknowledgment of differences and with efforts to find common ground and common cause. Degree of rapport varies within and between assessments.

This understanding of rapport was helpful in explaining to humanistic colleagues and to students of some years ago that rapport did not involve equality between participants, liking or approving of one another, confession of one's feelings, necessarily sharing the facts of one's life, nor siding against the establishment. On the other hand, this understanding of rapport has been helpful in advising psychometrists that they should be wary of assuming rapport in the everyday sense of harmony when (and if) they have in fact "established rapport" via a unilateral manipulation of the person. That is, most often rapport has been assumed, within a testing context, to be a controllable variable, having to do with testees' level of motivation to do their honest best. Having elicited this kind of test-productivity, however, does not insure that the assessee will take the assessor's conclusions seriously. Nor will the assessor know, in the absence of collaborative inquiry, the attitudes with which the tests were taken. Hence the assessor also will not know how those attitudes may be similar to and different from ones that are likely in those situations into which the assessor wishes to predict.

Finally, conceiving of rapport as mutual respect for the power of perspective, to open and to limit access, can be helpful to all of us as a reminder that even if we use "objective tests," we should consider enquiring into the perspectives with which the testee went about answering items. Test observations and test-taking are always situational, perspectival, relational. (An early version of the above conception of rapport appears in Fischer, 1969; elaborated and refined versions appear in Fischer, 1985.)

Privacy

Along with colleagues and students, I too had wondered how it was that individualized assessment could be so personal, and yet rarely leave me feeling intrusive or leave the client feeling that his or her privacy was being invaded. So once again I analyzed written descriptions of instances of "being in privacy." To my surprise, it turned out that privacy is very different from secrecy or even from guardedness.

Before reading the following structure of being in privacy, the reader may wish to recall such moments in his or her own life, perhaps moments spent in reading a novel, in serious discussion with a friend, in writing a note of condolence, or in reverie.

> *Privacy is when: the watching self and the world fade away, along with geometric space, clock time, and other contingencies, leaving an intensified attunement to the thematic object. This relationship is toned by a sense of at-homeness or familiarity, and its style is one of relative openness to or wonder at the object's variable nature.*
>
> (adapted from Fischer, 1971)

Now it became apparent that consideration of personal matters within collaborative assessment was not intrusive since that exploration occurred within shared privacy – a looking together in openness and wonderment at instances of the client's assessment comportment. That looking was not judgmental, in the pejorative sense. At the moment, the exploration was unmindful of what others might think of the revelation. True, a bit later, client and assessor would discuss the client's options and responsibilities, how readers might respond to the report, and so on. Still, the assessment exploration itself was one in which client and assessor were present to new understandings, and to the possibilities of growth from there. (See Neville, 1980, and Keegan, 1980, for similar understandings of privacy arrived at through a philosophical and a theological analysis; see Fischer, 1975, 1980b, for social implications of this understanding of privacy.)

The constructive, creative possibilities of privacy – conceived as an undistracted, nondefensive, open presence to events – are highlighted by the contrasting structure of disrupted privacy:

> *Attention is jerked from its prior object, and shifts repeatedly among the intruder, self as caught by the other, and the peripheral world, as well as the lost object. There is a jarring aura of control being still out of grasp, with return to privacy being in the hands of the intruder. Intentional relations are now in the styles of task, manipulation, or withdrawal. Time is lived in that future to be somehow achieved, or in helpless, fixed present or past. Both time and space thrust forth as inescapable contingencies, limitations to be suffered or reckoned with. As attention flits among its three focal objects, affect varies with felt ability and desire to do something about each of them. Specifically, the intersection of ought-must (do something) with uncertain can't is the location of such affects as irritation, anger, and impotent, frightened rage where the focus is on the intruder. Where oneself is the object (at the same intersection), the affect is unease, embarrassment, or shame as one finds oneself fixed. Finally, where the prior object is sought, the affect includes agitated despair, inadequacy, or anxiety.*
>
> (Fischer, 1971)

Now it is clearer that our societal concerns about protecting privacy have not focused on the "good" of what that state allows, but on the aversive nature of disrupted privacy. The guardedness and secrecy that often are mistakenly equated with privacy are in actuality states that preclude intrigued, un-self-conscious presence to the richness of phenomena.

These analyses of privacy and of disrupted privacy helped me to be explicit about how it is that one can directly explore personal matters and yet not also pry, offend, or hurt the client. Moreover, the analyses show us that in order *not* to be intrusive, that is, not to throw clients into distracted wariness, assessors must come to understand clients' personal worlds well enough to develop shared privacy – a looking together while phenomena begin to appear differently in response to open inquiry and exploration. For example, client and assessor together may come to discover that rushing through the Bender was unnecessary and that perhaps rushing through office work is similarly a personal style rather than a demand of the job. Note that tests allow both participants to witness unfolding comportment, rather than focusing on the person as such. It is the latter focusing, which necessarily is from an abstract and external point of view, that is likely to result in defensive self-consciousness.

Intimacy

At last, with all of the preceding as foundation, we come to address "intimacy in assessment." As mentioned earlier, in textbooks and in training programs, the assessment process has been a unilateral evaluation whose conclusions may or may not be shared with the assessee. In such a context, intimacy presumably is not possible and hence has not been an issue. However, since collaborative, individualized assessment does entail joint exploration of concrete, personally important comportments, people do ask if it does not also entail intimacy. Their concern, one also raised in regard to intensive psychotherapy, is for how professional distance and objectivity can be maintained when the assessor is so actively involved. To pursue this aspect of collaborative assessment, I again turned to solicited descriptions of everyday instances of the phenomenon under question, this time, intimacy. Again, such analysis, followed by reflection on its implications for the assessment context, revealed some misassumptions. Instead of necessarily being a close interpersonal relationship, intimacy turned out to be presence to an event placing one focally and awarefully in touch with a core aspect of one's being.

The following examples from research subjects, the resulting structure of intimacy, and parts of the discussion are taken from Fischer (1985). (a) A young man holds and reads a valentine poem he has composed for a woman friend, and realizes that the feelings it expresses are truer and deeper than he had allowed himself to know. In this moment, he also realizes that he has wanted to share their lives in a permanent relationship. (b) A married couple had brought a kitten home from a pet shop several days ago. They had enjoyed caring for it – naming it, setting up its food station and litter box, watching it tumble about during its play, and gently caressing it. But they were also worried that it hadn't eaten. It was as they looked into each other's faces upon hearing the veterinarian's terminal diagnosis, that they realized how deeply their affections had been tapped, that together they would again risk such affection, and that it would indeed be a risk. (c) A woman had told herself and her friends that she had applied for re-instatement to a graduate program only to demonstrate to her husband that this was no longer an option, that the faculty had rightly long ago judged her to be an unsuitable candidate. The day after receiving word of her reinstatement, she joyfully shared with a friend of longstanding her relief, excitement, and plans. Later, after having fallen silent for awhile, they spoke of how important the graduate program had always been to her, and of how, despite her protestations, acceptance by the faculty and later by the profession were critical to her sense of herself.

Analysis of such instances reveals that:

> *What we call intimacy is an open, acknowledging presence to essential aspects of one's journey through life. In the face of a concrete event, there is an unexpected sense of coming home to one's self, and of the giftedness of that return. There is quiet wonderment and reverence within an aura of gradual unfolding and then of profound immediacy at witnessing and owning without defense, a continuing, inevitable, perhaps universal, and yet also uniquely personal theme. There is awareness of vulnerability both in owning this deep caring, and in continuing – as one must – to care. The moment is recognized as an occasion for reaffirmation and/or for reflection on one's actions. Intimacy is thus a presence to one's own life, to one's simultaneous innocence and responsibility.*
>
> *That presence may occur in solitude, but often the co-presence of a knowing witness intensifies the significance of the moment. Intimacy may also be co-presence to the mutuality between or among lives. Poignance is intensified by a progression of symbolic ceremonial events (as at weddings) or of hurdles (as at Olympics or in daily struggles); in both cases, risk, vulnerability, and commitment are highlighted.*

The above description of intimacy helps to identify some common misassumptions that are particularly relevant to collaborative assessment practices. First, intimacy turns out *not* to be a relation between the assessor and client, although the assessor may witness the client's recognition of something as reflecting an essential aspect of his or her life. Second, intimacy is indeed a recognition about one's own life, and not necessarily a divulgement to someone else. Another assumption turns out to be correct, however; namely, that intimate presence is more likely to occur for a client within a collaborative assessment than in a more standard evaluation. This intimacy is not a goal of an assessment, but rather is a mode of presence on the client's part during the assessment, one that is likely to occur when that person genuinely explores, through concrete instances, who he or she is – where he or she has been and is going. I think that during all of my individualized assessments, I have witnessed intimate insights. However, momentary recognitions vary broadly in depth, extension, cognitive thematization, and frequency.

This understanding of intimacy helps the assessor to do the work of individualized assessment, that of exploring *who* the client is and could be, all the while engaging the client as far as possible as an active participant in this pursuit. When conducted within rapport and shared privacy, as reunderstood above, this exploration is not intrusive; it is not a disruption from an external, judgmental source. Neither is it a personal involvement, beyond the interest of assessment, on the assessor's part. Professionalism is not threatened by the client's being in intimate touch with his or her life. Rather, professionalism, in this context, comes into play as the assessor's responsibility to know when mundane testing events have put the client in intimate touch with his or her life. Care must be taken not to rush past these moments, and to instead assist the person to dwell with them, and then to integrate them into the assessment and into any action plans.

Summary

In summary, when we examine rapport, privacy, and intimacy from an experiential perspective, we discover that they are not so much variables or even states of being as they are intermittent modes of presence, respectively, between assessor and client, between these participants and the assessment events, and between the client and an essential meaning of his or her life. In the assessment context, rapport is necessary for shared privacy, which is necessary for witnessed intimacy. Understanding each of these modes of presence is important in four ways for effective assessment:

1. When appropriate, we can better foster these three relationships, thereby allowing relatively open self-exploration by clients. Therein, we also encourage responsibility and initiative.
2. If assessments are to be objective in the broad sense of not being merely subjective, and of being empirically based, sharable, and replicable, then the relationships through which the assessment findings emerged should be made explicit. This chapter's descriptions of rapport, privacy, and intimacy can serve as a starting point for such explicitations.
3. More specifically, if we are to anticipate and influence clients' comportment, we must have been mindful of the various modes of presence through which clients conducted themselves as they did, and through which they made particular discoveries. Similarly, if we are to communicate to other helpers how they, too, can engage clients in such exploration, then we must be attuned not only to clients' modes of presence, but to our own – through which we both perceived and engaged each particular client.

4. Finally, through attunement to presences we can more readily see beyond test products, and beyond presumably hidden secrets or dynamics, to process – to persons' habitual, defensive, creative, and intimate relations with their ever-unfolding worlds.

Acknowledgement

Discussions with Frederick Mertl have contributed to the understanding of intimacy presented in this chapter. Our discussions profited from readings of Bachelard (1964/1958).

Note

1 Reprinted with kind permission from Springer Science+Business Media: Fischer, C. T., Intimacy in Assessment, 1982, in M. Fisher & G. Stricker (Eds.) *Intimacy* (pp. 443–460). New York: Plenum.

References

Bachelard, G. (1964). *The poetics of space*. Boston: Beacon Press. (Original work published 1958.)

Dana, R. H. (1981). *A human science model for personality assessment with projective techniques*. Springfield: Charles C Thomas.

Fischer, C. T. (1969). Rapport as mutual respect. *Personnel and Guidance Journal*, 48, 201–204.

Fischer, C. T. (1970). The testee as co-evaluator. *Journal of Counseling Psychology*, *17*, 70–76.

Fischer, C. T. (1971). Toward the structure of privacy: Implications for psychological assessment. In A. Giorgi, W. F. Fischer, & R. von Eckartsberg (Eds.), *Duquesne studies in phenomenological psychology (Vol. 1)* (pp. 149–163). Pittsburgh: Duquesne University Press/ Humanities Press.

Fischer, C. T. (1973). Contextual approach to assessment. *Community Mental Health Journal*, *9*, 38–45.

Fischer, C. T. (1973). Intelligence contra IQ: A human-science critique and alternative to the natural science approach to man. *Human Development*, *16*, 8–20.

Fischer, C. T. (1974). Exit IQ: Enter the child. In G. Williams & S. Gordon (Eds.), *Clinical child psychology: Current practices and future perspectives* (pp. 333–350). N.Y.: Behavioral Publications.

Fischer, C. T. (1975). Privacy as a profile of authentic consciousness. *Humanitas*, *11*, 27–43.

Fischer, C. T. (1976). Undercutting the scientist-professional dichotomy: The reflective psychologist. *The Clinical Psychologist*, *29*, 5–7.

Fischer, C. T. (1978). Personality and assessment. In R. Valle & M. King (Eds.). *Existential-phenomenological alternatives for psychology* (pp. 203–231). N.Y.: Oxford University Press.

Fischer, C. T. (1978). Collaborative psychological assessment. In C. T. Fischer & S. L. Brodsky (Eds.). *Client participation in human services: The Prometheus principle* (pp. 41–61). New Brunswick: Transaction.

Fischer, C. T. (1979). Individualized assessment and phenomenological psychology. *Journal of Personality Assessment*, *43*, 115–122.

Fischer, C. T. (1980). Phenomenology and psychological assessment: Re-presentational description. *Journal of Phenomenological Psychology*, *11*, 79–105.

Fischer, C. T. (1980). Privacy and psychological development. In W. C. Bier (Ed.), *Privacy: A vanishing value* (pp. 37–45). N.Y.: Fordham University Press.

Fischer, C. T. (1985). *Individualizing psychological assessment.* Monterey: Brooks/Cole. (Reprinted in 1994 by Erlbaum.)

Fischer, C. T., & Wertz, F. J. (1979). Empirical phenomenological analyses of being criminally victimized. In A. Giorgi, R. Knowles, & D. Smith (Eds.). *Duquesne studies in phenomenological psychology (Vol. 3)* (pp. 135–158). Pittsburgh: Duquesne University Press/ Humanities Press.

Fischer, W. F. (1974). On the phenomenological mode of researching "Being anxious." *Journal of Phenomenological Psychology*, 4, 425–444.

Giorgi, A. (1975). Convergence and divergence of qualitative and quantitative methods in psychology. In A. Giorgi, C. T. Fischer, & E. L. Murray (Eds.), *Duquesne studies in phenomenological psychology (Vol. 2)* (pp. 72–79). Pittsburgh: Duquesne University Press/ Humanities Press.

Giorgi, A. (1975). An application of phenomenological method in psychology. In A. Giorgi, C. T. Fischer, & E. L. Murray (Eds.). *Duquesne studies in phenomenological psychology (Vol. 2)* (pp. 82–103). Pittsburgh: Duquesne University Press/Humanities Press.

Keegan, J. G. (1980). Privacy and spiritual growth. In W. C. Bier (Ed.). *Privacy: A vanishing value?* (pp. 67–88). N.Y.: Fordham University Press.

Neville, R. C. (1980). Various meanings of privacy: A philosophical analysis. In W. C. Bier (Ed.). *Privacy: A vanishing value?* (pp. 22–33). N.Y.: Fordham University Press.

PART II

PRACTICING COLLABORATIVE/ INDIVIDUALIZED ASSESSMENT

CHAPTER 9

COLLABORATIVE PSYCHOLOGICAL ASSESSMENT[1]

Psychological assessment has traditionally been an evaluation of a client by the psychologist. It has been the clinician's responsibility to establish rapport, administer and score tests, analyze the results, draw conclusions, and write a report. If the psychologist is the one to discuss the assessment with the client, he interprets those portions of the report for which he thinks the person is ready. That all sounds reasonable enough, especially since those practices reflect the tenor of our technological times in general as well as psychology's particular efforts to model itself after the physical sciences.

More specifically, in its efforts to be scientific, psychology has assumed that people should be treated as *objects* amenable to measurement, prediction, and control. But in fact psychologists do not have to limit themselves to the restricted view of object-psychology. Instead, they can rediscover, promote, and work with those characteristics of being human that render strict physical-science approaches inadequate. A proper science of humans should take into account that humans are also purposive *subjects* who behave in accordance with their experience of situations.

Definition of Collaborative Assessment

Collaborative assessment recognizes that the professional's understandings are not more real, valid, or influential within the client's life than are the client's. Collaborative assessment, then, is one in which client and professional *labor together* (from the Latin, *collaborare*) toward mutually set goals, sharing their respective background information and emerging impressions. They develop and try out alternative approaches for the client as they explore the particular circumstances and ways in which he or she has wound up in some sort of difficulty. Insofar as the client is able, he also collaborates on the formulation of any written report, adds his commentary and signature to the actual document, and advises concerning who may and may not have access to the report. In short, in collaborative assessment, client and professional are mutually informed and both are active participants.

Before going on to elaborate the practices and then the guiding principles of collaborative assessment, I will briefly overview the current assessment scene and the restrictive nature of psychology's traditional way of being scientific.

The Current Scene: "Yes, But" and "Never Mind"

Increasing numbers of professionals currently agree that a client ought to have greater access to the information about himself that is gathered by others. This agreement arises at a time of professional consciousness-raising in the face of public antielitism and demands for civil rights, accountability, and protection of consumer interests. Further impetus is provided by the recent state and federal legislation and court decisions that diminish obstacles to students' and clients' access to their files. Dissidents against the dehumanizing aspects of traditional physicalistic psychology call ever more strongly for "humanistic" reform.

Nevertheless, these "increasing numbers" are still decidedly a minority. In one study, 88 percent of the responding psychologists rarely or never gave written reports to their clients; half said that even upon direct request they would not consider giving the client a verbal account of the information (Vane 1972). "The Testee as Co-evaluator" (Fischer 1970) was apparently the first article to call for inclusion of the client as a full participant, including his or her reading and adding commentary to the report and designating who may receive it. Until then, and sometimes after that, my manuscripts (and presumably those of other authors) that were related to collaborative practices were rejected as being "too controversial," "irresponsible," and "unprofessional." Craddick (1975), Dana and Leech (1974), and Riscalla (1972) have authored three of the few publications with views similar to some of the themes in this chapter.

In the past five years or so, however, our legal system has challenged the tradition of professional secrecy. In Maine a superior court ruled that a rejected applicant to Bates College had a right to examine the records on which the decision was based. The youngster's parents then sued the high school counselor who had written an unsubstantiated derogatory letter. The United States Supreme Court has ruled (in *Gault* v. *Arizona*) that juveniles accused of delinquency should have access to their psychological reports prior to their hearings. In Pennsylvania a right to education act for mental retardates assures parents of their right for a hearing considering whether their children are receiving the education they require; as part of this right, they also are assured access to psychological tests and records. On the federal level, the "Buckley amendment" assures parents of right of access to their children's school records; this right of access passes to the students when they become 18 years old.

"Yes, but"

Here, we find the first "Yes, but" – that of "Yes, I know it's the law, *but* it's against professional interests." Some school systems, rather than open their files to parents and pupils, have considered dispensing with all evaluative records other than achievement test scores and final grades. A professional journal for college admissions counselors has carried an article advising colleges to devise an application form that would require the applicant to waive right of access to his files. The article admitted that such a waiver would not stand up in court, but that it might dissuade unknowledgeable students. This article has been abstracted in two newsletters for advisors of preprofessional undergraduates. More openly, many college career planning offices require students to check a box on their requests for letters of recommendation indicating to the prospective writer whether they have waived right of access to the letter.

Counseling centers and psychology services across the country are devising a system of dual files: the institutional file that is subject to the law, and the individual practitioner's private notes, which are not. This gambit keeps scores, diagnoses, undocumented suspicions and hunches, and other negative comments in the personal file to which the client cannot gain access. The personal file is bequeathed as personal property to one's replacement upon transfer to another job. And so on.

When one inquires of colleagues and assorted officials as to whether this means they do not believe that clients should participate actively in evaluating their own situations, the second "Yes, but" emerges:

> *"Of course, I believe in client participation, but as the expert, it is my responsibility to determine how much the client can understand or is otherwise ready for. Much of what is here in the records concerns unconscious or conditioned processes, which by definition the client cannot understand at his present stage. Besides, much of my report is just too technical for a layman to understand, even if I try to interpret it to him."*

Sometimes one can cut through part of this argument by making a case for not underestimating the client's strength. The next challenge to colleagues is that if they cannot say what they know in layman's terms, then they are not particularly clear themselves about what their esoterica mean. Here the third "Yes, but" emerges:

> *"Yes, I've felt that way myself, but surely all this technical know-how and information must be critical – what else is there that sets my work apart as professional? What would be 'expert' about talking in everyday language about things clients could already understand?"*

Variations:

> *"When I try to explain what I actually do with clients ... like ask them to copy geometric designs or draw houses, trees, and persons ... it seems embarrassingly simple"; "I do share my actual report with my private patients, but I don't think my clinic would stand for it"; "Our technology is not just a shorthand; it identifies the actual causes that underlie behavior. To refer to a client's obsessive-compulsive orderliness in any other way would dilute the precision of truth."*

In short, we professionals have not been trained to notice, explore, and work with everyday events in their own right. Instead we have been trained to see those everyday behaviors as signs or symptoms of something (for example, IQ, defense mechanisms, traits) presumably more fundamental or real.

We continue to utilize these reductive notions despite our own widespread criticism of the circularity of attributing explanatory powers to the name we give to behaviors (for example, "Roger's high achievement reflects his Superior IQ."). The precision and objectivity of our measurements and constructs belie the actual state of human affairs – their necessarily fluid and intersubjective nature. Put differently, we want to be relevant, humane, and genuinely helpful, but our traditional model of laboratory object science confounds our efforts. We are caught in the "Yes, but." We don't know how to be professional and yet deal with the everyday in its own right.

"Never mind"

The second movement on the current scene in effect says, "Never mind doing individual assessments; let's get right on with treatment." The first variation of the movement is a culmination of our longstanding efforts to emulate the technological efficiency of the physical sciences. This first thrust is now dominant in psychology doctoral programs, less than half of which still require PhD candidates to take courses in individual assessment. The assumption is that lower level technicians will accumulate scores which the PhD *consultant* or *supervisor* will interpret. Together with the research psychologist, he or she continues to develop categories and to accumulate scores and actuarial data. Computers can then predict behavior and assign treatment modalities even more accurately and efficiently than their human counterparts. There are, of course, many clinicians who protest that statistics should serve the professional rather than supplant him; but because they too have argued largely within the traditional *objectivistic* (scientistic) notion of how psychology is to be scientific, they have not been persuasive.

The second variation of bypassing individual assessment in favor of immediate treatment is more directly related to recent awareness of the destructiveness of the "medical model of mental illness" (Szasz 1961). That is, we are now aware that although our bodies are of course always involved, "mental health" problems most often are ones of getting along in life rather than ones that are primarily either "mental" or medical. "Mental health" professionals (now more appropriately coming to be called human services professionals) historically have reified their diagnostic creations through jargon, discrete categories, professional distance, tests, and social status.

In reaction, the humanistic psychologists in particular have opted for instant therapy, usually along the lines of self-help opportunities for expressing feelings, asserting oneself, and exploring one's ways of relating to other people (for example, sensitivity training, gestalt therapy, transactional analysis). Many of the persons who conduct these sessions are BAs and MAs or MEds whose training has not emphasized pathology patterns, personality theory, or research. Their jobs are an answer to a dual call: the antielitist spirit in which the community mental health movement was founded, and citizens' growing awareness of their problems and of hopes for their quick resolution. Personally, I welcome much of this trend and its emphasis on self-help and on positive growth. But I worry that the individual client's particular situation, goals, and style are not adequately taken into account, and that relevant, sometimes critical, professional knowledge is ignored to the client's detriment. Antitradition and proclient enthusiasm are not enough.

Finally, there is a third variation of the movement to bypass traditional assessment. It has arisen from a dissatisfaction with the limited usefulness of both object science assessment on one hand and subjectivistic (nonempirical) assessment on the other. In their place it has evolved practical, atheroretical means of addressing clients' problems in living. For example, "problem-oriented" psychiatric and general hospital charting spells out concrete problems and then lists specific explorations and actions, as well as points of reformulation, to be taken until resolution is attained. In some settings, the client or his family has access to these relatively self-explanatory charts, particularly where choices involving risk and personal values are called for. These charts serve the interests of general informed participation as well as those of professional accountability.

Psychologists and counselors in private practice similarly are finding that their clients now demand understandable accounts of what the professional has to offer. Many of these practitioners have discovered that, free from the constraints of institutional tradition, they can in fact meet these requests. Several have argued that all of us should draw up contracts with our clients specifying what the professional must provide or forego payment. Contracting also has arisen within clinical behavior modification, where (its contradictory deterministic theory notwithstanding) clients help to work out a set of goals and contingent rewards or penalties. Note that not only does the client participate in setting goals, but these goals are more closely related to his everyday life than were the older diagnostically oriented recommendations. The newest development within clinical behavior modification is that of "self-control behavior modification" wherein the client manages his own program, which the professional has helped him to develop.

Government insistence on program evaluation has led to the recording of clients' expectations and degrees of satisfaction, which in turn has required informed participation by clients in evaluating their own circumstances and progress. Thus far, such clients have expressed marked satisfaction.

The client involvement in this emergent thrust is promising. But it is still restricted by insufficient acknowledgment of the power and importance of the client's experience. Objectified units of client behavior are still plotted against actual or assumed time/space grids, whether on hospital progress notes, program evaluation sheets, or behavior modification charts. These records give priority to the professional's perspective as more objective and useful than the client's. Full client participation in assessing his circumstances and in shaping, trying out, and reevaluating new plans requires a transformation not only of human services practices but of theoretical assumptions.

Collaborative Assessment Practices

This chapter now will address collaborative practices, each of which is grounded in the belief that the client (although always constrained by context) behaves in accordance with his or her own experience of situations, as do the assessor and reader. To be fully effective, the assessor must grapple directly with the client's realities, letting his or her scientific abstractions serve only as searchlights into these powerful realities. Moreover, each of the assessment practices is intended to assist the client himself to develop alternative ways of reaching his goals. These "ways" are not merely decision-making strategies or socially conditioned patterns. They are a person's styles of experiencing and forming his own unity with the milieu through which he travels en route to his destination. No matter what or where, styles both limit access to some futures and open the way to others. Collaborative practices acknowledge this process and assist the client in developing alternative routes that provide greater latitude and probability of successful arrival.

Practices

Situating the referral. When I receive a formal referral from another professional, I note the wording so that I can later speak into that frame of reference, since it is meaningful to the referring person. For example, "Distinguish between paranoid personality and schizophrenia"; "Assess for emotional disorder"; "Test for IQ." But I do not accept such abstractions as the focus of the assessment. Instead, I speak personally with the referring person, and ask him what decisions he is faced with that he requires a psychological assessment. Typical responses: "Well, I don't know whether he is dangerous and should be placed on a locked ward"; "I'm trying to decide whether her problems are primarily situational or personal… Should I suggest a change in job placement?"; "Timothy just isn't keeping up with the other children… Maybe he belongs in a special education class."

Then I go a step further and ask for examples of the events that have led to these questions. During this conversation, I ask for more detailed descriptions of the broader *situation* or *context*.

For example, upon reflection Timothy's teacher told me that he falls behind his classmates in new "one shot" projects like making a calendar or answering questions about how to give directions for getting to the hospital. These activities required that the student work or think by himself while only one teacher was available to give instructions to an entire class. As a final step in situating or contextualizing the referral, I encourage additional reflection on the "when nots" of the problematic events. In Timothy's case, it turned out that he caught on to new requirements readily enough when they grew out of familiar routines and when classmates and teachers could provide repeated examples. It is from such "when nots" that Timothy could expand his effectiveness into previously problematic areas.

This situating of the referral is already an assessment. Frequently, the referring person finds that this opportunity has already answered his questions, and no further services from the assessor are required. For example:

> ***Unit psychiatrist:*** *The patient is nearly always suspicious of other people's motives, but now that we're talking about it, it's clear that he has been verbally abusive and blatantly irrational only when he's been taken by surprise. I think I'll advise the staff both to see if this does seem to be true, and to give him early gradual notice of upcoming changes. This way he may be able to stay on the open ward.*

In other instances, with permission from both the other professional and the client, I may drop by to see the client in his or her own setting so that I can help to make concrete just what the focus might be. For example, I ate breakfast where Irene Kugel waitresses. There, I observed that the clientele are a rushed and impolite lot and that the short order cook bellows for her to pick up orders immediately, no matter where she happens to be. These are indeed situational stresses, ones to which Ms. Kugel responds with increasing fluster and disorganization, which in turn eventuate in further demands from customers and bellows from the cook. As the breakfast crowd thins out, I see that Ms. Kugel now appears more efficient: she answers each call as it occurs until the work is done, whether the call is that of the cook, a customer's motion for his check, or a counter with dirty plates. Ms. Kugel and I wave, and I later telephone her counselor to suggest that they might explore some of the other "whens" and "when nots" of these ways of being. Perhaps they will indeed find a more suitable work setting; but they will also explore ways through which she might address calls before they become shouts.

In still other instances, the referring professional, the client, and I carry out the above explorations as a threesome. This requires more total hours, but in this way we all know firsthand the concrete referents of our assorted understandings and abstractions.

Engaging the client. In the case of a self-referred client or when the above contextualizing requires further exploration and reflection, the client and I pursue the assessment ourselves. I briefly inform the client of the other professional's original and concretized/contextualized referrals, and then ask him to fill me in on his understanding of why we're getting together and what the referral is about as he sees it. At first the client responds in a socially perfunctory manner, awaiting my further questions from which he assumes I will draw my expert conclusions. This expectation is disrupted as I refuse to deal for long with generalities or actuarial facts, instead respecting the client's expertise about his own life. My role is to guide him, through my specialized training, to engage actively in delineating the ways and occasions in which he gets into difficulty as well as the pivot points already available for trying out alternatives.

However, even with the self-referred client, the initial "presenting problem" is usually as overgeneralized and abstract as that of the professional referral. For example: "My inferiority complex has caused me to fail all my job interviews"; "I just hate myself… I've never been any good to anyone"; "I want you to give me an IQ test to see if I should apply for a management position." So here too, we begin by concretizing/contextualizing. I might ask, "Tell me about the last time you 'failed an interview.'" Together, we try to discover what was similar among several of these occasions, how the client comported himself into and through these, what other situations were similar (perhaps being turned down by a potential date), and when he managed to comport himself through kindred situations successfully (as when he asked an apartment neighbor to return a favor). Sometimes this sort of discussion provides the client with all he needs to experiment with some alternatives on his own, with or without return visits for follow-up assessment/counseling.

Since our primary data are his actual life events as he reconstructs them for us and as he lives new ones in our sessions, the client understands that his active, responsible participation is critical. He now frequently interrupts to share new recollections that modify one of our earlier understandings. We both experience ourselves as working progressively toward useful comprehensions rather than as looking for causal explanations or precise truth. As we enter this stage I tell the client that all of our time will be spent in this same manner, even as we use test materials, make field visits, perform role-play options, or whatever. I also tell him that before I write a report (if one is required), I will share what I have in mind and it will be up to him to let me know of any problems that my formulations might involve with particular readers. Later, he will review the entire report.

Using test materials. Often, the client and I talk our way to a certain point of understanding, but aside from some truisms, we still don't know what could be done. At that point I decide to use test materials, not so much to obtain scores as to go beyond talk into joint activity. As I observe the client copying Bender gestalts (geometric designs) or solving intelligence test arithmetic problems, I am open to being surprised by the client's particular way of doing these things. Even while I view through my experience of what other clients have done and what my books and journals have told me, I find that this person both does and does not fit my expectations. If my observation seems relevant to our focal interest, my remarking upon it may raise to awareness something the client has taken for granted. For example, I interrupt Ms. Kugel, the waitress (referred for continued assessment), to ask how it is that both the parallel lines of the last drawing are turning out to slant. "Oh," she says, "well I didn't notice that the first one wasn't straight, and I just used it to copy for the second line." Sure enough, we discover that that's how the earlier columns of dots gradually changed direction of slant from the original drawings. Moreover, Ms. Kugel laughingly suggests that she "Benders" her way through her apartment on the way to work; each completed task points to the next one. If she happens to catch sight of her uncombed hair on the way to the bathroom, she may forget to brush her teeth as she goes on to put on her make-up after arranging her hair. So too in the restaurant she follows the lead of dirtied tables and impatient glances rather than that of a prearranged plan.

Awareness of these habitual ways of getting about allows us to try out different ways of moving through the test materials, to discover viable alternatives. More about that in a moment. The tests are not used to uncover traits, but to provide situations similar to others in the client's daily life. The assessment events can serve both of us as a living metaphor for structurally similar past events, which become more readily available to us in these concrete ways. We are attuned to the unitary fullness of events rather than to their intellectualized aspects such as "cognition," "affect," "emotion," "motivation." An example is the sixth grader who couldn't explain how he managed to turn in "messy" spelling papers even when he knew all the words. After looking from his Bender copy to the card to me, and back to his copy, he grimaced, and began erasing and resketching. "Spelling!" I said. "Yes! Just like with Mrs. Morrison! My stomach hurts, I don't feel very sure, the letters don't look neat enough, so I erase..."

Locating assessment events in daily life. Several examples of this practice of collaborative assessment already have been provided, but it bears emphasizing and saying again that assessment events simply are specialized instances of the client's past and future comportment.

Besides locating, that is, identifying and contextualizing, events similar to those that occur during the assessment, the client and I also identify those occasions when he or she does not get into such difficulty (the "when nots"). For example, Irene Kugel mused that she *has* carried out a planned agenda, and in a relatively undistracted manner, on at least two recent occasions: when she took over care of her preschool niece during a family emergency, and when she planned a two-week vacation tour for herself. Eventually we concluded that in these circumstances she had experienced herself as the only person who could handle the task if it were to be done properly, and that, unlike most situations, there had been few opportunities for others to gradually pick up responsibility or for her to slip into just letting things happen.

As the client engages in this sort of exploration, he discovers in a powerful way that his life is indeed in his own hands, that things don't have to be the way they have been, and that change can be self-initiated. Compare this with Irene Kugel's statement early in our session that she had thought that I might find out what "makes" her become rattled and distressed at work. She assumed that the counselor would then "work it out" (that is, "fix it"). There is a liberating power to this informed participation by the client in contextualizing the whens and when-nots of his or her difficulties. It is dramatically illustrated in the following summarizing comment by a woman whose circumstances we had just unfolded as being precisely those in which she had attempted suicide on three other occasions: "You know, I feel so relieved and hopeful. I don't *have* a 'self-destructive' tendency after all; I've just been trying to kill myself." (We followed up with a set of concrete environmental changes, to be overseen by a therapist, through which this woman could move herself out of her suicidal situation.)

Trying out alternatives. Collaborative assessment necessarily assesses not just the client but options available to him or her given his or her particular goals, perspective, style, and situation. Since there is no absolute psychiatric portrait from which to prescribe diagnosis-specific treatment, the client and assessor themselves devise and try out alternatives that fit the client's particular circumstances. This process of developing understandings and then options is a spiraling one, in which the nonviability of what looked like a reasonable alternative leads to revised understandings which in turn serve to suggest new alternative routes, and so on.

The trying out can occur in a variety of forms: different approaches to taking the intelligence test, role playing variations of a problematic event, imagining and describing several versions of a scenario, and specification of concrete actions the client will try out on-site.

Let us return to Irene Kugel. We started with a "when not" of her "Bendering" her way among demands, with the hope of expanding that style into other situations. Specifically, she described in detail how she had planned that vacation trip so that it would be sure to meet her expectations. I suggested that she describe for us just how she would like the Bender to turn out if she were to do it again. She floundered for a while, saying that she didn't know what she should want. We nodded in recognition of a habitual pattern, and then Irene agreed to plan the Bender as though she were still the adventurous worldly vacationer who had brought just the right dress for every stop on the itinerary. The Bender was to be executed in light but unretraced lines. She would try to copy the patterns with quick approximations, paying more attention to the original design than to her own pencilings. She would draw five down the left margin, and then four down the right margin. As she began, we discovered something else about the context in which she is able to keep an advance plan in mind: it was easier when no one else was watching her. Nevertheless, I stayed, and she finished, surprised at how well it turned out. I next presented her with pictures of designs she was to build from colored blocks. As she finished the first one, she looked at me, as though for approval or instructions. Again we smiled in recognition, and this time Irene announced that for the rest of the designs she was going to decide for herself how to attack each design, and to know when she was satisfied with her own solution.

We continued in similar manner through several tasks, until we both knew that Irene could now recognize the feeling of letting developments tell her what to do next. On her own she could find a bypass to a now increasingly familiar place from which she could pause to plan the rest of her journey. Note that we were dealing not merely with physically visible sequences, but with the client's lived ways of traveling and experiencing her own terrain. My personal observation of the sequences alone would not have been adequate for helping her to modify *her* style.

Joint formulation of reports. Rather than writing a report about Irene Kugel, I called her counselor while she was still in my office and described in detail our successes and their evolution. I advised him that Irene was in favor of looking for another job, still waitressing, but where she could get a fresh start at planning her waitressing. During the ensuing weeks they used the assessment exploration as a point of reference in discussing Irene's newer ventures. Later, they also reflected on the similarities to (and differences from) Irene's social relations and their own relationship.

Sometimes my report is in the form of a letter to the client, summarizing what turned out to be the thematic moments of our session(s) and reminding him of the concrete on-site tryings-out upon which we had agreed. If a copy of the report is to go to another professional, I remind the client (in the letter) of that person's concerns and of how our assessment work is relevant to them. Rarely is there anything in the letter or report that the client and I have not already discussed. If I do have an afterthought, I label it as such.

In short, before the client leaves me, he or she is already informed about what I think are the critical points to be recorded. Occasionally a client will request that I not divulge some particular fact, such as a homosexual encounter. If I agree that it does not seem essential to our goals, I ask the client to provide me with incidents that make the same point with different content.

So long as I formulate the report in terms of everyday life, there is no need to disguise my findings. Most clients regard our conclusions in this manner: "Nothing really new, although I never thought of it this way before; and now I can do something about it." Thus I have included diagnostic labels while discussing with patients their neurological impairment, paranoid delusions, suicidal state, and so on without undue disturbance, defensiveness, or surprise on their part. Although the labels may be politically deleterious, operationally they are simply gathering devices for difficulties with which the client is already quite familiar.

I write my reports in first-person form, and try to let the reader see who I was and how I contributed to the conclusions that emerged between the client and myself. Where possible, I include the client's actual words, so that we may all stay in touch with his sense of things rather than with my abstractions. There is no unexplained jargon. Test behavior is reported only as an introduction to similar everyday events, which in fact make up most of the report. Everything that is mentioned must meet the "so what?" criterion for practical implications. In other words, overall my reports strive to embody my beliefs that truth, even scientific truth, is necessarily perspectival and value laden, and that the professional knowledge that advises and guides me is not more fundamental than the life events as they are lived by the client. Moreover, it is only within life events that the client and his significant others can intervene constructively. There is a marked contrast between these reports in which life events are the data and already tried out alternatives are the results, and the traditional reports in which test scores are the data and traits and diagnoses are the results.

Client's commentary and instructions. Where there is a formal record or report, I ask the client to read it, and to add his comments and signature. If the assessment process itself has been collaborative there is nothing new in the report. Any corrections are usually along these lines: "The part about my family is true, but it seems a bit overemphasized"; "Actually, my mother died when I was nineteen. It's my stepmother we were talking about"; "I don't want it to appear that these problems dominate my life; they're important, but I'd like to emphasize the part about my also being a successful salesman and a contributing member of my lodge." Although these changes are usually minor, the fact of the client's involvement as a commentator is powerful: first, it encourages the assessor to stick as closely as he can, in his own formulations, to the client's experience; second, the client knows for sure that he continues to be seen as responsible for participating fully in directing his life. When I believe that the client understands the interpersonal and nonfinal nature of the report, I provide him with his own copy. Along with his written commentary and signature, the notation about the client's possessing his own copy of the report goes a long way toward impressing other readers with the client's readiness to participate actively in any further helping relations. Moreover, client and readers alike share common referents, namely actual events, as they discuss further implications of the report. Again, the professional's competence here lies not in his knowledge of scientific notions, but in how well he helps the person to cope with his own daily life.

The client's commentary also informs the assessor and readers of discrepancies, beyond those already noted in the report, between the client's and assessor's views. For example:

> ***Mr. Ruckles's commentary:*** *Dr. Fischer has accurately portrayed my tendencies to create a hostile environment through my defensive aggression. However, she has failed to give adequate attention to the conspiracies that are spawned even in my absence. She made no mention of my therapist being in the employ of the Communist Party.*

Whoever works with Mr. Ruckles will have to contend with Mr. Ruckles's perspective while keeping in mind the understanding that he nevertheless developed with the psychologist. In less dramatic instances, the client may point out a previously implicit difference in values: "I'm already working on our recommendations for initiating conversations, but it still seems to me that social relations are not as important as how well one does his work."

Sometimes the commentary indicates growth since the writing of a report. For example:

> ***Joan's commentary:*** *I've already begun to take time out when I find myself plunging into things (like on the ink blots). But I've discovered that I can seek my own counsel best when no one else is around. So I'm going to practice with school work and housekeeping before trying out in social settings.*

This last excerpt also illustrates that the commentary phase is an occasion for continued assessment, as are the client's tryings out in his daily life. The report is not an x-ray of immutable traits, but a progress report on changing comprehensions, growth, and suggestions, similar to therapy or counseling notes.

Additional excerpts

The following excerpts are all from one report, written for a state mental hospital on a 54-year-old retired coal miner. In answer to the diagnostic referral, I concluded that his delusions were not schizophrenic but were related to brain damage suffered in (documented) mining accidents.

> *As I found myself lapsing into swapping social pleasantries with Mr. Clark (for example, recipes for frying rabbits, soil conditions for cantaloupe, reputation*

> *of the hospital), I realized that for the moment I had forgotten his delusions about being a six-star general, and that he could no longer correctly add four plus four. I suspect that in a similar way his family and neighbors often either forget, or find it seemingly inappropriate, to check out with him his understanding of new plans or agreements...*
>
> *Mr. Clark worked attentively with the Kohs blocks for much longer (ten minutes on one design) than most testees will. He said that it felt like puttering in his workshop) – he'd keep "fooling" with it until the "danged thing" worked out. Sometimes, when he's available, Mr. Clark's (adult) son has been called on for advice about a resistive project. But sometimes Mr. Clark has shouted and argued, thrown tools around, and insisted that his son is disobedient, that he (Mr. Clark) is the "commander-in-chief." He described such incidents when I asked him when else had been like "just now, with me (psychologist) pushing you to go faster, the nurse interrupting us to say that you have to miss garden assignment to take medication, and your leg hurting." I'm not clear about what his household variations of these conditions are; perhaps Mrs. Jayson (unit social worker) could develop some leads on this with the family...*
>
> *Mr. Clark and I eventually named this sequence "impatience," and practiced his "standing for [his] rights" by asking for clarification or assistance whenever "impatience sets in." We practiced this on the Bender, where he finally "stood" for his "rights" by asking directly if he were doing okay, and in a "pretend" interview in which he finally announced that he was "confused" and "impatient" and that I would have to get help from someone else for my answers. Ward staff and family could continue this terminology and practice with Mr. Clark to help him bypass those situations in which confusion, frustration, and what I suspect must be a sense of impotence, have led to delusional assertions of competence.*

These excerpts illustrate several of the themes from above: the assessment context, including my own kind of presence and approach, is represented; test performance is presented as instances of the patient's daily comportment and as my vehicle for trying out alternatives; the language we used in the sessions is made available for continuity in relating with the patient; and finally, the report tries to evoke a sense of the patient's living of his world – its fluctuating physiognomy for him as he moves through it in variations of his way. While physically visible events are the touchpoints for the patient, myself, and his other helpers, we must try to reach him "where he lives" if we are to help him to recognize those changes in the face of his terrain that ought to announce: "Danger: Take Alternative Route."

Mr. Clark did not comprehend several of the sentences and the thrust of the report. So I focused on his understanding of our concluding set of recommendations and of how the staff would behave with him. In addition I tried to clarify for him his understanding of why he was in "the loony bin." I assured him that he did not have a "split personality" (his definition of "crazy"), but that it was his familiar periods of "confusion," "filling in" or "exaggerating," and "getting in trouble" (his characterization of fighting with a storekeeper, threats of violence to his family, and so on) that had led his son to hospitalize him. I explained that his difficulties in "recollecting" and planning started with damage to his nervous system sustained in the mining accidents, and that although medication and periodic examinations might help, it was up to him to learn to live with this "unfairness" as he had other "hard times"; others could help him, but "staying out of trouble" was still largely up to him. Of course this message had to be represented in multiple, repeated, and consistent ways by staff and family, but Mr. Clark again understood and experienced himself as "[his] own man, like in the old days."

Tallent (1975) has published a full psychological report that I wrote several years ago. It illustrates most of these collaborative assessment practices. Additional lines of discussion and examples can be found in Fischer, 1969, 1970, 1972a&b, 1974, and in Fischer and Rizzo, 1974. Before going on to respond to some questions typically raised about collaborative assessment, let me mention that all that I have said about psychological reports also holds true for other records. If the above practices are followed, client access to files should present no problem.

Elaboration

As Mr. Clark's case illustrates, the nature of the client's informed participation varies drastically from person to person. Admittedly, the earlier illustrations were from verbal, fairly reflective persons – always the easiest with whom to be a clinician! On other occasions, when the client cannot help me himself, I ask his significant others to help me locate the "whens," "when-nots," and pivot points. In short, the *practices* are malleable in order to meet each situation. But the *theoretical principles*, to be summarized in the next section, serve the goal of all cases: for the client to expand whatever experience he has of himself as sharing a world in which he can participate in shaping his own life.

Collaborative assessment does require more time than traditional assessment. In the long run, however, it is more efficient. The outcome includes not only a portrait of the client, but already tried-out entries into his daily life, and a first-stage set of concrete recommendations. The client already is feeling better able to cope with his situation. If he is referred or returned to a longer-term therapist or counselor, the transition is a smoother, more efficient one than in the past. Client satisfaction is higher, recidivism is lower, intensive individual therapy is assigned more judiciously, and staff's sense of achievement is greater.

The data and notions developed by objectivistic approaches, whether MMPI (Minnesota Multiphasic Personality Inventory) profile predictions or psychoanalytic interpretations, should not be overlooked. They too should guide the professional's understandings and queries. But they are realms of reflection, not of some truth underlying or causing behavior and experience.

This sort of common sense approach does result in a loss of mystique about psychology. I frequently hear from my graduate students' clinical supervisors that their reports were received enthusiastically by all involved as maximally useful, but that "they really weren't very psychological." Collaborative assessors learn to accept being ordinary, and earn their prestige on the basis of accomplishment with clients. This does require that the professional be much more than the technician he often has been in the past. It is his or her opinions that are presented, not "what the test says." Scores are starting points; they are not "results." The professional is answerable for his own values and assumptions, which must be reexamined as he confronts each new client. In a way, he is a consultant to clients, offering his impressions and suggestions, and perpetually refining and correcting procedures as his clients let him know the extent of his usefulness.

There are indeed touchpoints with other contemporary trends. For example: contingency management client contracts, self-control behavior modification, client participation in program evaluation, and humanistic psychology's therapies and workshops on self-discovery and self-help. Where this particular approach to informed participation differs, however, is in the theoretical foundation that allows it to go beyond the just-mentioned techniques to respect and work with the person's humanness, especially his lived world, in a fuller and more sustained manner.

Guiding Principles

Because most practitioners are more interested in successful techniques than in theory, this chapter has emphasized actual practices. At this point it seems important to review the human-science framework and to name explicitly the principles that guide the practices of collaborative assessment. This may attenuate readers' tendencies to yea-say the practices, or to reject them out of hand, without critically comparing them to their own assumptions and practices.

Human-science psychology in general

To summarize, psychology as a human (versus object) science takes explicit account of the individual's goals, values, and ways of forming and experiencing his milieu. Objectifiable physical conditions are also taken into account, but not as independent, more real, or as causal. Human science accepts the complexity involved in respecting the multiperspectival character of human reality. It forsakes the precision of object-science methods in the interest of staying in closer and more effective touch with the necessarily ambiguous and fluid structure of human affairs, including the inherent unity of experience and behavior. Ambiguity and flux are not chaos, however. There is order, but one for which the goals of anticipation and influence are more appropriate than those of prediction and control.

This human science approach allows professionals to be both scientific (rigorous, empirical, reflective, disciplined) and humanistic (promoting personal growth and capacity for experience). It encourages us to bring the idealistic preambles of our assorted codes of ethics (for example, "respect the dignity and worth of the individual") into consonance with our explanatory theories. A human science approach allows us to bypass the "yes, buts" and "never minds" to address the individual client in his own right while still being guided by general knowledge of human expression, options, and limitations. Finally, such an orientation necessitates the client's active involvement as an informed participant.

Among the relevant writings of the increasing numbers of existential, phenomenological, and humanistic authors, the ones addressed most directly to psychology as a human science are Giorgi's *Psychology as a Human Science* (1970) and volumes one (1971) and two (1975) of *Duquesne Studies in Phenomenological Psychology.*

Guiding Principles for Collaborative Assessment

I have named my own practice of human science psychological assessment in terms of the *collaborative*, jointly responsible, relationship between the client and assessor. But it also is characterized by several other interrelated guiding principles; collaborative assessment is *descriptive, contextual, structural, and interventional.*

Its data are on-going events from daily life and the assessment sessions, *described* as well as possible without recourse to reductionistic abstractions. Such descriptions try to present the *context* of the event – the observers' perspective and participation and at least an evocation of what seems to be the client's vantage points and involvement. Human-science assessment comprehends *structurally* rather than causally or reductively. That is, we understand an event in terms of its all equally essential, distinguishable but inseparable components rather than as a product of underlying forces. (For example, we understood Ms. Kugel's "Bendering" as occurring *when* she has no personally appropriated plan and standard for action, *when* there are others around to direct her, and *when* she perceives others as expecting her to be her old self; we did not attribute her conduct to "dependency," "social immaturity," or "impulsiveness.") The structure is understood in terms of the participants' situated experience rather than in terms of one privileged observer's objectifying perspective. This approach acknowledges that any assessor necessarily influences his client's participation in the assessment as well as his own perception of that participation. Finally, it encourages planned *intervention* within the client's accustomed ways of dealing with tasks. Thus we surpass identification of restrictions to explore personally viable expansions.

If the reader does not follow these or related principles in his or her professional work, then that person should specify just how his or her practices do take into account any human differences from objects. If he or she sees no significant differences, then shouldn't prospective clients be informed of that fact? For those readers who do find themselves in general agreement with a human-science approach to psychology, perhaps these guiding principles can help to bring practices into closer consonance with beliefs.

Note

1 Copyright 1978 by Transaction. Reprinted with permission. The official citation that should be used in referencing this material is: Fischer, C. T. (1978). Collaborative psychological assessment. In C. T. Fischer & S. L. Brodsky (Eds.). *Client participation in human services: The Prometheus principle* (pp. 41–61). New Brunswick, N. J.: Transaction.

References

Craddick, R. A. (1975). Sharing oneself in the assessment procedure. *Professional Psychology*, *6*, 279–282.

Dana, R. H., & Leech, S. (1974). Existential assessment. *Journal of Personality Assessment*, *38*, 428–435.

Fischer, C. T. (1969). Rapport as mutual respect. *Personnel and Guidance Journal*, *48*, 201–204.

Fischer, C. T. (1970). The testee as co-evaluator. *Journal of Counseling Psychology*, *17*, 70–76.

Fischer, C. T. (1972). Paradigm changes which allow sharing of results. *Professional Psychology*, *3*, 364–369.

Fischer, C. T. (1972). A theme for the child-advocate: shareable everyday-life events of the child-in-his-world. *Journal of Clinical Child Psychology*, *1*, 23–25.

Fischer, C. T. (1973). Contextual approach to assessment. *Community Mental Health Journal*, *9*, 38–45.

Fischer, C. T. (1974). Exit IQ: Enter the child. In G. Williams & S. Gordon (Eds.), *Clinical child psychology: Current practices and future perspectives* (pp. 333–350). N.Y.: Behavioral Publications.

Fischer, C. T. & Rizzo, A. A. (1974). A paradigm for humanizing special education. *Journal of Special Education*, *8*, 321–329.
Giorgi, A. (1970). *Psychology as a human science: A phenomenologically based approach*. N.Y.: Harper & Row.
Giorgi, A. Fischer, C. T., & Murray, E. D. (Eds.). (1975). *Duquesne studies in phenomenological psychology (Vol. 2)*. Pittsburgh: Duquesne University Press.
Giorgi, A., Fischer, W. F., & von Eckartsberg, R. (Eds.). (1971). *Duquesne studies in phenomenological psychology (Vol. 1)*. Pittsburgh: Duquesne University Press.
Riscalla, L. M. (1972). The captive psychologist and the captive patient. *Professional Psychology*, *3*, 375–79.
Szasz, T. S. (1961). *The myth of mental illness*. N.Y.: Harper & Row.
Tallent, N. (1975). *Psychological report writing*. N.Y.: Prentice-Hall.
Vane, J. R. (1972). Getting information from school and clinical psychologists. *Professional Psychology*, *3*, 205–208.

CHAPTER 10

ASSESSING PROCESS[1]

The word "process" is derived from the Latin *procedere*, meaning to advance, to progress, to move onward. Individualized assessment directly addresses progressing. From the point of view of a human-science psychology, tests are simplified and specialized versions of challenges that also face clients elsewhere. They are challenges to clients' progress – to their continuing the courses of their lives. Clients cope with the challenge, whether defensively, offensively, or routinely, as they cope with similar events in similar situations. For certain other forms of evaluation, it is sufficient and appropriate to address only the milestones that have been passed, the achievements left behind. Sometimes such data are used to predict what other milestones and achievements might be reached in the future. Some evaluations regard test profiles as products of various cognitive styles or psychodynamics, and thereby attend to process, albeit indirectly. Assessors can, of course, look to test scores and patterns for clues to process, which then can be pursued directly with clients.

Witnessing and Exploring Process

Whether studied in clients' environments or in an assessor's office, the process through which a person approaches, goes through, influences, and is changed by situations, is most accessible when the person is directly observed coping with challenges and then discusses what it was like, and how it was similar to and different from other situations. Clients, however, may offer explanations for what has happened rather than describing events directly and holistically. A major part of the assessor's task is to encourage the client to present events phenomenally – as they were lived at the time. A person progresses, after all, through a simultaneously affective/cognitive/actional engagement with the world.

To begin to explore process, the assessor first must be present to it. In particular, one does not ask "why," but instead asks, *who* is this person? Where is she or he going? What is her or his world like? Within that world, which things are seen as obstacles and which as invitations? What assumptions are made? What futures are possible from such positions? Process may seem to be internal to the client, but his or her travels are inextricably engaged with the worlds we share – the physical world, the world of past common experience, and the world in which our respective projects touch, clash, or cooperate. We know each other by what we do and where we go. Process becomes visible as style through first-hand encounters with the client's pathways, sequences, strategies.

To enhance sensitivity to process, the assessor should make conscientious use of her or his own biography and experience while with the client. In particular, it is appropriate to pay attention to one's associations, so long as they are not a continuation of an unrelated personal preoccupation. Even though the associations are the assessor's, they occur in the client's company and provide one avenue for understanding that person.

Explicit anticipations of where the client will go next allow the assessor to be surprised, to direct well-grounded requests for clarification to the client, and to reformulate. Throughout, the purpose is to continue reformulating, reunderstanding, until the referral can be answered in terms of this individual's life and until recommendations can be tailored. There is no need to search for absolute categories or explanations. It may be appropriate to judge, for example, whether one person is brain-damaged or whether another person fits the Borderline Personality Disorder designation. But to the extent that the assessment is to be individualized, greater priority is given to how the person lives her or his life – what the person's world looks like, and how the person perpetuates problems and perhaps could modify them.

An assessment is not intended to be a total portrait; the assessor does not look for themes or categories that would explain a person completely. The assessor remains open to complexity and to the diverse meanings that co-exist. Early confusion should be allowed to continue until the assessor discovers that a certain sense of things has begun to evolve. Actually, the assessor's presence, or attention, moves through many vicissitudes: openness to impressions, reflection, calculation, recollection, back to openness, and so on. The point is that unless the assessor becomes an access to the lived world of the client, calculations and deductions cannot lead to an individualized assessment.

During the assessment, meanings may occur to the assessor before their source is identified. For example, one may experience a client as evasive even though she or he is providing immediate, enthusiastic, elaborated answers to inquiries. The assessor should trust the impression long enough to search for its source and appraise its significance. In one case, the assessor recognized that the "evasiveness" of his client was his own impatience with the client's lengthy answers, which were tangential to the *assessor's* unspoken concerns. It was he who had not yet come to the point.

Another assessor experienced a client as haughty. He located that impression, after a while, in her turning away and tilting her head upward when he expressed concern for her. Then he noticed that the client's knuckles were white as she clutched the books in her lap. He realized that although she appeared to be haughty, she was also feeling tense and uncertain. He could now share both impressions with the client, pointing to their sources in what was visible and in his own differing reactions. This is another important reason for locating the source of impressions: The client can then "see" what others see, and can discuss what the observed event was like from the actor's perspective.

At other times, the assessor notices details that seem somehow meaningful even though the specific meaning is not clear. A lapel stickpin worn at an odd angle may be noticed early, only to gestalt much later with other "off center" ways that the client establishes independence. During discussions and in the report, a concrete example such as the stickpin can serve to collect or to recollect other instances of referral-relevant themes.

Ambiguity should be regarded as possibly inherent to phenomena rather than necessarily a deficient or confused form of knowing. This approach helps the assessor to accept both sides of apparently contradictory observations. The haughty woman was *both* disdainful of the assessor's solicitude *and* anxious about what they might discover. Apparent contradictions are in fact the dynamics of a person's moving toward goals.

While observing two graduate students making a class presentation, I noted that Pat directed Kevin and that she waited for Kevin's agreement. Upon reflection, I saw that her *way* of taking charge considered others' perspectives and desires; but this solicitude occurred in a context of being the leader. That Pat is experienced by most acquaintances as both pleasantly serious and quietly dynamic has to do with the tension of her living toward both goals (directing and waiting) concomitantly.

There are many ways to be present to process. In general, one should remain open, not interpret too readily, not reach closure prematurely, not explain away what one has witnessed. To keep myself attuned to process, rather than becoming sidetracked in a search for explanations, I ask, "How could this event have come into being?" I ponder the evolution of a completed Bender (the task that asks the client to copy freehand nine geometric patterns) much as one ponders footprints along a beach. One might guess the owner's height, weight, and gender fairly accurately. But where was this person going? Perhaps just for a walk; the prints follow the tide's edge as though the goal were to follow the tideline rather than to reach some particular destination. Yes, the prints are relatively flat – unlike those where the hurried walker's heels have struck the wet sand sharply. Perhaps the walker was on a nature stroll. But look at all these intriguing shells that the stroller left unturned and the huge horseshoe crab he did not investigate. How could a nature lover ignore these things? Perhaps they are familiar; maybe he was just walking home along an habitual route. Perhaps he ignored these marvels because he was preoccupied – I wonder about what? Here, the tracks veer to avoid walking through a child's small, crumbling moat. Although preoccupied, the stroller noticed it and cared.... This form of presence to process enriches perception and helps one to address meaningful questions to the client.

Other queries that I pose to myself and later address to the client include: Where does this experiaction bring the client? How and when does it work for him or her? When not? What is the short-term outcome? Long-term? Is the person winding up at places that were not intended? Where else is the person going? And coming away from? And avoiding? Because people often are not focally aware of all these facets of their travels, the assessor must be all the more alert to those moments when the client is in touch with a pertinent aspect of his or her movement. Those moments are entry points for joint exploration. In general, the assessor accepts a client's account *as the client's account*, and then suggests additions and modifications as they become apparent. Even these revisions are revised as the session goes on. When the client resists a line of inquiry, the assessor has failed to begin that inquiry within areas of the client's world that he or she experiences as familiar and traversable. Common ground was not adequately established. Sometimes, however, clients for their own reasons or because of severe disability do not allow the assessor access to more than end-product data. In all cases, as long as one's impressions can be documented with primary data, they should be retained and reported, even if the client does not agree, or does not understand. The client is an expert about what he or she remembers, and about what he or she is now concerned about and believes; but the assessor's differing impressions may be just as valid in a broader sense. Both views are important for understanding and planning, and both should be reported.

Table 10.1 illustrates the collaborative exploration of process. Many of the excerpts forerun activities illustrated in Table 10.2, on developing viable options. In actuality the activities of exploration and option-development are not so distinct. Both sets of excerpts illustrate the functions of tests that were outlined previously and the guiding principles of individualized assessment presented earlier.

Table 10.1 Witnessing and Exploring Process – Excerpts

The client is a 28-year-old program monitor, a woman, self-referred for career guidance.

Assessor: Sandy, what was your turning the paper horizontally about? [The client's Bender drawing paper is placed vertically, but was repositioned twice by the assessor after Sandy moved it.]

Client: I don't know. It just seemed better that way.

Assessor: Most people just leave it the way it's placed. You moved it to suit your preference. Is that like anything you've done at work that Mr. O'Pake might have seen as "going off on your own [part of the referral issue]"?

Client: No. It's just that the cards run this way [horizontal], so I thought the drawings would fit better if my paper were running the same way.

Assessor: Oh! So perhaps what Mr. O'Pake and I have seen as persistent individuality may be instead your effort to be even more conscientious than other monitors have been? [Sandy then describes how her work has been demonstrably more thorough and more timely than that of all others in her office, but superiors in her present and prior jobs have criticized her for unorthodox, sometimes defiant, sometimes lackadaisical work habits.] Well, you know we already talked about how surprised I was when your copies of the designs turned out to be so precise. As I was watching you, taking your time but not erasing or otherwise appearing to me to be concerned about accuracy – you were chatting with me most of the time – I expected the copies to be haphazard. At the end I still had that feeling, even though each design had turned out just fine. I think I'm beginning to see what Mr. O'Pake may be responding to.

Client: [Long pause] Well, that's it in a nutshell. I guess I've just got to find ways of letting my supervisors see that I am in fact doing exactly the job they want done. I'd hate to do it, but maybe I should ask them to check my work en route so they can see *it* instead of *me*. At least that would be easier than changing careers!

The client is a 19-year-old college junior, male, referred to the Guidance Center by a business law professor for trouble in attending classes regularly.

Assessor: You seem to enjoy the challenge of these test items. I have trouble imagining you being bored with Dr. Pressinger's course?

Client: That's why he said I should see somebody. When I'm in class, I enjoy it and I participate. And like I said, I write the papers. On other days I get up early, but on business law days I often just sleep in. I know I ought to, but...

Table 10.1 (cont.)

Assessor: Ought to? Who says people should go to early classes? [Client: You just should.] What happens to people who go to their early classes?

Client: [Laughingly] They get good grades, get elected to offices, and grow up to be responsible executives.

Assessor: And who wants you to grow up to be an executive?

Client: I do. Well, I mean it's expected, and I do have the skills and the opportunity....

Assessor: Who's doing this expecting? [Discussion continues, as the client discovers that he feels as though he has been pushed into his father's career line. An appointment is made for career advisement assessment, through which the client could make some informed choices, including possibly his present business major.]

The client is a 41-year-old marketing manager in a corporation-sponsored manager-development assessment.

Assessor: Many people who score as high as you did on these two scales have been described as stubborn. [Personality Research Form, high dominance and endurance scales.]

Client: Well, it's sure right about that! My wife would tell you that!

Assessor: Yes? What would she say?

Client: Well, that I'm not satisfied until something is finished, till it's done right. [Assessor: Like?] Like putting up the dry wall for our driveway; took me all summer a couple years back, but ours is the only one that didn't buckle during these severe winters we've had recently.

Assessor: Your approach certainly paid off. But what do people call your being stubborn when they don't like it?

Client: What do you mean?

Assessor: What do your kids, or your subordinates at work, say about your being persistent?

Client: Oh, I see what you mean. I'd say the boy and my daughter don't much notice unless I'm after them to do something right. Then they say I'm picky. [Assessor: And at work?] Perfectionistic. [Long pause] I guess we're onto something. This seems to relate to what we were saying before – about my having trouble delegating authority. Like you said, it's not a question of my knowing how to analyze a problem and break it out into assignments. I just don't like to let go until I know it is done right. Lord, I just remembered [smiling] – my house painter told me he was going to increase his charges if I didn't get out from underfoot!

Assessor: Okay. Tell me some times when you *do* get out from underfoot.

Client: Do you mean like at home? [Assessor: Okay – whenever.] Well, it would never occur to me to interfere with my wife's cooking. And of course I don't insert myself into the sales manager's side of things. If anything goes wrong there, everyone knows it's got nothing to do with me.

Assessor: Is that similar to when you were copying the designs [Bender-Gestalt]? You said you hadn't been "assiduously careful" since you didn't see what they had to do with your intelligence or your management competence? [Client nods.] Then so far it seems that being persistent and proud of a job done right has been an asset except in those situations when you're afraid that someone else's work will reflect badly on you? Is that a key to when you haven't "let go"?

Table 10.1 (cont.)

Client: I guess that's fair to say, although I'd never thought of it that way before.
Assessor: As we go along, let's keep an eye out for what else might be involved.

The client is an 18-year-old college freshman, woman, self-referred for academic problems.

Assessor: I noticed just now [on the Bender-Gestalt] that you started out very carefully – checking the card several times, making small drawings. Then toward the end you only glanced at the cards, and the drawings became bigger and somehow more casual. Do you recognize that as something you've done before?
Client: I've never done this before [the Bender].
Assessor: I meant have you done other things in the same way? For example, if you're cooking with a recipe, do you start out double-checking the instructions, and then toward the end just trust your inclinations?
Client: [Laughs] That's exactly what I do! Unless it's a recipe I've done several times. Then I just review it once.
Assessor: What was it like while you were doing the drawings? How did it become different when you began to draw them on your own? Somehow you looked both more confident and more impatient at this juncture [pointing to the BenderGestalt reproductions].
Client: I wouldn't say "confident." I just decided it was pretty silly to take something so simple so seriously.
Assessor: Okay. Is that what has happened on your English term papers? Maybe your instructor was partly right – perhaps you didn't follow the instructions carefully, especially if you've already done other papers. And I bet since you *did* study the instructions very carefully at first, you assumed you remembered them.
Client: Oh my!

The client is a 60-year-old male stroke (CVA) victim, a lawyer, assessed for recovery of function.

Assessor: This graph [WAIS-R profile] shows how well you did on each of the sections. Here's Vocabulary and here's the section with the items about the mailbox and getting out of the forest. You earned about the same score on each of them, and I think it's probably at your prestroke level. Does that square with your experience? You didn't feel as though you were at a disadvantage on these, did you?
Client: No. Do they [scores] compare favorably with other lawyers'? [Assessor: Yes] Except the one with copying of the figures [Digit Symbol]?
Assessor: Yes, you're right, your score on it is way below where it probably used to be. This one [pointing to profile] has fallen significantly too; could you take a guess at which one it is [Digit Span]?
Client: The one with the blocks?
Assessor: Here's Block Design. That's in the middle range of your scores. I really don't know whether it was much higher before or not. But you felt disadvantaged while working with the blocks?
Client: Toward the end I was feeling nervous – my insides knotted up.
Assessor: Okay. And how about when you repeated numbers to me?
Client: I managed to forget that. Yeah, that really scared me. Where's that one [on the profile sheet]?

Table 10.1 (*cont.*)

Assessor: Here. Now let me ask you: How did your insides do on this [holds up Trail-Making B test sheet]?

Client: I figure I did all right. I just was careful to slow down. But I don't like that; it feels like I'm a kid in school just learning his letters and numbers.

Assessor: Again, you're right on target. You made very few mistakes, but you took as much time as a schoolboy to do it. Let me tell you what I think is involved on all these tasks where you had trouble. They all look pretty simple at first, but they're things you don't do every day, things that require you to figure out and then remember the principle. Especially when you realize that in earlier years you could have done these tasks more or less automatically, you become "scared" and tighten up.

Client: Yes, but that's preferable to faking answers – or throwing things [which he reported he had done].

Assessor: Indeed. And as we agreed before, you seem to acknowledge these new limitations and cope with them honestly when you are with somebody who knows about the stroke. We can make this recommendation to your wife and partners: Whenever you're confronted by something that's a little new for you, family or staff should be around. Another recommendation is that when you go back to work, you've got to limit yourself to things you know how to do by heart, things that don't require you to think on your feet. I imagine title searches and wills wouldn't give you trouble…?

Client: But what about numbers? These tests all had numbers.

Assessor: I don't think it's numbers as such that throw you. See – here's where you scored on Arithmetic; that's not at all bad. And your wife tells me that you're back to balancing the checkbook, and that you come within pennies of estimating the grocery checkout total.

Client: That's true. You know, I vacillate between extremes: One minute I'm afraid I can't do anything, that I've no business thinking about going back to the office. The next minute I'm furious about being restricted to jobs any punk law clerk could handle.

Assessor: And sometimes you worry that you're getting worse, that your brain is deteriorating? [Client looks up, surprised, and nods slowly.] The only danger of that is if you had another stroke. You've probably recovered about as much as you're going to from the damage you have, though. [Long silence] You *will* have to restrict your assignments. For example, you shouldn't argue trial cases in court anymore; you'd probably miss some of the abstract points or unfamiliar lines of argument, like you did on this Concept Formation Test. [Extended discussion of other tasks at work and at home that he could or should not undertake, followed by a discussion of his embarrassment at returning to what he felt was "clerk status."] You've already come a long way in coping realistically with your stroke. Frankly, I admire your courage and honesty. But as you said, there will be a lot of ups and downs as you develop ways of accommodating at work. You'll make some mistakes, but a good way to minimize them is to respect those signs that you're moving into dangerous zones. What are the signs?

Client: Knotted insides! And feeling impatient and wanting to dismiss obstacles. Or feeling like a schoolboy – that precedes impatience.

Assessor: Yes, it's important to catch yourself there, before you became impatient. And what were our suggestions in that regard?

Client: Here, I made notes on that too. (1) If there's time, just slow down as I did on "follow-the-dots" [Trail Making]; (2) if not, or if I'm not sure I'm getting it right, go to someone for consultation.

Table 10.1 (cont.)

Assessor: Right. Of course, these steps are new for you, so you'll have to go slowly with them too! Seriously, it will take considerable practice. But since we'll work this out with your family, partners, and staff, they'll understand what's going on. Let's ask your wife in now, to explain our progress and then continue our discussion. All right?

The client is a 24-year-old man, arrested for car theft, referred by his lawyer.

Assessor: You mentioned that your parole officer accuses you of not planning ahead? [Client nods.] And that other people have said that too, but you disagree? [Client nods.] Well, I don't know yet whether I agree with them, but I'll bet we've got an example right here [Bender-Gestalt] of what they're talking about. You did all of these [pointing to early designs] accurately and efficiently, but look how these later ones had to be squeezed in on their sides. Could that be an example of not planning ahead? What I mean is, you could have figured out the space ahead of time, especially since I mentioned how many designs there would be.

Client: I don't waste time planning for easy things. I just know what to do without thinking. Corsky [parole officer] says that's impulse; I say it's intuition. If you don't have it, don't knock it. Besides you said yourself it [Bender copy] was pretty good.

Assessor: Yes, it is. So I guess going by intuition worked pretty well this time. Tell me some other times it worked well.

Client: Like what?

Assessor: Well, I don't know. I need for you to tell me. But I would imagine that another example would be getting ready to come here today. Some guys would lie awake planning what to say. I'll bet you thought about it a little, and then figured you'd know what to do when you got here. [Client nods approvingly.]

Assessor: Okay; so can you think of other times when somebody else might have to do a lot of figuring, but you don't have to?

Client: Sure, all right. I did some boxing at Haywood, and everybody said I was a natural. [Assessor writes that down and nods.] Or if I'm going out drinking, the way to do that is you must flow with the tide. Have a good time. This one time I wound up on the other side of town in this executive's penthouse. To this day I don't know how I got there, but I helped myself to breakfast.

Assessor: Tell me about times you've wound up someplace by surprise, but it didn't work out so well. [Client looks startled. "You mean… "] Yes, go ahead.

Client: [Avoiding assessor's gaze] Well, I guess that's like how I wound up getting arrested. I mean we was all in the car, and I was driving, but I didn't mean to steal it.

Assessor: Right. So generally, going by intuition works quite well for you. But it doesn't work all the time. When it doesn't work is when people say you didn't plan?

Client: [Slowly] Yeah, I guess. But see, I plan by taking things as they come, one day at a time. [Picking up speed] See, I knew this fellow…

Assessor: Hey, hold on. I want you to tell me about times you *have* planned – perhaps planning what to take on a trip, or calculating how many months you have left on parole.

Client: Well, yeah. What the ___does Corsky know. I probably have planned more than he ever knew how! [Assessor: Give me some specific instances.] Once I took this shop course, and the instructor really knew his stuff. I made this wood-based lamp, and gave it to my mother. [Assessor: And that required a lot of planning?] Oh, yeah, lots. You have to use a template and measure and check. And choose a die and figure what you had to get done before the shop closed.

Table 10.1 (cont.)

Assessor: Okay, so the point is that you can plan, and in fact often do so quite well. But you don't plan "when to plan": You get in trouble when a situation calls for planning, but you keep going on intuition.

Client: When you put it that way, it's true.

Assessor: Okay, as we go on here, let's keep one eye out for signs that might tell you when to shift from intuition to "planning to plan." Mr. Corsky probably could be more helpful to you if he knew those signs too.

The client is a 35-year-old self-referred graduate student in a Humanities Department, who wants to know if he is "officially paranoid" or whether his university's faculty and administration are in collusion against him.

Assessor: You know, I think I know how that woman security officer [at his university] felt when you were explaining your complaint. *You* knew that what you were saying made sense, but until the very end, she didn't. Just now [during copying of the Bender-Gestalt] I couldn't imagine that this design [twelve three dot parallel slanted columns] was going to come out right. I've never seen anyone do it that way. [Client smiles.] Most people draw an entire row or column at one time. You were all over the place – a dot here and one there. I was amazed when it all came together. I think she and I were both confused [client nods, smiling broadly], and I think you thoroughly enjoyed and abetted our confusion. At this point I find this intriguing, but I'd guess that in her shoes I'd have felt used. No wonder she began avoiding you, and being short with you on those other visits. What do you think – are we onto something?

Client: Yes, that is an astute and accurate assessment. People have to learn to appreciate the internal beauty of the universe. Instead, the sheep...

Assessor: Yes, well, I see that you regard me as one of your sheep.

Client: A likely proposition, but one that remains to be proven.

Assessor: Well, if you have repeatedly told your advisor, chair, and dean, in one way and. another, that they are all sheep, you thereby make it impossible for them to want to spend their time with you. I suspect that you make us into sheep by nipping at our heels, and lurking behind trees waiting for us to be caught off guard. [Client nods, smiles derisively.] Let's see what else we can learn together. [Rorschach, including inquiry, is completed.] What struck me most here is that even though you appeared to be relaxed and fairly low key, in fact you were very actively searching through each card, looking for connections, building up a story that would take everything into account. Many people just say what this part or this one looks like [pointing to areas on card] and just let the rest alone if it doesn't seem at first glance to fit in. I have a better appreciation now of why you have insisted on receiving the full year's syllabus, and why you don't want anyone to interfere with any one step on your worksheets.

Client: That's correct. They don't see that there's an entire system involved. So you tell me who's schizo.

Assessor: Let's talk about that. It's clear to me that you do not match the official category that we call schizophrenic. You don't experience hallucinations, or see or understand things in bizarre ways. You're not crazy. But there are some categories that you do match and these categories do include the word *paranoid*. Not crazy, but paranoid. What does that word mean to you?

Table 10.1 (*cont.*)

Client: If it doesn't mean crazy, what does it mean? It's a label for not having to deal with people who are different.

Assessor: As always, you do have a point there. But there is also some worth to this label; it refers to being suspicious, competitive, angry in a certain pattern, one in which a person tries to read other people's motives at the cost of letting them be.

Client: I let others be! What else can I do as a "mere" student?

Assessor: Let's look at this card [Rorschach] again. You put together an image that was complex, didn't leave anything out, and so on. It was quite amazing, very unusual. And you enjoyed doing that and impressing me. That's the "good news"; the "bad news" is that while doing all that, you missed what most people notice, namely that this whole thing [holds card up and out at a distance] strikes most people as a bat. Or here, this part strikes many persons as a woman.

Client: [After a moment of silence] I'm not most people! I don't give a rat's ass what they see! It's got nothing to do with me.

Assessor: They're all sheep? Look, your creative side is admirable, but your way of being creative puts others in a one-down position. You've been doing it to me ever since we started. Even though I'm trying to be objective, and even though I don't know what actually happened on your campus, I find it very easy to sympathize with the faculty and administrators. [Client starts to protest.] No, let me answer the questions you brought to me. (1) You're not schizophrenic; (2) but if you took the university to court [client's reason for consulting the assessor], the lawyers, judge, jury would all see your complaints as paranoid – they would see from the way you would treat them that you probably did the same thing with university representatives. That is, that you did not look at their side, that you ignored usual protocol, that you made it difficult for them to be sympathetic to your complaints, that you looked everywhere for evidence of their inferiority and their disregard for yourself. Whatever validity there is to your complaints, and I'm sure there must be some, the judicial system would probably find in favor of the university. You would be your own worst enemy in court. [There ensued an hour's discussion, in which the assessor stood by the above conclusion, but pursued what she felt were the client's worries about undergoing some kind of breakdown in the future, and his deep (albeit vehemently denied) longings for approval, support, and love. The assessor spoke of ways the client might moderate (not give up) his aggressive stance, just to take some pressure off himself. She also said that she felt he deserved an opportunity to explore his concerns with a therapist – somebody who would hear him out, who could be sympathetic without taking sides, and who could offer a place of refuge. About a month later, the client entered therapy with another psychologist, although he attended erratically. He backed off his threatened lawsuit against his university, and settled into a more or less workable relation with his professors. Of course he maintained his basic defensively competitive stance. He refused to pay for the assessment he had contracted.]

The client is a 22-year-old male, accused of attempted rape, referred by his attorney.

Client: [During Rorschach.] Jesus, you must be making something of all these insides I'm seeing. [Assessor: I am a little surprised; what do you think is going on?] Maybe you think I'm falling apart. [Long pause] Maybe you think I think women are just anatomy.

Table 10.1 (cont.)

Assessor: There's probably something to both of those points, but not quite that severe. Back here [Card VI] you mentioned "muscles tautened" [sic]. Tell me what about the card helps give that appearance?

Client: The way they are. See, they're knotted and straining. This darkness shows how they're stirated [sic]. This is a larger section but it looks smaller because it's behind this section.

Assessor: I don't think you're breaking down, but I do think that you're doing a lot of struggling – trying to keep things in perspective but feeling caught, maybe held immobile, when you'd like to just do something. [Client nods incredulously but vigorously.] Okay, tell me – just let your thoughts go wherever they want to – of a time, any time, when *your* muscles were like that.

Client: Okay, but I don't know if this makes sense. [Assessor nods and shrugs.] I think of when my father chased my mom around the kitchen table with a butcher knife. He cut her too. She went to the hospital. [Assessor: And you were where?] In the corner, God, was I scared. I wanted to save my mother, but I was too little. My father and I, we respect each other now; but we keep our distance. He didn't come to my wedding. [Assessor: That must have hurt, and made you mad too.] Naw. Well, yeah, it did.

Assessor: I know it was different too, but were you feeling "knotted" the day you picked up that woman?

Client: Yeah, at least all afternoon. [Client tells that he was tired that day, had been teased in front of the secretarial staff, and had collected his pay check only to spend it all at a local bar on pinball machines and buying drinks for his "buddies," who left him there after his money ran out. Further discussion reveals that in his own way the client recognizes the dynamics of his having struck the woman who refused to go with him that night, but that he does not know what he could have done instead.]

Assessor: Tom, let me tell you what I'm going to say to Mr. Letterman [lawyer] in my report. I'm going to say that in fact it is possible you could threaten or hurt a woman again in similar circumstances, you know – if your manliness and competence are severely challenged as they were that day: being fired, the men laughing at you, the woman calling you a "kid." [Client nods, looking to the floor.] But I can also say that you don't want it to happen again and that there is an unusually good chance that, if you see a psychotherapist regularly to explore other ways of handling challenges, you won't show up in the judge's court again. I'll also write to Mr. Letterman about the vocational options we have discussed.

The client is a 24-year-old male arrested for reckless driving and resisting arrest, referred by his attorney.

Assessor: [After Rorschach] You know, I can see just from how you sit back, keeping your distance [assessor gestures between herself and client] as you go through these tests that most people must see you as laid back. Is that true? [Client: Yeah.] But I can also imagine that there are a lot of situations when you also feel vaguely restless, kind of tense, like you wish you were going somewhere, but you don't know where.

Client: [Wide-eyed, but slumps further back into his chair] Where did you get that?

Table 10.1 (cont.)

Assessor: Well, like this card [Card VI]. It's hard for many people to see that this skin could be stretched out and pulling against the nails while it's drying, unless they know what it's like to be stretched that way.

Client: I don't let nobody push me around.

Assessor: I understand. But sometimes there's no person there, and you still feel that way, right? [Client: I guess.] Maybe, since you're already feeling held down, you're sort of ready to strike back if somebody crowds you.

Client: Yeah, I guess. But that's the way it has to be.

Assessor: Not if you had a sense that you were getting somewhere, that you were on the way somewhere.

Client: I *am* going places. I *am* somebody.

Assessor: Uh-huh, [gently] you're somebody who's going to jail. You're somebody who smarts off with police officers instead of keeping cool.

Client: That's what you have to do. I'd rather do that than get pushed around.

Assessor: We have to stop in a few minutes but we'll finish tomorrow. I want to leave a thought with you today. I think that in a vague, kind of haunting way, you long to be more of a somebody than you already are, that you long to be on your way, and that you wish people would help you instead of getting in your way. [Client: Nah, that's shrink stuff.] We'll have to agree to disagree about this. I really don't know how to be clearer about what I'm talking about. But I do know that whenever you're feeling "nailed down," you're aware that life could be different for you, that it would be nice if everybody could be more gentle with everyone, and you could take care of yourself without having to fight back. [Client sighs and sits quietly for a full minute, then leaves without a word. The next day he showed up early for his appointment.]

The client is a 31-year-old technician, being screened for employment at a nuclear facility.

Assessor: Considering the reason we're doing this evaluation, I don't think I should use the word "explode" in my report. [Both smile.] What's another term for that feeling you've had when different supervisors have given you conflicting instructions?

Client: It [the explosive feeling] only happened when it went on for a long time and when there wasn't anybody, except my wife, I could talk to about it.

Assessor: Yes, but it's happened twice, you say? [Client nods.] Anyway, how shall we describe the feeling?

Client: Torn apart. Like if I'm not going to wind up in shreds, I'd better quit the job or keep on drinking. I did each once.

Assessor: Okay. That's the language we'll use. I'm going to tell the New York office that you do meet their criteria for clearance under special supervision; that they should advise your company's personnel section of what you consider to be stressful work conditions, and that you would appreciate an early opportunity to discuss with your superiors your concerns in this regard. The idea is that you'd like to have an advance, agreed-upon strategy for handling any such conflicts.

Client: I wish I had done that on the second job. [Discussion follows of the ways the client could cope with disagreements.]

Table 10.1 (cont.)

The client is a six-year-old girl, referred for "gifted student" evaluation.

Assessor: I'm going to tell you two things you said, and you tell me what's different about them: (1) "I don't know. There's some. Is it five pennies?" and (2) "It's when there's snow. It's a season." [Client's tone is imitated.] What's different about you in those two answers?

Client: I was smart about winter. [Assessor: And what about the number of pennies in a nickel?] I was ignorant about pennies.

Assessor: Ignorant? Who says "ignorant"? [Client, giggling: Eddie, he's my brother. He's in fifth grade.] But you knew the right answer; five is correct. What's ignorant about that?

Client: I didn't know if I was sure. I didn't know ahead of time if it was right. [Assessor: If I hadn't kept at you, do you think you would have guessed by yourself?] Nope, I mighta made a mistake.

Assessor: Here's a new test [Stanford Binet]. This time the rules are that you're supposed to guess, even if you might be wrong. Okay? [Assessor continues with the S-B, documenting that client in fact has been earning misleadingly low scores because of her fear of looking ignorant.] Marie, you know what? I think you were "smart" when you guessed. I'm going to suggest to your mother and father that they tell Eddie that sometimes it's "ignorant" not to guess. What do you think about that?

Client: Eddie says you're not allowed to guess at school or kids make fun of you.

Assessor: Maybe they do sometimes, especially if you're being silly. Let's practice some more guessing, and see if you can tell when it's silly and when it's not.

The above clients were not unusually responsive or reflective. The transcription does, however, make the tempo seem faster than it was. At the time, there were many pauses within and between sentences and between interchanges. For the sake of economy, these excerpts do not show the gradual evolution of the dialogue. In addition, the false starts, unintelligible mumblings, and "uhms" and "ahs" have been deleted. The excerpts do not show the long periods of working and observing, during which the participants do not converse.

The assessor does not mention everything that seems interesting; interjections are carefully selected and timed, are calculated to reach clients at their present state of awareness, and are all referral-relevant. (The brief identifications of clients preceding the excerpts are not the clarified referrals, but are meant only to provide the reader with a brief orientation.)

The assessor's Rorschach remarks were not mere intuitions, but were based also on empirical research, most often that reported by Exner (1974, 1978). This research is particularly useful in that it reports the relations of test patterns to actual life events, such as going through a divorce or waiting for the results of a gross anatomy examination. The remarks addressed to clients are not based only on a single, just-observed comportment. Rather, prior observations of similar comportment have suggested that it would be productive to share these related impressions with the client.

One does not simply "dream up" daily life parallels to clients' test comportment as one goes along. Comportment has been observed directly from the moment the client knocked on the office door. The person's knocking, greeting, and way of walking into the room and taking a chair are all life events. Comparing these to test comportment helps the assessor to look for parallels with preassessment events.

These direct observations also provide a link for my graduate student assessors with two of their training exercises. First, each time a student encounters a distinctive production (DAP or Bender, for example) with a volunteer "client," the student later reproduces that drawing several times. The student tries different approaches and notes his or her own posture, breathing, attention, and so forth, as for instance, one draws tiny, light figures in the lower comer of the page, and later draws large, bold, one-per-page figures. This exercise attunes one to what it may be like to be the client in those moments. The light lines, for example, may be tenuous, delicate, or evasive; all are (nonexclusive) possibilities. The second exercise is to notice how people go about everyday tasks, such as short-order cooking, waiting tables, mowing a lawn, driving, carrying on a conversation, conducting a media interview, and so on. Assessment attunement develops as one has imagined how the cook, waitress, mower, driver, whatever, would approach a DAP, Bender, or Rorschach.

I have developed a stock of common tactics people employ in carrying out school and household tasks and in entering new social situations. After observing a copy Bender evolve, I might remark that "I'm reminded of a friend who cleans house by starting with windows, discovers a cobweb in the casing, begins dusting all comers, discovers fingerprints around a light switch, goes to the closet for a sponge, and is surprised to find the windows only half done." I would then indicate the step-by-step parallel with the Bender's evolution. This client might respond, "No, no. I always stick to one thing at a time till it's finished. But I do go back to wipe up streaks in the midst of washing another pane. My husband says I'm deceptively unmethodical for being such a meticulous person." It does not matter if my comparison is not accurate, so long as the client can use it as a starting point for providing actual instances similar to the Bender performance.

Finally, reading excerpts such as those in Table 10.1 often dissolves assessors' reservations about sharing written reports with clients. What makes a difference is the way the assessment was conducted. Its findings were not just judgmental, but rather took into account the person's own view of the situation. The person's approaches were not viewed as good or bad in themselves, but as working for the client in some circumstances and for some purposes, and against him or her in others. The assessor's focus on actual events – primary data – allowed the client to be an active, genuinely informed participant. The written report reviews this collaborative assessment; it does not surprise, offend, or mystify the client. The assessor need not fear the client's response to reading the report.

Developing Options

Table 10.1 has illustrated how an assessor can help clients to see that existing patterns may not be necessary patterns, that clients can author their lives differently. However, these discoveries are rarely sufficient to initiate change. A person must find himself or herself already functioning in a different way before that possibility is fully experienced as personally viable. Therefore, trying out alternatives during the assessment is intended to serve three related functions: (1) to explore just what is personally viable – what fits the person's sense of who he or she has been and where he or she wants to go from there; (2) to help the client recognize landmarks – signs that one is moving toward trouble – and to locate pivot points where the client could shift to an optional route to reach the destination; and (3) to practice taking that optional route, so that it feels familiar and reliable and can be taken again on other journeys.

Efforts to develop options continue the assessment of who the person is. The client may discover further aspects of his or her circumstances that should be taken into account. For example, a secretary noted that she could indeed ask her supervisor to clarify instructions, but now she realizes that she could not ask in front of the other secretaries. Moreover, a client may encounter additional motivations that the old comportment served. While practicing drawing Bender designs with lighter strokes and less concern for perfection, another client remarked: "You know it is frightening to feel the heaviness of having to do it just exactly 'their' way; but up here [lightly skimming over the paper instead of darkly tracing] I realized that I'm free to take 'their' demands lightly, and go my own way. But I don't know what my way is." TAT stories later elaborated on the ways the client had resented the burden of others' demands and yet had diligently answered them rather than risk failure on her own. It is in these practicings of alternative approaches that self-deceptions, incompatible goals, and other previously nonfocal concerns – in short, unconscious motivations – become concretely available for collaborative exploration. These pursuits usually occur after the assessment is well under way. Earlier phases of assessment typically emphasize discovering and describing *what* the client does. Previously unexamined assumptions and habitual, taken-for-granted comportment become apparent well before conflicted, dynamic comportment is evident.

Trying out alternatives early in the assessment serves to explore which of these options are already available for the client. I find it helpful to ask myself the "when/when-not?" question as I notice the person taking some particular approach. To protect myself from assuming that what I am witnessing is the only approach this person takes, I consider the client's present circumstance and how different circumstances might promote different comportment. This reflection leads me to intervene with suggestions that help to clarify where different alternatives should be developed. Although more practicing occurs toward the end of the assessment, it typically arises in earlier form as a "trying out."

I have purposefully used the term "different comportment," rather than "new comportment." For an optional route to be personally viable, it must be a variation of present approaches; it must branch off from where the client is now, and it must accommodate familiar action. Using the client's terms, such as "lightly," "heaviness," and "doing it their way" in the example above, can help the client to recognize what is familiar in a different approach. While inquiring into the "geography" of a client's journey – where he or she is going, away from what, among what, and so forth – I also ask "for whom?" Sometimes clients know explicitly; other times the answer remains vague. It may be helpful to ask, "Who would be proud to see you do this?" Or who would be surprised, jealous, or angry?

The excerpts in Table 10.2 illustrate the development of personally viable options.

Table 10.2 Developing Options: Excerpts

The client is a 32-year-old woman, referred for assessment of "chronic depression."

Assessor: Some people just automatically turn these cards over, but you waited for me to do it.

Client: Oh, I didn't know I was supposed to turn them. You didn't tell me to, did you?

Assessor: No. Either way is fine. But I was reminded of how you waited outside my door instead of knocking. What would you say was the same?

Client: I don't see anything wrong about waiting. I was taught to be polite.

Assessor: I see. And what would be the opposite of polite?

Client: Pushy. Getting what you want at someone else's expense.

Assessor: I wonder if being polite isn't sometimes at *your* expense? You must have felt a little apprehensive waiting in the hall, wondering if I was going to remember.

Client: No. [Assessor: What then?] Impatient. No offense, but frankly I heard you laughing on the phone, and it was on my time.

Assessor: I'll bet you were impatient that I was writing instead of turning the cards.

Client: Well, yes. But you're the psychologist.

Assessor: I'd like to try an experiment. Let's start over. [Assessor lays out the Bender cards and new paper.] But this time, turn the cards yourself if you feel like it. [Assessor repeats original instructions.]

Client: [After turning four cards] Are you going to tell me what this experiment is about?

Assessor: Sure. And by the way; your inquiry just now strikes me as quite appropriate, not the least bit impolite. I was wondering if turning the cards felt all right.

Client: Well, yes. You said I could.

Assessor: So it's not just a question of being polite, but also of waiting for permission. [Client looks startled and nods.] And waiting can be frustrating, especially when other people are not being considerate of your deference.

Client: My what?

Assessor: Deference – putting the other person's initiative or plans ahead of yours. I can imagine that sometimes you could become quietly teed-off? [Client makes a dismissing gesture with her hands, but nods.] Being polite while you're wondering if you're being taken advantage of can be awfully wearing. [Testing and discussion continue.]

Client: This [Block Design] was harder than the others. [Assessor: What seemed harder?] You didn't say whether you were counting errors or just timing me or what. I didn't know what to concentrate my effort on. I felt like quitting, but you're not supposed to.

Assessor: And being caught in that bind, you were also a little angry. You did hang in, but you were glaring at me from time to time. [Client nods hesitantly.] You know, in a different situation I might have tried to avoid you so I wouldn't risk having you mad at me.

Client: But I was the one on the spot. You were in charge.

Assessor: Granted, I'm in charge, but let's do another experiment to see how you can avoid being "on the spot." Maybe ask for clarification so you don't have to wonder, or choose what *you* think is most important. [After re-administering the Block Design subtest twice, up through the fifth design, the assessor pointed out that both she and the client felt more comfortable. Through the remaining subtests, the client practiced asking for clarification.]

Table 10.2 (cont.)

Client: [At the beginning of Rorschach inquiry.] You didn't tell me I was supposed to explain everything the first time!

Assessor: You weren't. Going back through the cards this way is standard procedure. What's interesting is that you assumed I was criticizing you. And in turn I felt just now that you were criticizing me for putting you in an awkward place. I'm beginning to see how both you and Marianne [neighbor] are right. I bet she *does* avoid you, leaving you politely waiting again, but that probably happens after she has sensed your unspoken criticism.

Client: Maybe so [silence]. But I don't see what you expect me to do. [Both laugh in recognition of a familiar theme.] Okay, as you've been telling me, I guess the question is what I expect and what I could initiate. But that is not easy to do, you know. [At the end of the session assessor and client summarize the ways the client can recognize when she is setting herself up to become resentful. They role-play successful interchanges with the neighbor. They agree that behaviorally oriented counseling might help her to avoid the trap of becoming resentful in nondirective therapy, and help her to take more responsibility for her own action.]

The client is a 16-year-old high school junior, female, referred for declining grades.

Client: This is horrid [DAP]. I can't draw. This didn't come out right at all.

Assessor: Okay. If you *were* an artist what would it look like?

Client: Like an artist's drawing! [Assessor smiles, gestures for client to continue.] You know, no erasures, confident lines, perfect rendition of an elegant woman.

Assessor: Uh-huh [both laugh]. So here we are again, with you comparing yourself to perfection! That sure is a rough thing to be doing to yourself so often.

Client: Yeah, and the worst part is that I don't know when I'm doing it.

Assessor: There's hope! You knew you'd done it this time! But I'd like to pursue something else here. If you could draw well, this drawing would have been of an elegant woman? [Client blushes, nods hesitantly.] Let's draw it with words. What about the arms – what effect were you after?

Client: This arm should be gesturing emphatically but gracefully. This one should fall easily to her side. [Client illustrates, although remaining seated.]

Assessor: Yes! Look at you! You're doing it. Granted, you're not standing, and it was just a quick gesture, but it was certainly more "elegant" than this woman [DAP]. Kind of symbolic, isn't it? Instead of trying out, practicing, being elegant, you and she [DAP] hide your hands behind your back? [Client and assessor chuckle.] Like a lot of young women, you're not sure whether or not to hide the fact that your breasts have developed? [Assessor points to erasures of lines indicating sizes of breasts. Client nods; after further discussion, assessor asks client to draw her elegant woman, even though it won't be perfect.]

The client is a 21-year-old female graduate student who volunteered for a practice assessment during class.

Assessor: So you have often behaved as though things were against you, as was the case in your TAT stories? [Student: I certainly have. This even came up in my peer counseling session last week.] All right. Do you have some concrete instances you wouldn't mind sharing with us?

Table 10.2 (cont.)

Student: Well, I barely could believe that I had actually graduated from college, and friends had to convince me that I should apply to a master's program. Now people are telling me I should apply to the doctoral program. I just never thought that I could be that sort of person.

Assessor: Wait a minute. That sounds more like "level of aspiration" than what we were talking about before. [Student: What do you mean?] I'm not sure yet. Tell us some more instances. [Student goes on with further instances until finally she rejects the "against me" theme and renames it "aiming low." Discussion also pursues the student's readiness to agree with others' opinions.] Do you remember this card [TAT #10]? Well, you told a story of two older persons quietly dancing together. Did you know that some describe the man as sneering down at the woman?

Student: Oh my! I didn't see that before. That surely could be.

Assessor: There you go again! [Student laughs and asks a classmate to recount a similar experience they have had together.] Okay, when does this "taking the other's stance" work out well for you? For example, I can see that your classmates feel you understand them and are gentle with them; and they in turn respect you. [Classmates offer other variations along these lines, plus instances of when she had given up her own point of view prematurely.]

Client: Let me summarize the "landmarks" of when I'm moving into "aiming low" or "giving priority to the other's stance." It's when I'm in unfamiliar territory and regard others as experts. I find myself pulling back, both figuratively and literally – like wanting to hide. And from there I find myself glancing into the faces of others, looking for cues.

Assessor: On this card [TAT 3BM], you described a young woman catnapping before finishing cutting out her pattern. Sounds pretty evasive to me! How about this gun here? [The object on the card is ambiguous.]

Student: Each to her own! [We all laugh in celebration.] No, seriously, I can see the gun – or maybe it could be a hypodermic in today's times. It surely could be a gun; maybe she's shot somebody or is thinking of killing herself. Yes, I can certainly see your point. But I think that for myself, I'll stick to my story. [More congratulations from the class.] Wow! This stuff is powerful. I mean I've known about those themes, but not in this way. I can do something with it now! Of course, there's a lot more to it that I'd rather not share in a group. But now I'm beginning to see more clearly how "aspiration" and "aiming low" goes way back into my family's dynamics.

The client is a nine-year-old boy referred for academic problems.

Assessor: Hey Timmy, what are you doing? [During Block Design of WISC-R]

Client: I made a wall [matter-of-factly].

Assessor: Did you make it so this design [pointing to card] is on your side?

Client: Uh-huh [starts to break them apart, to get ready for next design].

Assessor: Hold on! [Assessor gets up, walks to client's corner of the table.] From my side, I can't see whether you did what I asked. My word! You did indeed. [Assessor returns to her seat.] Tim, I'm beginning to see how Ms. Cunningham would say you don't pay attention, even though you say you do. Pretend I'm Ms. Cunningham, and I told you to make this design with these blocks. Okay? And so Tim says, "There, I did what she said." But come over here to Ms. Cunningham's side of the desk. Now look at the wall from her side! See, from her desk, it doesn't look like you did the design at all.

Table 10.2 (cont.)

Client: Oh! [Assessor: What do you think Tim could do so Ms. Cunningham could see that he pays attention?] Turn it around this way after I'm finished?

Assessor: Now that's a good idea. Let's try it. [Assessor administers the next card. Client makes a wall, and then turns it for assessor to see.] Yes, now I can tell that you did it right. Tim, could this be what happened when I was in your room this morning? The art teacher – what is his name? [Client: Mr. Simms.] Mr. Simms got a little impatient with you when he told everyone to clean off their desks. You said you did and he said you didn't. If you were Mr. Simms, looking across the room at your desk, what would you see?

Client: Pieces of construction paper. But I was saving that for recess; it wasn't garbage. I didn't spill any paste or anything, and I put the scissors in my desk.

Assessor: Is there anything you could have done so Mr. Simms could *see* that you followed his directions?

Client: I guess put the paper in my pocket.

Assessor: Sounds good to me. I think you already know what to do from now on so the grown-ups can *see* that you're following directions.

Client: Can we do some more [blocks]?

Assessor: Sure. [Later] If I told your mom about the wall and about the construction paper, would she know some other times like that at home? [Client gave examples. A conference was held with Tim, two teachers, and both parents, so all could hear about the examples, what Tim planned to do in the future, and how he would like the adults to help him.]

The clients are a married couple, in their late 20s, who had referred their six-year-old son for an assessment of "shyness." The following session was held at the family's kitchen table after the psychologist had met with the boy.

Husband: [Card I, Rorschach] Obviously this is a folk festival ethnic dance. Two men with capes swirling, a woman with arms raised in the middle. Yes, definitely. Ukranian, I'd say. That's it.

Wife: [Pausing, while walking past with coffee pot, to look over husband's shoulder] Oh, now I can see that. The woman is wearing a filmy dress. She's probably on her tiptoes.

Husband: [Card II] This one is more complex. These red parts should be integrated. It's a circus. These are dancing bears; this is an elephant's upturned barrel – the kind they balance on. This red is bunting – the overall impression of center ring.

Wife: [Chair pulled up beside her husband's] Oh my. The bears could be playing patty cake, couldn't they?

Assessor: [Presenting Card III] Miriam, pull your chair over here [to side of table diagonally from husband]. This time, you tell us first, what could this be?

Wife: Oh, well, I… I don't know what Dave would say. [Assessor: Go ahead.] Could it be more than one thing? [Assessor: Sure, there are lots of possibilities.] Would it be all right for these to be two native dancers?

Assessor: Why in the world not? Miriam, what's the worst possible thing you can imagine could happen if neither Dave nor I agreed with you?

Wife: I'd feel dumb. I'd be lost. Well, he'd help me, but I'd be afraid I was wasting time. Besides, he's always right, he really is. [Assessor asks if what just happened were familiar – that Dave organized a response, and then Miriam accepted it and filled in. They immediately provided such examples as Dave's buying their new

Table 10.2 (cont.)

house without Miriam's having seen it (although they had agreed in advance which criteria it should meet), and her then selecting wallpaper, rugs, and furnishings. The same pattern was identified in regard to raising their son, Ricky. They agreed that although Miriam and Dave generally found the pattern comfortable, Ricky's holding back until given directions and permissions was not working well for him.]

Assessor: I suspect that if Ricky saw you [Miriam] being more flexible – initiating plans yourself, and sometimes offering your opinions first, he would begin to do so too.

Wife: You know, I never thought of this before, but sometimes I see him [Ricky] holding back, and my heart just aches. I know what it's like.

Assessor: Holding back has been painful for you too, at times.

Husband: Honey, I sensed that too, even when you say it's okay.

Assessor: [Ricky peers around the kitchen doorway.] Hi, Ricky. You're just in time. Come sit here on your side of the table. Here's what we're going to do. Do you remember these pictures [TAT]? I'll show all of you a picture, and each of you will think to yourself what could be happening in the picture. Then we'll take turns being the first to tell what we thought. [All four tell a story to each card, taking turns being the first. Assessor points out that nobody was wrong, that there were many possible stories, and that Dad feels okay about all this.] All right, let's see some other times when Ricky and Mom could "go first." Mom, tell Dad some ideas for this year's vacation – just some random thoughts about what would be nice. [Laughter and apologies are followed by suggestions. Ricky is then asked to pretend the assessor is his teacher, and to make a request for which morning song the class should sing. Other practicings follow. Assessor acknowledges that the family's pattern works very well in many circumstances, but suggests that they all continue the exercise for a week, and then decide whether they would like further guidance from a family counselor who would conduct similar sessions with them.]

The client is a nine-year-old retarded boy, referred by his EMR teacher for reevaluation of his intellectual level.

Assessor: Milton, let's practice that. Tell me how the boy makes a happy ending [TAT card 1BM].

Client: His name is Sammy – Sammy rides my bus. This is one of those things you play [violin]. Sammy doesn't know how to play it. [Assessor: What can he do to make a happy ending?] He does what his teacher says to, and once upon a time he makes a song come out. [Assessor: Good. That's a happy ending. What will Sammy do to make a happy ending if Brooks teases him?] Brooks says, "That's gross! That's baby noise." Sammy says, "Go away. My teacher says I play it good."

Assessor: Okay! [Handing Milton his human figure drawing of himself] What can Milton do to make a happy ending?

Client: Milton tells the lady at MacDonald's that he wants a big French fries. She tells him it's not enough money. [Assessor: That's not happy! What will Milton do?] He'll cry.

Assessor: Milton, what would happen if Milton said, "What do I have enough money for?" and the lady said, "A small French fries," and Milton said, "Okay, I want a small French fries," and then he told his mother that he didn't cry and that he did everything by himself?

Table 10.2 (cont.)

Client: Milton's mother would go back to her job and Milton would have to live by himself. All alone with Walpole – that's our cat. [Further practicing of "making good endings" confirms Milton's fearfulness that being competent may result in his being abandoned or overwhelmed by increased demands for independent accomplishment.]

Assessor: Let's talk to Mr. Remy [teacher]. I'll bet he would understand if you told him when you were afraid of "too much." [Milton brings Mr. Remy back from the classroom. Assessor retells Milton's stories and explains his fears. They role-play Milton telling Mr. Remy that he wants to finish just one page, so the work won't become "too much"; that is, escalate too quickly. Mr. Remy reassures Milton that nobody will move him to Mr. Bono's class without discussing the move with Milton, that he will visit the class first, and that after transferring he may come back to see Mr. Remy. Similar discussions were later held with Milton and his parents.]

The client is a 55-year-old housewife, self-referred for job guidance.

Assessor: [As client begins to tell a story for TAT card #9GF] Hold it! You're about to tell me that this woman up here looking from behind the tree is thinking that the woman down below running on the beach is going to get somewhere first, that she got a head start!

Client: [Taken aback at first] No, you got there first! I'm not going to give you the satisfaction of telling you how accurate you were! [Both laugh.]

Assessor: That's a nice twist – my getting there first. I'll bet you could imagine all kinds of other stories here. Try a few. Yes, go ahead.

Client: Well, this one [behind tree] could be plotting how to stop the other one. [Assessor: Sure! What else?] Or she could may be be thinking how to follow her footsteps, so to speak, to get to the same place. [Assessor: Right. I wonder if you could tell me what's happening for this woman who's running?] She probably doesn't even know someone's watching. She's probably just trying to get somewhere on time. You know, I just realized, she looks worried, but determined [laughs]. Pretty tricky! I see what you've just done! But it's true: Whatever I do, whether it's keeping up with volunteer work from home or getting a salaried job, I'll still be worried and determined. So I might as well be getting paid!

Assessor: Okay, so try that out with this picture. Tell me the story here [#17BM].

Client: [Long pause] He's on the way up this rope in some sort of Olympic competition. He's decided it's not so much whether he wins or loses medals, but that under the circumstances he does his best. And how about this: and that he enjoys it!

Assessor: Quite a difference from the story on Card 1! By the way, when you told that first one, were you aware that there were different potential stories?

Client: Intellectually. But none of them occurred to me.

Assessor: I'd say that you came to me already prepared to try out some different perspectives.

Client: I guess so, in a way. But I didn't realize how much it was me holding myself back. I guess I'd be willing to try that job interview role-play now. But you promise to help me with cues?

Table 10.2 (cont.)

The client is a 24-year-old woman bank teller, referred by her counselor for differential diagnosis between neurotic depression and borderline personality disorder.

Assessor: [Client has been protesting that she wants to be more independent but that people won't let her be so.] Look how lightly you've done all your pencil work; it's barely visible! [Assessor holds her penciled notes up by way of comparison.] Here, how about retracing these [Digit Symbol from WAIS-R], making them darker? Press harder, keep going. What's it like to press harder?

Client: It feels good. And nothing's getting messed up.

Assessor: Let's do these again [Presents Bender cards and fresh paper.] Okay. But putting pressure into what you do doesn't have to be laborious. Go faster; you've been here before! Okay, and how shall you sign your name? Ah-ha! Well, I imagine that you could practice putting more pressure into other things you do too. It's like putting yourself more firmly into whatever you do. Let's try that out another way. Let's move over here to these chairs, and pretend I'm Dr. Caligny [counselor] telling you that I want you to see a psychologist, and you tell me just what you think about that. [Role-plays ensue.]

The client is a 23-year-old heroin addict, assessed at a methadone treatment center as part of intake procedures.

Assessor: So this turned out to be worth your while after all?

Client: See, I talked to this shrink at the lockup, and that was nowhere. And my girlfriend, she's had four different therapists, no offense, but they were nothing. Thought they knew it all, and they didn't know nothing.

Assessor: You've met Tom Walker? [counselor; client nods.] Well, after you and I have read and made any changes in my written report of what we learned today, we'll ask Tom to join us. He'll have a copy of the report. We'll tell him what changes we've made, and he'll ask us questions to be sure he understands. Then the two of you will continue where we've left off. You can work out different goals as you go along – as we did – and role-play, and he'll tell you what impressions you're making. I don't think he'll use tests, but otherwise counseling can be very much like what we did today.

Client: That Walker fellow seems okay... See, I thought therapy was getting lectured at. And I get to keep a copy of my own of the suggestions, the same ones he'll have?

The last excerpt in Table 10.2 illustrates how the assessor may encourage a client to enter counseling or therapy with positive expectations. The client's success during the assessment is compared with therapy activities to show the client that therapy would be an extension of what he or she is already familiar with (if that would in fact be the case). The absence of any tests in the excerpt is a reminder that assessment does not necessarily involve continuous use of tests. Interviewing, counseling, and therapeutic techniques also are prevalent, but Tables 10.1 and 10.2 focused on testing examples because the other individualized techniques are well known.

The options developed in these excerpts are only those that clients are ready for at the time of the assessment. Often further restructuration will require protracted professional assistance. The assessment report's suggestions may include recommendations for treatment, further evaluation, and environmental changes, in addition to the tried-out options. In addition, many of the assessor's shared observations slowly germinate as the person later goes about his or her life, proving to be helpful at some later point.

The assessor makes use of technical and diagnostic knowledge even when it is not presented as such to the client. These secondary data are the assessor's tools for exploring primary data – how the client approaches the assessment tasks and similar daily life situations. Informed observation of these primary events is the most productive information to share.

It is not always necessary to obtain a completed assessee production, such as the "other gender" drawing in the "elegant woman" DAP excerpt in Table 10.2. Just getting started on a task often puts the person in touch with his or her inclinations, resistances, concerns. These responses and their pivot points into options are then available for joint exploration. In an individualized assessment, such exploration, rather than completed "productions," is the point of using test materials.

Finally, in those instances where individualized assessment is appropriate; that is, where testing is not merely for establishing comparative levels of achievement or category of best fit; assessment certainly is broader than administration of tests. Individualized assessment is also a testing of optimal environments, interventions, and ways clients can help themselves.

Note

1 Reprinted from Fischer, C. T. (1994). *Individualizing psychological assessment* (pp. 85–107). Mahwah, NJ: Erlbaum. (Originally published 1985 by Brooks Cole. Now available through Routledge.)

CHAPTER 11

COLLABORATIVE, INDIVIDUALIZED ASSESSMENT[1]

Collaborative, individualized assessment is an approach to psychological assessment in which the assessor and the client work together to develop productive understandings. Collaboration is a means of individualizing the assessment – its process, resulting suggestions, and written accounts. In this approach, life events are regarded as primary data. Test scores, categories, and related research are used as bridges into a particular life and as tools for then exploring that life. This article, an invited Master Lecture presented at the 1999 Society for Personality Assessment (SPA) meeting, presents examples of contextualizing, intervening, describing in life-world terms, and writing individualized reports with suggestions. Historical struggles to promote individualized assessment and current openness to its practices, especially within SPA, are mentioned. A hermeneutic approach to impression formation is described.

There is no other group with whom I would more like to have this opportunity to share my work. I truly thank the Society.[2]

I will speak first about principles and practices of collaborative, individualized assessment, about its history and current trends, and about individualized report writing. At the end, I will speak a bit about the philosophical assumptions and the process of impression formation that, for me, ground the practices. However, psychologists from diverse orientations have practiced in similar ways.

What is collaborative, individualized assessment?

Collaborative, individualized assessment is an approach to psychological assessment in which the assessor and the client work together (*co-labor*) to develop productive understandings of this *individual client.* Collaboration is a means of individualizing the assessment – its process, resulting suggestions, and written accounts. In this approach, life events are regarded as primary data, and test scores, categories, and related research are regarded as secondary data derived from life. Test scores, categories, and related research are used as *bridges* into a particular life, and then as our *tools* for exploring that life. In short, the *life world* is given priority in individualized assessment.

This is an approach to assessment for when we choose to go beyond answering a request limited to classification (e.g., is this person psychopathic, brain-damaged, gifted?). I think that most of us, when we have deemed it appropriate to go beyond classification assessment, have engaged in some or all of the following practices, at least to a degree. I hope to encourage fuller adoption, adaptation, and innovation. Almost needless to say, this approach, like all others, works best with clients who are interested in exploring their lives and options. It works least well, again like all other approaches, with persons who are limited in their reflective skills or who wish not to reveal themselves, as in many forensic situations. Nevertheless, I find that to the degree that I manage to individualize the assessment, to that degree I assist all parties in understanding the assessee as a person.

Principles and Examples of Individualized Assessment

The following principles overlap and imply each other. They are practiced throughout the assessment.

Collaborate

Client and assessor discuss the purposes of the assessment and then co-labor to reach useful understandings. This is not merely feedback by one person at the end of an evaluation. Instead, both parties may work together throughout the assessment to revise their evolving impressions. The client is engaged as an active agent.

For example, in a workshop demonstration of collaborative assessment practices, a participant, John, presented a problem to explore:

> *I see myself as methodical and responsible, but my supervisor just marked me down for being "disorganized and inefficient." He says that each time he walks through my area, I'm not being serious about my work. This kind of thing has happened to me before; I just don't get it.*

After we discussed other instances, as well as times when John had been seen as methodical and responsible, we began with the Bender-Gestalt. John indeed looked as though he was not taking the task seriously, what with his legs stretched out in front of him and his closed left hand supporting his left cheek as he drew with only his right hand. We workshop participants watched, puzzled, as John copied the designs in most unusual ways. On the first design, he completed half of the circle, then the far corner of the diamond, a quarter of the circle, and then one line of the diamond, and so on, to completion. All the designs were copied similarly in what seemed to be a casual, haphazard manner. To the observers' amazement, the finished page was neat, precise, and completed in only five-and-a-half minutes. I confirmed to John the precision and efficiency of his effort, and added, "But I'll bet we've just seen what your supervisor sees!" I shared my earlier confusion about what he was doing and my surprise when the designs turned out so well. We went on to talk about specific ways in which he could let his supervisor know that in fact he is on his way to the desired work product.

The following is an excerpt from a discussion with a client. It begins with a hunch from her Rorschach (low *Afr*, and $Zd = -4$):

Assessor: From some of your scores, I wondered if you have often avoided complex or emotional situations?

Client: No, that's *not* it! – What it *is*, is that I have the *courage to hang in.* I just choose something to hold on to 'til I get through the situation.

Assessor: Like you pressed so hard on your pencil but didn't check back against the card [Bender-Gestalt]? (Client nods slowly.) So what we called "being determined" is also a way of keeping things simple, of getting through?
Client: (after a long pause, then laughing) Like a horse with blinders plodding straight ahead!

Contextualize

Earlier, the assessor has asked the referring party for some of the actual events and their contexts that led to the request for an assessment. Often, the ensuing discussion obviates the need for a formal assessment. To begin the assessment, the assessor also asks for the client's understanding of the referral. In the case of Ms. Seale, a therapist asked for an assessment of suicidality. The context of the referral turned out to be that Ms. Seale was very quiet in sessions, seemed despondent, and would not answer the therapist's questions about whether she was feeling "self-destructive." When I asked Ms. Seale about her therapist's concerns, she explained that she had not understood that self-destructive referred to suicide. She did sometimes think that she could not wait much longer for life to get better but had not thought of killing herself. After a little more discussion, we agreed that we had answered the therapist's question.

When I asked Ms. Seale if she had questions of her own, she said that she wondered if we could find out why she is slower than workmates at learning new procedures. We then used tests to explore when and how that relative slowness might occur. We found through a Wechsler Adult Intelligence Scale-Revised subtest (Digit Symbol) and the Bender-Gestalt that Ms. Seale waited for others to take initiative when she felt that they were supposed to be in charge. Whether from supervisor, therapist, or assessor, she waited for instruction rather than either asking for clarification or jumping in to try out her hunches. We discovered that she was also slow to act in other unfamiliar circumstances, finding herself afraid that she might be criticized. However, we identified *when nots* of this problematic approach: Ms. Seale reported that she "roughhoused" with her little nephews, argued with her younger sister, and initiated new arrangements of the candy bars in the movie theater where she clerked. By looking into life contexts, we discovered some ways in which Ms. Seale surpassed, as well as exemplified, her therapist's characterization of her as being passive-dependent. Then, through role-playing revised beginnings of the Digit Symbol subtest, the Bender, and a therapy session, we developed starting points through which she could ask me and her therapist for clarification and could even venture her opinions. Ms. Seale spontaneously noted that from then on, when she used the same active approach in her job setting, she would no longer be slower than all her officemates to learn new tasks.

We have seen in these examples from John's and Ms. Seale's assessments that exploring contexts allows us to reach people in their worlds, from which they extend, grow, and change. Indeed, we are reminded that just as we are not static as we engage our clients, so too are they in lively flux – they are not an assemblage of traits or even of set patterns of dynamics.

Intervene

To collaborate, the assessor may interrupt standardized procedures at natural breaks, such as at the end of a subtest. The assessor also may interrupt the client's movement to explore alternatives. In other words, the goal is not just to describe or classify the person's present state, but to identify personally viable options to problematic comportment. For example, Ms. Plock's initial Thematic Apperception Test stories were all about characters who were stymied by outside factors. After handing her the next card (10, which shows a man and woman perhaps dancing or otherwise close to one another), before she could begin, I interjected, with a grin, "He's not going to move, because *he doesn't know* what she's up to; she's not going to move because *she doesn't know* what he's up to; so they'll just be *there forever.*" Ms. Plock looked at me quizzically, fell silent, and then challenged me to tell a different story. I suggested that the card might show a couple in a quiet moment, both thinking about news they had received about their son. Then, again grinning, I said, "Your turn." Ms. Plock sighed and said she guessed she was supposed to figure out something other than her usual reactions; with that she told a story of a couple in a retirement community, dancing after dinner in the dining hall. I congratulated her and presented further cards. In the process, she began to recognize her habitual inclination to look for danger rather than for opportunity. On Card 14 (the silhouette of a man at a window), she smiled meaningfully at me, and announced that the man was thinking of the serenity prayer, and trying to acknowledge that he has to be alert to real danger but that he can also be open to trusting at least some people. Thus, rather than just documenting Ms. Plock's vigilance, we also assessed her readiness to try to move on, and we developed some ways that she could begin to do so. We spoke of her learning to recognize that pulling back suspiciously is a landmark indicating that if danger is not confirmed, she could then venture toward opportunity.

Describe

While collaborating, the assessor uses clients' words, in part to deepen clients' efforts to communicate their own meanings but also to help the assessor to feel his or her way into clients' worlds. For example, "Tell me what you already understand about how this 'dirty bastard' has gotten you so worked up." However, when clients use abstractions, especially constructs, the assessor asks clients to provide concrete examples so that they both are addressing life events. For example, when an undergraduate, Karyn, said that what she wanted to explore in the assessment was how to overcome her procrastination, her graduate student assessor said: "Uhm. Procrastination. Tell me about some times that you have procrastinated." During the ensuing narration, the graduate student continued to word her reiterations and understandings in verb form, so both were describing actual past actions rather than relying on a construct. For example, the assessor said, "So 'putting off your English essay and 'putting off writing the Dear John letter have been typical of what we want to explore?" Gradually, Karyn, too, spoke in terms of representative actions rather than in terms of traits or causal dynamics.

Later, written reports also describe situated action. Explanation through constructs is not necessary. I will share some excerpts from reports shortly.

Respect Complexity, Holism, and Ambiguity

All of the preceding examples of interaction with clients seem pretty simple, and in a way, they are. However, they respect the complex interrelations of our lives; they do not reduce lives to a variable or to any system of explanation. The goal is understanding rather than explanation. Although never complete, understanding via an assessment is adequate when it assists interested parties to similarly comprehend a situation, and when specific, viable individualized suggestions for change have been developed.

Communicating via concrete, contextualized examples evokes listeners' and readers' own lives, which allows fuller communication beyond the assessor's sentences. Carefully described incidents can convey a holistic sense of how a person lives his or her past on the way to a future, dealing with perceived obstacles, dangers, and invitations en route. That much of the person remains ambiguously implied is not necessarily a reflection of deficient knowledge, but is rather an accurate reflection of human ways of understanding before we impose artificial, categorical clarity. A judicious mix of these two modes generally best serves the interests of our clients and colleagues.

I do struggle to find ways of speaking that reflect the life world and yet do not mystify. For example, I am inclined to avoid speaking of *behavior*, which can be taken to be separate from affect, cognition, motivation, and so on. Instead, I may speak of *comportment*, etymologically implying, as in the French *se comporter*, to carry one's self, which implies style, burden, direction, and so on. Unfortunately, for many people, comportment instead means good or bad behavior for which they received grades in grammar school! Most often I use the term *action*, which I hope implies beyond behavior, selection, purpose, cognition, and accompanying affect.

Individualized Assessment: Then and Now, Now and Then

Now that I have provided a sample of individualized assessment practices, before going on to provide an excerpt from a written report and some related principles, let me briefly address my history with individualized assessment and some broader current developments.

I think that many if not most psychologists have practiced some if not all of the principles and practices that I have just reviewed. However, surveys indicate that very few have done so systematically. Hence, publications on report writing continue to plaintively urge that reports be client oriented and reader friendly rather than being test oriented.

My own route into collaborative assessment was one of becoming dissatisfied with what I had at first enjoyed, in my graduate training in the 1960s, about piecing together parts of puzzles, finding an immediate utility of psychoanalytic theory, and delivering a logically derived laboratory report. Although I was proud of my skills, I gradually acknowledged to myself that the reports often were not particularly helpful to the patients. Even more gradually, I began to acknowledge that both the assessment process and the resulting reports were often destructive to patients' self-respect. Clients were indeed called *patients* in those days, and our job was to administer tests, whose pattern of scores would explain what was wrong with that patient. The bottom line, literally, of our reports was "diagnostic impression" (psychiatrists pronounced *the* diagnosis). To arrive at the diagnostic impression and at psychodynamic understandings, even kindly psychologists put a patient through hoops, all the while observing and taking notes. This approach, it seemed to me, implied to the patient that elicited and emitted responses would tell us all we needed to know and that aside from reporting history and symptoms, the person did not have anything important to say about what was wrong.

Indeed in the late 1960s, when I first began submitting journal manuscripts about including clients as co-assessors, the rejection letters were inevitable, fast, and brief. Editors informed me in stark prose that my practices were unprofessional, unethical, and harmful to patients. Some editors asked me not to submit future manuscripts to their journals. Most said that it made no sense to talk to patients because they did not know the real nature of their problems; depending on the journal, it was assumed that pathology was caused by learned response patterns, unconscious dynamics, or neurological impairment. Editors believed, without reading the full manuscripts, that assessment reports could only be written in jargon and could only emphasize pathology and limitation, with a few "strengths" tossed in; hence, patients who read reports would not only not understand them but also would be harmed. Some reviewers commented that we psychologists no longer would be respected as experts if we collaborated with "testees" (as they were called), especially if we wrote in ordinary language.

In 1970, the *Journal of Counseling Psychology* published my article, "The Testee as Co-Evaluator" (Fischer, 1970 – Chapter 1 in this volume). I think that the counseling field, being less involved with pathology, and being conversant with Carl Rogers' work, was more open to collaborative work than was clinical psychology. After that, I heard from other psychologists who were relieved to find the article; its being in print, especially in an American Psychological Association journal, legitimized their own similar inclinations. Nevertheless, as you know, a ground swell for life-oriented, collaborative assessment practices did not occur.

Still, being able to cite the co-assessor article, it was much easier for me to publish such papers as "Paradigm Changes Which Allow Sharing of Results" (Fischer, 1972a – reprinted here as Chapter 2), "A Theme for the Child-Advocate: Shareable Everyday Life Events of the Child-in-the-World" (Fischer, 1972b), "Contextual Approach to Assessment" (Fischer, 1973), and so on. Then, while taking a Comprehensive System workshop with John Exner and Irving Weiner, I found myself in a conversation with them at a break, and Exner asked me to say more about where one of my questions had come from. I spoke a bit, and he and Weiner (then editor *of Journal of Personality Assessment* [*JPA*]) suggested that I submit an article. They seemed serious, but still I was incredulous. But lo, in 1979, *JPA* published "Individualized Assessment and Phenomenological Psychology" (Fischer, 1979 – reprinted here as Chapter 7). This was the first time that I spelled out fairly fully what the approach was. (Other representative publications on psychological assessment from the 1980s to the present include Fischer, 1980, 1982, 1989, 1994a, 1994b, 1998b; articles on underlying philosophy and theory include Fischer, 1977, 1998a.)

Moving on, in 1985, Brooks-Cole published my textbook, *Individualizing Psychological Assessment* (Fischer, 1985/1994a). However, they marketed it only through their counseling series. By 1993, the run was depleted, and they gave me back the copyright, saying that the book was not a large seller (which I knew!). When I mentioned to Phil Erdberg, at a Society for Personality Assessment (SPA) meeting, that I was just going to let it all go, he suggested that, right at the conference, I "talk to Larry," who turned out to be Larry of Lawrence Erlbaum Associates, Inc. The book was quickly reissued along with a contract to publish a second edition; Erlbaum has been very patient with my delays.

In the meantime, in the early 1990s, I met Steve Finn at an SPA meeting. While at the University of Minnesota, he already had been looking for ways to use the Minnesota Multiphasic Personality Inventory (MMPI) in particular but also assessment in general, explicitly for therapeutic purposes. My own efforts had been geared toward humanizing the assessment process, making it less harmful, making it more useful for all parties, and allowing clients to grow through the process. I had not thought of it as therapeutic, in that I reserved that term for its older meaning of thorough-going transformation. By now, with the advent of short-term therapy and with Finn's innovations, I fully agree that collaborative assessment is indeed therapeutic. Sometimes it "just" helps clients focus on the impact of habitual or taken-for-granted styles; at other times, it leads to profound insight. Very often, as clients later follow suggestions from the assessment, they develop further understandings and revise their comportment accordingly.

At any rate, when I met Steve Finn, he told me that he had been pleased to find my work and that he had based the workshop he was giving at that SPA meeting partly on material in my book. I accepted an inch-thick handout from him and that night dutifully flipped through it. Hours later, now reading and rereading every page, I discovered that my eyes were welling with tears as I encountered his wonderful, depthful, caring examples of what he came to call *therapeutic assessment*. Even where he had borrowed, with credit given, from my work, he presented my narrative text in flowchart form, which proved to be clear, appealing, and useful. His workshops, with videotape illustrations, and the training he has provided at the Center for Therapeutic Assessment in Austin, Texas, have introduced hundreds of psychologists to this approach. Moreover, he has published and encouraged systematic research that has shown that clients report less distress, more hope, and higher opinions of themselves after receiving collaborative feedback on MMPI testing. Such research, along with some of his videotapes, convinced several large managed care organizations (MCOs) to allow Finn to bill portions of psychological assessments as psychotherapy. These same MCOs also refer clients to the Center for Therapeutic Assessment. Moreover, clients now come directly to the center with their own requests for what they would like to explore via assessment.

Other psychologists, although not identified with collaborative or therapeutic assessment as such, have been working in similar ways. Paul Lerner and Len Handler for several decades have practiced, taught, supervised, and written about experience-based, or "experience near," assessment. Their reports are immediately helpful in understanding the worlds of their clients. (Paul is presenting at this conference on report writing and presenting feedback.) Phil Erdberg regularly relates Rorschach constellations to possible everyday life situations. Anna Marie Carlson and Thomas Lindgren, our Swedish SPA colleagues, are developing an empirically based client checklist of behaviors and experiences that might be related to the client's Rorschach scores. Phillip Caracena's most recent RorScan program includes a list of life-related statements that can be checked directly with clients. Most current MMPI books suggest "nonjargony" ways of providing feedback to clients. Steve Finn (1996) published a handbook devoted to individualizing MMPI feedback (see also Finn & Tonsager, 1997). This morning, members of Exner's Research Council reported their pursuit of research involving "reasonable life criteria" and "ecological validity."

I am aware of many other instances, but I would greatly appreciate your letting me know of your own related approaches, examples, and of literature references to your own work or to that of others, so that I might include them in that next edition of *Individualizing Psychological Assessment.* I am also interested in collecting further instances of what we now call *collaborative* or *therapeutic assessment* that you encounter in the writings of our founding assessors. I noted several in an earlier award ceremony honoring Dr. Piotrowski. Many of our early personality theorists and assessment founders were more life- and person-oriented than is often recognized by contemporary psychology.

There still is no ground swell of individualized assessment out in psychology at large; indeed, it is still *now and then.* Nevertheless, I think that as psychology has proven itself as being both scientific and useful; its practitioners are becoming more comfortable about addressing the life world directly. Moreover, society's expectations are shifting: citizens want straight talk, MCOs want client satisfaction and life change, and APA's Psychological Assessment Work Group (Meyer et al., 1998) called for development of assessment that all parties readily see as immediately useful. Of course, I think that the practices we have looked at here fit the bill.

Individualized Report Writing

Now I return to specific practices, namely writing individualized reports. I tell my students that if they cannot write their reports in terms of everyday events, they do not yet know *what in the world* they are talking about. Our assessments and reports are not just *experience near* but are *life near*; they address past events that were explored during the assessment as well as events that occurred during the assessment.

Some reports are written as letters to the client. For children, we sometimes write fables ("Once upon a time there was a little boy, about five-and-a-half years old, who lived in a cave..."). Even if the report is written for others, clients may read and add comments directly on the report. Reports sometimes designate certain impressions as being ones about which client and assessor have agreed to disagree.

We write in first person, active voice, using verbs rather than constructs. If technical terms are necessary, they are explained parenthetically. We write in past tense so that it is clear that particular comportment is not inevitable but rather did occur before. These reports put all participants "on the same page" with regard to characterizations of the client; we are all talking pretty much about the same events.

Here is an excerpt from a letter to a woman who undertook an assessment with me, to explore why other people often misunderstood her and to explore how she often managed to sabotage her own progress. We had already discussed these themes during the assessment; the letter and report were meant to serve as a record of our findings for her and her therapist. The report begins with some images I recalled of her:

> *Sometimes you sat in quiet reflection, slouched back in the chair in your roomy shirt. I knew that you were open to what I had to offer as well as to your own musings. I was struck by the contrast between that potentially vulnerable posture and what strangers might take as the (defiant?) boldness of your 1/3" haircut, nose stud, and single large earring.*
>
> *A second recollection: There were your immediate, vociferous protests (as in "NO WAY!!!") to some of my suggestions, such as that you might be depriving yourself of being taken care of.*

A later section of the report read:

> We also saw clear indications that both your developmental years and recent life have left you with a different way of reading situations and of dealing with them. We agreed that you often have confused other people, and in turn found yourself confused about the difference between their and your perceptions of you... It seems that your way of dealing with new, complex, stressful situations has been to leap in, just keep on going, and to sort of force details to fit into your quick overview (remember our discussion of the woman on the raft on the inkblot?). When you're caught up in this style, it's next to impossible for you to be analytic, which you have done very well at other times.
>
> *A suggestion here would be that* ***when you recognize yourself moving into a new, complex, stressful situation, that you pause and ask yourself how other people in the scene might view it, and what their concerns might be.*** Actually, you did this with me throughout our sessions. At least you readily slowed down and considered my comments and questions, and genuinely helped me to understand... ***So maybe the implication is to slow down in these circumstances and ask yourself what other people's questions might be, even before they ask you.***

Please note that using first person, active voice, past tense for past events, and verbs instead of constructs attuned all participants (client, assessor, other readers) to the client's actual life and to her choice points and possibilities. We also see hints of how the collaborative process already had been helpful.

Some Comments on Practices

While clients are engaged in an assessment task, drawing Bender designs, or whatever, they are living out a situation similar to others in their past. Those past situations become available in ways beyond words. Similarly, concrete events mentioned in reports evoke more than cognitive recall for the client. What is more, the contextually and concretely described events reverberate with readers' similar past happenings, allowing their own lives to be a resource for understanding more than is said. Likewise, the assessor uses his or her own life and current experiences of the client as a resource for understanding. Examples of the assessor's participation are included to help readers to see aspects of the context in which clients emerged as described by the assessor.

I hope I have illustrated how individualized assessment enters the client's life, within which corrections to assessor impressions can be made, and where client and assessor can locate landmarks that the client recognizes as signs to change his or her course in ways that have already proven to be personally viable.

Foundations and the Process of Impression Formation

In general, individualizing practices are consistent with contemporary respect for the notion that humans can know the world only in human ways. This means in turn that our knowledge is always perspectival, always formed in part by our times, interests, values, and methods. Humans are always in relation to the world; we can know it only through our relations to it. The goal of science in a contemporary philosophy of science, then, is not to arrive at truths about an independent world. Rather, the goal is evolve coherent patterns of understandings with perspectives and interests specified. So although materialism and logical positivism served their purpose in their time, they no longer serve as the only philosophy of science. *Empirical* now includes its early meaning of "evident to the senses" – evident through viewing and listening.

In contrast to speaking of clinical inference based on logical induction, deduction, and statistical inference and decision making, I think in terms of impression formation and of open-ended efforts to revise and expand understandings. I regard assessment reports as progress reports of joint understandings of the individual and of the success of suggestions to date.

The method of developing, reforming, extending, and refining impressions is hermeneutic. That term refers to interpretation but not in the sense of "this means that." Rather, it refers to a long, scholarly tradition of the searcher's developing his or her understanding by circling repeatedly from an observation back to context or to larger prior comprehensions, then back again to observation. Each movement transforms understandings of what was observed, the context, and earlier comprehensions. The circling continues until the scholar's efforts have achieved a usable or otherwise desired level of articulation and coherence. What is observed could be a printed text, like the Bible or Freud's writings, the text of a conversation, or aspects of a person's life as presented to an assessment psychologist. When I am engaged in an individualized assessment, the question I pose to my "texts" is, How is this person co-authoring his or her world, and what options are available within that world?

The hermeneutic quest moves repeatedly among the presented issue, the client in front of the assessor, theories of development and personality, research studies, statistical norms, the client's history, diagnostic traditions, previous clients, and the assessor's own life. Impressions and questions form and reform, both thematically and vaguely. Eventually the assessor – and in collaborative assessment, the assessor and the client – reaches useful, coherent understandings of the presented issue. The assessor, however, is responsible both for being able to document the sources and coherence of impressions and for being disciplined, especially in regard to using his or her own life as a resource. Assessors should be trained as are therapists in self-awareness.

By way of concluding, let me say that much of what I have presented is, as my first-year students tell me every year, *common sense.* I hope and anticipate that we will continue to find ways to talk about and develop such practices so that they become more *commonplace.*

Notes

1 Originally published as Fischer, C. T. (2000). Collaborative/individualized assessment. *Journal of Personality Assessment*, 74, 2–14.
2 I also thank SPA President Sandra Russ for her kind introductory comments, for her characterization of my early work as pioneering, and for noting its relation to my similarly grounded efforts in the area of qualitative research.

References

Finn, S. E. (1996). *Manual for using the MMPI–2 as a therapeutic intervention*. Minneapolis: University of Minnesota Press.

Finn, S. E., & Tonsager, M. E. (1997). Information-gathering and therapeutic models of assessment: Complementary paradigms. *Psychological Assessment*, 9, 374–385.

Fischer, C. T. (1970). The testee as co-evaluator. *Journal of Counseling Psychology*, *17*, 70–76.

Fischer, C. T. (1972a). Paradigm changes which allow sharing of results. *Professional Psychology*, *3*, 364–369.

Fischer, C. T. (1972b). A theme for the child advocate: Sharable everyday life events of the child-in-the-world. *Journal of Clinical Child Psychology*, *1*, 23–25.

Fischer, C. T. (1973). Contextual approach to assessment. *Community Mental Health Journal*, *9*, 38–45.

Fischer, C. T. (1977). Historical relations of psychology as an object-science and subject-science: Toward psychology as a human-science. *Journal of the History of the Behavioral Sciences*, *13*, 369–378.

Fischer, C. T. (1979). Individualized assessment and phenomenological psychology. *Journal of Personality Assessment*, *43*, 115–122.

Fischer, C. T. (1980). Phenomenology and psychological assessment: Re-presentational description. *Journal of Phenomenological Psychology*, *11*, 79–105.

Fischer, C. T. (1982). Intimacy in assessment. In M. Fisher & G. Stricker (Eds.), *Intimacy* (pp. 443–460). N.Y.: Plenum.

Fischer, C. T. (1989). A life-centered approach to psychodiagnostics: Attending to the life-world, ambiguity, and possibility. *Person-Centered Review*, *4*, 163–170.

Fischer, C. T. (1994). *Individualizing psychological assessment*. Mahwah: Lawrence Erlbaum Associates, Inc. (Original work published 1985.)

Fischer, C. T. (1994). Rorschach scoring questions as access to dynamics. *Journal of Personality Assessment*, *62*, 515–525.

Fischer, C. T. (1998). Phenomenological, existential, and humanistic foundations for psychology as a human science. In M. Hersen & A. Bellack (Eds.), *Comprehensive clinical psychology: Vol. 1, Foundations* (pp. 449–472), London: Elsevier Science.

Fischer, C. T. (1998). The Rorschach and the life-world. In L. Handler & M. Hilsenroth (Eds.), *Teaching and learning personality assessment* (pp. 347–358). Mahwah: Lawrence Erlbaum Associates, Inc.

Meyer, G. J., Finn, S. E., Eyde, L. D., Kay, G. G., Kubiszyn, T. W., Moreland, K. L., Eisman, E. J., & Dies, R.R. (1998). *Benefits and costs of psychological assessment in healthcare delivery: Report of the Board of Professional Affairs Psychological Assessment Work Group, Part 1*. Washington, DC: American Psychological Association.

CHAPTER 12

INDIVIDUALIZED ASSESSMENT MODERATES THE IMPACT OF HIPAA PRIVACY RULES[1]

In this comment, I express appreciation of Erard's (2004) review, and urge psychologists to continue to protect test security. I disagree with Erard's belief that the Health Insurance Portability and Accountability Act of 1996 (HIPAA) is salient for nonhealth forensic issues. I then review some ways in which individualized assessment practices can moderate the negative impact of the HIPPA privacy rules. Assessors can use tests as a ground for joint exploration of the client's experience, behavior, and their contexts. Clients may later ask for a review of test data and collaborative life findings, but they rarely are interested in acquiring test records. Attorneys, after discovering that assessment conclusions are based largely on events/contexts provided by the client and others, are less interested in acquiring test records that the psychologist used as tools rather than as evidence for conclusions.

In this comment, I (a) express appreciation of Erard's (2004) sophisticated reassurance and guidance in regard to the Health Insurance Portability and Accountability Act of 1996 (HIPAA) requirement that psychological test data and reports generated in health settings be provided to clients who request them; (b) urge psychologists to do all that we can to protect test security in that record forms often contain the stimulus items; (c) take issue with Erard's prediction that in practice, forensic assessment will not be exempt from HIPAA rules; and (d) at greater length describe the advantages of individualized, collaborative assessment practices in both clinical and forensic settings. As Erard suggests, sharing with clients greatly lessens the odds that they or their attorneys will formally request copies of their test data. Collaborative practices also promote client well-being and growth and most fully meet our American Psychological Association's Code of Ethics requirement that assessors explain findings to clients. Finally, individualizing and collaborating provides life examples of test patterns; these examples are less contestable in forensic situations than are abstract characterizations based on statistical probabilities.

Continue to Protect Test Security

Erard's article is wonderfully clear and sage, leaving me with that sense of "I knew *that* (sort of)." Reflecting on Erard's (2004) analysis, I realized that HIPAA does not threaten to change the status quo as hugely as I had feared.

I agree with Erard (2004) that an enterprising attorney or client can find most test items and many interpretations in libraries, bookstores, and online. However, psychologists still should not make stimulus items or other previously "secure" material readily available to less enterprising clients and attorneys. Aside from invalidating intelligence tests and others of similar format, the major issue is that laypersons readily draw false inferences from their reading. For example, I have encountered Rorschach clients whose percepts of humans were of poor Form Quality because the clients were searching for Human Movement responses, having read variously that high M would result in their being seen as being imaginative or interpersonally adjusted. Clients have said variations of "Oh, I've been waiting for this one; it was in my Intro Psych book. I decided I would call it …." A custody evaluation client reported that after reading a list of Minnesota Multiphasic Personality Inventory (MMPI; Hathaway & McKinley, 1943) critical items in her previous report, she would know how to answer them the next time. Although psychologists can sleuth our way through much of these efforts at beating the system, we should continue to do what we can to minimize them to maintain valid use of norms. Hence, I hope that test publishers will pursue copyright remedies, that our professional organizations will continue to alert text authors and publishers not to reprint sample items, and that as individuals we all will continue to protect test security, creatively but within the law. I agree with Erard that heroics typically are not required.

Despite Erard's (2004) understandable misgivings about the probable success of efforts to maintain test security while also abiding by HIPAA rules, I believe that psychologists indeed should record client responses separately from stimulus items or delete ("redact") that material from copies of client data, and in forensic situations appeal to attorneys and judges for permission to pursue various ways to serve justice while protecting tests. I appreciate Erard's review of the many steps we can take to preserve the integrity of test material in forensic situations.

Sustain the Forensic Exemption

I disagree with Erard's (2004) opinion that forensic work not involving prior health care will likely also be covered by HIPAA, that is, that psychologists will be required to release test data directly to the requesting client (and attorney). HIPAA is a "Health Information" act, not a psychological assessment act; we should strongly reinforce this position. The health care client's interest in his or her test data usually is quite different from an attorney's adversarial interest in challenging the psychologist. I do not imagine that my own county courts will veer from the tradition of releasing assessment data only to another qualified psychologist who is agreed upon with the client's attorney.

Nevertheless, client requests for records that originated outside of court proceedings will most often have been instigated by an attorney. As Erard (2004) suggests, in the absence of an attorney's motivations, most clients' concerns will be addressed satisfactorily by open discussion. In either case, client well-being and test security are both well served by individualizing the assessment process.

Individualize Psychological Assessments Through Collaboration

Increasingly, psychologists are individualizing at least parts of their psychological assessments – using nomothetic data as starting points that the client and psychologist review together and then explore in terms of what they might indicate about this person in particular. To further individualize the assessment by contextualizing behavior, the assessor and client also can collaboratively explore the situations in which these test-derived descriptions pertain and those in which they do not. In the following, I present detailed examples to convey some ways in which the psychologist's findings are not so much deductions and inferences from scores but rather patterns of actual behavior and experience that have been affirmed by the client. With these results in hand (reports are written to be read by, and sometimes kept by, clients), clients usually have no interest in possessing the test data, which served client and assessor as a tool rather than as evidence. At most, the client may ask to again review test data and its relation to earlier or new concerns. Said differently, following the assessment, client's interests are not so much in test data as in a record of the clarifications that they led to. Attorneys similarly realize that test records will not be useful in a cross-examination when they were not used as indicators of a psychological "Truth" but as starting points for assessor–client discussions. In addition, it is difficult for the attorney to argue with actual behaviors, which are the assessment findings.

Principles and examples of individualized collaborative assessment may be found in Fischer (1985/1994, 2000, 2003) and in Finn (1996) and Finn and Tonsager (1997). Finn (2003) published a full case study of Therapeutic Assessment in which clients participated in an assessment as a means of making decisions, resolving conflicts, and coming to understandings that open the future.

Example of Individualized, Collaborative Assessment

Here is a recalled example with a mother in a custody dispute. Both parents had taken the MMPI–2 (Butcher, Dahlstrom, Graham, Tellegen, & Kaemmer, 1989), Sixteen Personality Factor questionnaire (16 PF), Personality Assessment Inventory (PAI; Morey, 1991), and a sentence-completion form. I had observed each parent interacting with their two boys and had already discussed the father's test patterns with him. In that discussion, we explored both the wife's claims that he is domineering and test profile suggestions that he may be impatient and quick to irritation when he encounters obstacles.

Fischer: [after looking together at the 16 PF profile] I found some other indications in your test profiles that you might be like people who are kind of passive. That reminded me of your husband saying that you have been "remote" with the boys, and that it is he who provides "affection." Can you help me to understand what he means? Would you say that you've often been passive?

Mother: Well, I don't know. Is it okay if I sort of disagree with what he said? [Fischer nods] He does rough house with the boys, rolls on the floor with them, throws them in the air. They do love that. They jumped all over him when he came home. I take care of them by keeping their clothes clean and feeding them properly. I don't feel comfortable about it, but I'm the one that meets with the childcare teachers. I'm not sure what "passive" means, but I don't like for people to see me as pushy. It's me that the kids come to when they're hurt or scared or just want to cuddle.

Fischer: Okay, that helps. John's test patterns and comments have led me to think he's pretty energetic and outgoing, and that between you he's more likely to take the initiative in making plans. [Gestures for comment.]

Mother: Does "passive" mean I think more? [like what?] Well, sometimes I'm still thinking when he gets impatient, and says "Then let's just go to Pizza Hut!"
Fischer: The last time that happened, how did you react?
Mother: Sometimes what he decides is fine with me, but he knows I don't like Pizza Hut because I can't get vegetables there. [And?] Well we went, but I was kind of mad and he knew it.
Fischer: [a little later] Could you give me an example of when *you* took the initiative?
Mother: Do you mean like when I called you and asked if you could meet on another day?

We continued to discuss instances, when-nots (counterinstances), and contexts of behavior, affect, and dynamics suggested by test scores and by my direct interactions with both parents. In the mother's case, we came up with examples of her preferring structure and being a follower but resenting "being pushed." She came to agree that "passive–aggressive" described her resentful response. We smiled in sad recognition of the fuller dynamics between the couple. Later, I brought them together and presented each person with a list of reported events that illustrated their respective parenting and interpersonal styles. They clarified some examples and after a while recognized that some of the same themes had been tapped in an unsuccessful mediation session. In my office, they now were communicating with definite regard for each other. I encouraged the couple to return to mediation with their lists and said that we would bypass a court hearing and full evaluation report unless later necessary.

Most individualized assessment is indeed therapeutic in process. Clients discuss how they have been participating even in "what happens to" them, and they recognize that they already have alternative ways (the counter examples) of coping. Even when there are issues that we agree to disagree about, clients inevitably experience themselves as better able to be responsible for themselves. This outcome is remarkably different from those cases in which clients read psychological evaluations whose conclusions seem to be based on indicators of traits, diagnostic categories, and other abstract classifications. Finn and Tonsager's (1992) research showed that even when given general feedback, including negative information, clients are more satisfied with psychological assessment.

When assessments are undertaken at the client's own or the client's therapist's request and when the assessments are pursued in a collaborative manner resulting in client insight and viable personal options, then perhaps over time these records will qualify under HIPAA as therapy notes, not directly available to clients (more to the point, to their attorneys). Use of the term *therapeutic assessment* in the referral and in any reports would lend credibility to the argument.

Individualized Assessment Reports

In the preceding example, an assessment report could mention the test patterns that led to the findings – patterns of past behavior relevant to the issues posed to the assessor. An individualized report to a third party includes the usual headings and information. However, the "Behavioral Observations" section carefully contains descriptions that presage the assessment findings by including variations in the client's comportment noted directly in interactions in front of or with the assessor.

The entire report is client oriented rather than test focused. When test patterns or diagnostic categories are referenced, they are presented not as findings but as useful technical material that led to life-world findings, which constitute the bulk of the report.

For example, a report might say,

> *Elevations on the MMPI–2 scales (4 = 66; 9 = 61) opened the way to discussion of Mr. Dinsdale's having grown up amidst adults who punished him unpredictably and rarely praised him. Although surprised by the characterization, he agreed that he continues his youthful reactions: pretending he doesn't care about punishment, lying to avoid confrontation, and "getting over" on the "system" as a means of balancing the justice scales. In contrast, Mr. Dinsdale later told a Thematic Apperception Test story about "a little boy being lonely and daydreaming about a big brother returning home from a corrections facility to take care of him, protect, and teach him neat things." That story led to a discussion of how much he enjoys being an uncle with seven-year-old Raymond; he reported teaching him to play catch and to take care of his dog and taking him on walks and to the movies.*

These concrete instances convey both Mr. Dinsdale's dyssocial orientation and his capacity for interpersonal empathy. Anticipations and suggestions based on these descriptions are more credible than those that appear to be justified on test scores alone.

Individualized reports may be prepared for clients who self-refer or for the whole range of third-party referrers. When appropriate, individualized, numbered suggestions can be developed with and for the client. For example [to a court-mandated resident of a substance abuse facility]:

> *(1.) Amber, next time you find yourself tempted to just leave an assignment, recall how much more comfortable you were after you asked me questions about those drawings [Bender Gestalt], and that you hung in and did just fine. Also recall that summer job you mentioned where you somehow dared to ask the manager what you needed to know, and again you did fine.* ***When you want to flee, instead find someone to answer your questions.***

Again, clients who have been helped in this way are unlikely to be interested in later acquiring the data nor are attorneys going to be inclined to argue with suggestions based on behavior rather than on test scores alone. Please note that individualized assessment obviates any need for "feedback" or "explanation"; collaborative exploration has already provided the client with joint findings and understandings (including agreements to disagree). Summary discussion and written reports or reminders conclude the assessment.

In the case of a client who had participated in a traditional assessment and who has now requested records, meeting to personally review test profiles, explain findings, answer questions, and address other apparent concerns, as Erard (2004) suggests, typically would be satisfactory for the client (unless there is an attorney behind the request). However, I believe that all parties usually are better served to the degree that the assessment is collaborative from the beginning.

Summary and Conclusions

HIPAA's privacy rule requiring release of test data on request of a client is indeed, as in Erard's (2004) subtitle, a "raw deal" in that it involves extra difficulty in protecting test material and clients. It is also "a half-baked idea" in its classification of client responses as on par with X rays and blood tests. However, the rule turns out, in light of Erard's review and numerous suggestions, to be what psychologists could call a fairly "doable deal." Nevertheless, it is necessary for psychologists to continue to be vigilant in protecting the security of our tests and in protecting clients from potential misuse of data. It is also incumbent on us to try to bypass adversarial stances and instead work cooperatively with clients and their attorneys for the client's best interest.

Individualized assessment, the trend of exploring test profiles directly with clients to access what this data might point to in actual life, provides findings useful to all parties with less emphasis on test records themselves. The test record is not regarded so much as evidence as it is regarded as instances of the behaviors and the contexts to which the collaborative exploration led. Attorneys will find themselves preparing cross-examinations with less emphasis on the validity of tests and their scores because the tests were regarded as tools rather than as indicators of truth. Judith Armstrong has spoken to me in recent years of the power, in contending with cross-examination, of providing the analogy of looking out the window to see if it's raining rather than relying solely on probabilistic meteorological data. However, as assessors become known not just for expertise in psychological tests but for their expertise in using tests to gain access to life events, then psychologists rightly are expected to gather what in custody work is called "collateral" data: reports of behavior from other observers such as teachers, employers, and neighbors, of course with consent provided. Gathering reports from a range of observers also prepares us for that frequent courtroom question: "Would you change your mind if you knew of [such and such behavior]?"

Individualized, collaborative practices are possible with a wide range of clients, including neurological and dementia patients, involuntary populations, and special needs children (see Fischer, 2002). Working with these folks presents an extra challenge of finding entry into these clients' different worlds, but the task is a variation of individualized assessment.

There are some assessments of the decision-making rather than descriptive sort for which minimal individualizing is necessary. However, I find that even intelligence testing for gifted child or mental retardation status is enhanced by some contextualizing and therapeutic exploration and reporting. Yes, the more thoroughly collaborative and life-world oriented our assessments are, the more time they require. However, they are helpful to all readers of reports who find themselves picturing behaviors in particular contexts and readily seeing positive points of intervention, and they save a lot of later effort at minimizing HIPAA problems.

Note

1 Originally published as Fischer, C. T. (2004). Individualized assessment moderates impact of HIPAA privacy rules. *Journal of Personality Assessment*, *81*, 35–38.

References

Butcher, J. N., Dahlstrom, W. G., Graham, J. R., Tellegen, A., & Kaemmer, B. (1989). *MMPI–2: Minnesota Multiphasic Personality Inventory–2: Manual for administration and scoring.* Minneapolis: University of Minnesota Press.

Erard, R. E. (2004). Release of test data under the 2002 ethics code and the HIPAA privacy rule: A raw deal or just a half-baked idea. *Journal of Personality Assessment, 82*(1), 23–30.

Finn, S. E. (1996). *Manual for using the MMPI–2 as a therapeutic intervention.* Minneapolis: University of Minnesota Press.

Finn, S. E. (2003). Therapeutic Assessment of a man with "ADD." *Journal of Personality Assessment, 80*, 115–129.

Finn, S. E., & Tonsager, M. E. (1992). Therapeutic effects of providing MMPI–2 test feedback to college students awaiting therapy. *Psychological Assessment, 4*, 278–287.

Finn, S. E., & Tonsager, M. E. (1997). Information-gathering and therapeutic models of assessment: Complementary paradigms. *Psychological Assessment, 9*, 374–385.

Fischer, C. T. (1994). *Individualizing psychological assessment.* Hillsdale: Lawrence Erlbaum Associate, Inc. (Original work published in1985.)

Fischer, C. T. (2000). Collaborative, individualized assessment. *Journal of Personality Assessment, 74*, 2–14.

Fischer, C. T. (Ed.). (2002). Humanistic approaches to psychological assessment. *The Humanistic Psychologist, 30*, 3–236.

Hathaway, S. R., & McKinley, J. C. (1943). *The Minnesota Multiphasic Personality Inventory.* Minneapolis: University of Minnesota Press.

The Health Insurance Portability and Accountability Act of 1996 ("HIPAA"), Pub. L. No. 104–191 (1996).

Morey, L. (1991). *Personality Assessment Inventory.* Odessa: Psychological Assessment Resources.

PART III

TEACHING COLLABORATIVE/ INDIVIDUALIZED ASSESSMENT

CHAPTER 13

RORSCHACH SCORING QUESTIONS AS ACCESS TO DYNAMICS[1]

This article consists of scoring questions posed by students, answers adhering to conservative scoring criteria, and the main theme of this article – suggestions alerting students and readers that the scoring dilemma may reflect the client's dilemma in contending with the inkblot. The client's dynamics in going through the Rorschach are representative of his or her dynamics in going through broader life. From this perspective, discussions with clients, as well as the ensuing written reports, can go beyond technical jargon to address directly the individual's inclinations and choices in daily life.

This article invites readers to consider the possibility that the psychologist's Rorschach scoring questions and dilemmas may reflect the client's psychological dynamics. The viability of this possibility is illustrated through a series of examples. Each example presents the Rorschach response and inquiry, the scoring question, a conservative answer in accordance with Exner's (1986) Comprehensive System, and some imaginable dynamics on the client's part as she or he contended with the card's options. Suggestions are frequently made for exploring these possibilities directly with the client. Because such exploration is about broader life instances rather than about the Rorschach choices per se, future administrations are not jeopardized.

Although several psychological theories could frame this approach, the one that for me grounds the examples and suggestions to follow can be characterized as *practical theory.* Here, "practical" has a double meaning. The first refers etymologically to ordinary practices and actions in the everyday world. I view the client's ways of dealing with each card as instances of his or her going about life and being confronted with dilemmas – choice points among routes, goals, commitments, dangers, surprises, ambivalences, and ambiguities. This practical approach is holistic. In clients' responding to the Rorschach cards, we find that motive, perception, association, affect, cognition, and action are mutually implicatory, just as they are in everyday life. Clients' journeys through the cards give us access to their complex, multidirectional, and multidimensional travels through life. Dynamics are not only intrapsychic, but are also always between the person and his or her world.

The second sense in which this approach to the Rorschach is practical is its usefulness. As emphasized earlier, we have access to the client's world beyond the assessment situation in that his or her practices (typical actions) in coping with the Rorschach can be understood as instances similar to others in his or her everyday world. The client can be asked about such possibilities directly, without reference to separate, technical indicators of perception, cognition, affect, and so on. The Rorschach becomes immediately useful for addressing the client's actual life.

For me, this practical approach is grounded philosophically in phenomenological psychology (e.g., Merleau-Ponty, 1945/1962, 1942/1963). Within that frame, I work my way toward understanding a client's dynamic responses through the usual resources, including an earlier review of records, a clinical interview, and other test data. In regard to the Rorschach, I reflect on Schachtel's (1966) descriptions of the properties of each card, and on which life situations might present the client with similar "stimuli." I observe the client's nonscorable ways of relating to the Rorschach situation, including his or her impact on me. I note the client's positions among Exner's norms for the general population and for diagnostic groups. I draw on developmental studies and on psychodynamic theories. I recall Rorschach lore. Particularly helpful as I move from general and abstract impressions and begin to imagine what they might tell me about the client's actual life are the empirical studies that have correlated codes and ratios with life events. For example, inanimate movement responses increased among Israeli seamen aboard a small boat in a severe storm (Shalit, 1965), and *m* also rose among paratroop trainees on the evening before their first jump (Armbruster, Miller, & Exner, 1974). The combined use of these various resources promotes a contemporary scientist-clinician stance, one that makes use of technical procedures, research empirics, psychodynamic approaches, and a life-world orientation.

The body of this article is composed of my responses to students' questions about coding. By using answers to student questions I hope that the theme of this article will be clear for readers of all levels of clinical experience. Toward the end of the examples I include a student's contribution, and I bypass the question-answer format to present some examples from my own Rorschach administrations. In responding to questions, I first address the scoring criteria, affirming the student's concern with scoring precision. Then I alert students that even the quickly resolved coding dilemma may point to the client's dynamics in dealing with the inkblot, which in turn may be an instance of how the client contends with larger life. Dynamics are always about one's efforts to deal with the world. Students thus develop a fuller clinical presence to the client prior to studying the structural summary. Class discussion often sensitizes us to alternative dynamic understandings and to diverse ways of exploring those understandings directly with the client. Sometimes we try out this approach in class by exploring possible student dynamics implicit in a repeatedly presented scoring question. For example, Sandy discovered that his questions about including additional codes (overscoring) was similar to his writing overinclusive psychology term papers. It turned out that Sandy prefers a simple comprehension of events, but in both of these instances he complexified matters to avoid being judged naive about clinical matters. Sandy later reported that this simple discovery had been profoundly helpful in several areas of his life.

In the following excerpts the subject's (S's) response is followed in brackets by S's inquiry phase elaboration.

Questions and Dynamics

RESPONSE: "A volcano ready to explode." [This colored part would be melted lava rising. (?) I think they explode after the lava goes over the edge.] SCORING

QUESTION: Should we score this inanimate movement active or passive? The lava is passive, but "ready to explode" sounds active. ANSWER: I'd say passive. S does not describe strong tension; when asked, he tells us his knowledge of volcanoes rather than telling about pressure building to the point of exploding. POSSIBLE DYNAMIC: Just as S, in providing this response, appears to back away from an initial perception of possible eruption, so too in other situations he may talk himself into focusing on process rather than being caught up in possible explosiveness. This shift could be useful or limiting depending on the situation.

RESPONSE: "Sideways it's nice, but I can't say what it is." [Oh yes. Nice colors. The shape has delicacy without being overly delicate. It's delicate without sacrificing substance.] SCORING QUESTION: Score *CF? AB?* ANSWER: No. This one isn't scored at all; S is doing "card description" rather than providing a percept. S did not name colored content; she is being abstract but has not named abstract content, such as an emotion. But I'm glad you recorded this rich material. POSSIBLE DYNAMIC: We certainly wonder what S is up to here – is she using the cards as an opportunity to tell us something about herself that she wants us to know? Colorful, substantive delicacy may be characteristics she values in herself. You could ask her about that directly after the inquiry. I also wonder what she's in touch with when she leaves a task to engage in aesthetic commentary, and when that shift works for her and when it does not.

RESPONSE: "Two women met after shopping." [They both have shopping baskets. (Help me see the two women just as you did) See, here's the basket – the shape of a basket.] SCORING QUESTION: should *M* be scored? – Movement is implied in having met, and the women must be holding the baskets. ANSWER: No. Past action is not scored for movement; and no present tension or activity is specified, so we score conservatively. But S certainly is relating to the possibility of action in an interesting way. POSSIBLE DYNAMIC: Especially in that most people picture these figures as active, we note S's and the perceived women's nonengagement. Does S often find herself on the edge, not quite engaged, uncommitted? Does she experience other people as "just there"? Do things then "just happen" in S's world? On the other hand, was she drawn to the possibility of two women at last simply resting? Or did she see interactive potential that she preferred to back away from?

RESPONSE: "A distorted Popeye cartoon." [The nose is too big.] SCORING QUESTION: Should I score the distortion as Morbid? ANSWER: I think not, because the "too big" nose is not hurt, deteriorating, etc. But our inclination to score *MOR* does point toward a tension. POSSIBLE DYNAMIC: I wonder if S is attuned, both here and in broader life, to the possibility of things being wrong, out of proportion, distorted, but keeps this possibility on the edge of full consciousness – here in the realm of the not really real, the realm of cartoons instead of actual people.

RESPONSE: "Two bears touching." [They're fighting. Hurt. (?) Blood on their fur.] SCORING QUESTION: Can I score the blood, given that it emerged only after I introduced a question in the inquiry? ANSWER: Yes, so long as you're reasonably sure that S did see the blood during the free association and is not now associating to blood for the first time during the inquiry. POSSIBLE DYNAMIC: Your alertness to the scoring question allows us to watch for other instances of S's speaking sociably at first, only later addressing negative themes. I imagine that this approach could be a useful delay in most social circumstances, but that if the elaboration were not shared, then other persons could feel confused by contradictions between

S's initial statements and his later dissonant behavior. On the other hand, if S were aware of the blood for the first time only during the inquiry, then we may have an example of his unknowingly blocking fuller perception until he's out of the original situation and is looking back on it.

RESPONSE: "A flower garden – beautiful display of colors." [It must be flowers; that's the only colored things that would be near all this dug up stuff. I guess this dirt was fertilized, that's why it's discolored.] SCORING QUESTION: Do I score *ALOG* for inappropriate logic? The original percept isn't at all arbitrary, but the statement in the inquiry is strained logic. I didn't prompt except to repeat the original percept. ANSWER: Yes, for the latter reason, we score *ALOG*. POSSIBLE DYNAMIC: I wonder when else S has been attuned to beauty when he was viewing from a panoramic distance, but then became attuned to things being disturbed and not quite right when he looked more closely. Scoring *ALOG* reminds us that he may lose touch with consensual perspectives when he becomes involved with this closer look – which we don't yet know enough about.

RESPONSE: "A woman falling and clutching her purse tightly." SCORING QUESTION: Score *M* active or passive? ANSWER: I would prefer to score both: $M^{a\text{-}p}$, capturing that unusual co-occurrence. However, Exner instructs us to score $M^{a\text{-}p}$ only if there are two separate humans, one in passive movement and one in active movement. Here, Exner's criteria call for scoring the stronger component, Mª Nevertheless, the tension in the response is indeed remarkable. POSSIBLE DYNAMIC: Even while subject to outside forces, the reported woman exerts herself, but in an inward, "holding on" manner. S seems familiar, either personally or observationally, with being tenacious even when things are not in her control. My own association to its being a purse that the woman holds onto is that S may be familiar with pulling in and holding onto her possessions and characteristics when they are endangered. That would be an advantage in some situations and a drawback in others.

RESPONSE: "Blood all over the place." [It's just there. There, there, there. (?) I can't say anything else about it; it's just blood.] SCORING QUESTION: Score Morbid? ANSWER: No; S doesn't specify illness or injury, so we conservatively do not score *MOR*. POSSIBLE DYNAMIC: This response reminds me of a similar one where it turned out that the client was indeed attuned to destruction and death, but was so overwhelmed by the perception that he couldn't bring himself to speak it. The implied but non-scorable *MOR* paradoxically pointed to a heightened concern with injury and threat.

RESPONSE: "This shading represents ovaryitus." SCORING QUESTION: At first I scored this *DV* because I thought it was a made-up word. It turned out that the client had said, "ovaritis," which is an inflammation of the ovary. How can I tell when a word is a deviation or a relatively esoteric word I just don't know? ANSWER: If the clarification doesn't occur during standard inquiry, you can ask S about it directly after the entire inquiry is completed. If necessary you can later consult a dictionary. POSSIBLE DYNAMIC: As with persons who give *DV* responses, this client was not concerned with whether the use of an unusual term might confuse you. If this occurred only once, we might wonder about what is going on in S's life that she found an inflamed ovary in the Rorschach. If there are several instances, then we wonder whether S tries to impress people in authority with her special knowledge, perhaps especially when she's in unfamiliar situations. If so, I suspect the gambit doesn't work well in that, like you, the other person feels used and/or confused.

RESPONSE: "Furry wings." [Yes, hairy, but not long hair. See? (traces around edge of wing)] SCORING QUESTION: Should this be scored for texture? ANSWER: No; S neither rubbed the interior of the card nor specified shading as a determinant. However, S did seem to back off from an initial attunement to texture. POSSIBLE DYNAMIC: You might want to see if S finds himself drawn to affectionate or sensual contact and then backs off to a more formal distance, perhaps through intellectual discussion or through structured roles. At any rate, I'm curious as to when else S stays on the edge of *T* and when he embraces it.

RESPONSE: "An undersea ball. Dancing fish – dancing pairs." [Yes, dancing. But on the other hand, they're trying to tear something. These creatures are eating each other.] SCORING QUESTION: This is *M* for human movement. But is it *COP* for cooperative activity or *AG* for aggression, or is it both? ANSWER: We try to score what the person was seeing during the free association, so the *AG* material would not be scored. But it was certainly wise to note this "additional response." I would not score *COP* because S did not stress dancing together; we are not told of an effort to achieve something through joint effort. POSSIBLE DYNAMIC: We wonder whether S scans for danger after encountering pleasure, recreation, mutual activity, or whatever the dancing means for him. You could have gone back after the inquiry to ask what the mood of the dancing fish scene was at the time. We should look back through the protocol for other instances of shifts from pleasure to attack. S might have been able to provide similar examples from his interpersonal relationships.

RESPONSE: "Two dogs that are looking in a mirror on their hind legs." [Here's the head and paws. (Mirror?) There was no mirror – I was just imagining.] SCORING QUESTION: Is this response scored for reflection? ANSWER: Yes, I'd score *Fr*, for S's clear response during free association. But the momentary scoring dilemma puts us in touch with S's inconsistencies. POSSIBLE DYNAMIC: S not only reneged on the reported mirror, thereby being internally inconsistent, but also was not in consonance with what most persons would construe: one dog seeing itself. So here perhaps we have a person about to enjoy a mirroring – a self-involvement – and maybe even the basking of determined performers. But he quickly turns away from that option, with a glib dismissal. We wonder when else he has turned away from such opportunities and whether he experienced them as dangerous or perhaps as somehow socially improper.

RESPONSE: "This is a caterpillar about to metamorphize." [See the wings are just starting to come out. It's going to take off.] SCORING QUESTION: Is this animal movement, and is it passive or active? ANSWER: Yes, the tension state qualifies it as animal movement. I'd code it as passive because so far the metamorphosis is simply evolving, much like "grass growing"; the caterpillar is in a state of readiness. "It's going to take off" might be scored active if it were in the present scene, but here S is telling us about something that will occur later. POSSIBLE DYNAMIC: Our pause to consider the scoring question alerts us to S's attunement to things just happening, much like the waiting that so often is reflected in inanimate movement responses. After the entire inquiry, you could have gone back to ask S if he could recall his sense of how the butterfly would take off (uncertainly, lazily, awkwardly, gracefully, determinedly?). You might have asked S whether he could associate anything in his life right now that might be similar to this metamorphosis; most people can tell us what delays in their lives are keeping them in a state of waiting, and of how they'd like to "take off."

RESPONSE: "A spider. He could be eating something." [Well, I can't tell. Whatever it would be isn't there; it might be eating something or not.] SCORING QUESTION: Should movement be scored? ANSWER: Yes, in that our task is to score what S reported during free association, and S was perceiving eating. I thought you also were going to ask about coding for aggression; S doesn't tell us whether the eating is feeding or preying, so we conservatively refrain from coding *AG*. POSSIBLE DYNAMIC: This woman probably declines to commit herself to readings of other situations too. I'm wondering whether she knows that spiders eat only trapped insects, and if here she is avoiding having to acknowledge aggression and morbidity. At any rate, sustaining awareness of conflicting possibilities can be a wearing process; I wonder what positive purposes this stance serves, and I wonder how aware of the process S is. Post inquiry you might have asked her if she recalls what it was like to report the spider and whether she was consciously making choices about what to commit herself to. If she could, then she probably also could tell you about similar life situations.

RESPONSE: "A bright fire – multicolored. These witches with green capes are casting a spell around it." SCORING QUESTION: I want to score this *CF.FC*, but I think I'm supposed to score only the stronger use of color: *CF.M*[a]? It seems to me that we're missing something by not including the *FC*. ANSWER AND POSSIBLE DYNAMIC: I agree. In the Comprehensive System we score only the stronger of the color codings. But I think you're right to note that S can subordinate color to form even while also giving color dominance over form. This reminds me of someone who can invite the other person to respond to one's emotional outburst, or someone who can give himself or herself over to spontaneous dancing even while keeping beat to the music.

RESPONSE: "Snooty girls." [Condescending attitude toward each other. (?) Chins are projected forward like this (demonstrates).] SCORING QUESTION: This is human movement, but is it active or passive? ANSWER: The attitude alone would be passive, but although the projected chins emerged late, I'd score them active for intention and sustained effort. POSSIBLE DYNAMIC: The scoring dilemma may reflect S's own dilemma in regard to taking action. Because it is only *Hd* that is moving, and because the movement isn't "going anywhere," of course I would guess that S sometimes restricts her own interpersonal progress through passive-aggressive postures. After the entire inquiry, you might have asked her about her associations to the snooty girls on the Rorschach and about their relevance in her present circumstances.

(Note: The following items depart from the earlier format.)

DILEMMA AND POSSIBLE DYNAMIC: I finally just stuck with the form quality tables and criteria and did resolve my numerous questions about whether one client's responses were FQ_u or FQ_-. However, given that I haven't experienced such repetitive difficulty with other clients' Rorschachs, might it be that my quandaries were a reflection of S's seeing situations in ways that often border between just a bit offbeat (unusual) and quite idiosyncratic (arbitrary)? ANSWER: Yes, that's a good bet. I also bet that you haven't been the only person who has been caught between going along with S and suddenly being confused or derailed during interaction with him. You might want to report your experience during the Rorschach to him, to test whether he is able to take consensual perspectives into account. After asking him for similar examples from his daily life, you might practice ways for him to check whether he's "being arbitrary" and whether he might want to help the other person to see his perspective.

RESPONSE: "Spider head. It's up to something evil." DILEMMA AND POSSIBLE DYNAMIC: At first I scored this as animal movement; then I realized that evil is a human attribute, so I scored it as human movement. Throughout the Rorschach administration I was aware of this fellow being on the lookout for danger. It was in the midst of this scoring revision that I realized that he never attributed harmful intent to his human percepts. In discussion following the *TAT* we discovered that he wants for people to be "nice," and treats them nicely, but secretly he worries that people covertly wish him ill.

DILEMMA AND POSSIBLE DYNAMIC: I've found that people whose records leave me perplexed as to whether to score monsters and creatures as human or as animal turn out to ignore the full humanness and individuality of their involved others. That is, these people see others as just organisms much more often than most of us do. Similarly, I've found when I'm weighing whether to score an animal or human percept as mythological that my Rorschach client turns out to often vacillate between relating to people on their own terms versus relating to them in terms of protocol, roles, or fantasy.

RESPONSE: "This is a priest praying." [You can see the gown they wear.] DILEMMA AND POSSIBLE DYNAMIC: I decided to score human movement because it was clear in the free association although S did not return to the human in the inquiry. I decided against *ALOG* because the gown wasn't given as a strained justification, even though it was only a partial explanation. I did not give in to my inclination to score *(H)* for the costume/role quality of the priest and instead scored *H*. But my decision process made me aware that S may relate to people in terms of their roles rather than in terms of their own involvements and intentions. As I looked back on the assessment session, it occurred to me that indeed Mr. Smith never engaged me as an individual, but only as a tester, and that only in regard to the court order.

RESPONSE: "Oh what beautiful colors! This is pretty, my favorite card. This could be a flower." [It's just shaped like a spring flower – see the stem, the bloom, and this could be the leaves.] DILEMMA AND POSSIBLE DYNAMIC: At first I wanted to score color, but then I knew that S had not said the flower was colored. My momentary wavering led me to speculate that S might enter other situations too with a show of affect and then retreat to more cognitive interaction.

RESPONSE: "Two mermaids holding hands, dancing around each other with a crown on." [They're both dancing. Here's the crown.] DILEMMA AND POSSIBLE DYNAMIC: I expected to score cooperative movement but finally decided against *COP* because S did not sustain a percept of dancing together. In later discussion, this client affirmed that she often follows expected form in social interaction but then backs off from genuine involvement. An instance was that she had filled out intake forms neatly and completely, but then drew blanks when I asked her to elaborate on goals and to give examples of her self-characterizations. Another instance was when she and her new roommate agreed to go shopping together to coordinate purchases for their room; S, however, wandered off and bought her own bedspread without consulting the roommate. Her rationale at the time was that the unilateral action had seemed "more efficient." We agreed that similarly she often has been more comfortable with mythical (fantasied) rather than with real people.

Summary

Psychoanalytic psychologists have, of course, made some of the above sorts of interpretation for decades. Also, since the advent of Exner's Comprehensive System, we have scored more consistently, and with his research tradition we have made use of the direct relations between structural summary features and behavior patterns. The contribution of this article is its emphasis on retaining the noted progress while systematically regarding how the person copes with the Rorschach as a sample of how he or she gets through other situations too. Coding dilemmas often reflect clients' dilemmas.

This article invites readers, in their own practices, to consider a range of possible client dynamics that might be reflected in scoring questions. I do not claim that a particular scoring dilemma necessarily points to any one dynamic. As often as not, the possible interpretation remains just that. Fortunately, however, having just traveled through the Rorschach together, client and assessor have an immediate sense of what it has been like to journey through similar situations. When asked, clients often readily share related instances of living out the dynamics of multiple, sometimes conflicting, motives, habits, and styles. Such discussion not only tests the validity of the assessor's impressions, it also can correct and refine those impressions through the client's provision of context and specifics. This checking of assessment impressions against a client's recollection of actual life events is a rigorous form of empirical validation. It also affirms clients' ability to investigate collaboratively their dynamic journeys through life. Psychological assessment reports, as well as discussion with clients, can focus on their life situations rather than on theoretical constructs and the technical features of the structural summary. The Rorschach thus can provide an individualized sample of clients' complex, dynamic lives (cf. Fischer, 1979, 1989, 1994).

Note

1 Originally published as Fischer, C. T. (1994). Rorschach scoring questions as access to dynamics. *Journal of Personality Assessment*, 62, 515–525.

References

Armbruster, G. L., Miller, H. S., & Exner, J. E. (1974). *Rorschach responses of parachuter trainees at the beginning of training and shortly before their first jump*. Unpublished workshop (Study No. 201). Rorschach Workshops.

Exner, J. E. (1986). *The Rorschach: A comprehensive system: Vol. 1. Basic foundations* (2nd ed.). N.Y.: Wiley.

Fischer, C. T. (1979). Individualized assessment and phenomenological psychology. *Journal of Personality Assessment*, 43, 115–122.

Fischer, C. T. (1989). A life-centered approach to psychodiagnostics: Attending to the life-world, ambiguity, and possibility. *Person-Centered Review*, 4, 163–170.

Fischer, C. T. (1994). *Individualizing psychological assessment*. Hillsdale: Lawrence Erlbaum Associates, Inc. (Original work published 1985.)

Merleau-Ponty, M. (1962). *Phenomenology of perception*. N.Y.: Humanities Press. (Original work published 1945.)

Merleau-Ponty, M. (1963). *The structure of behavior*. Boston: Beacon Press. (Original work published 1942.)

Schachtel, E. G. (1966). *Experiential foundations of Rorschach's test*. N.Y.: Basic Books.

Shalit, B. (1965). Effects of environmental stimulation on the M, FM, and m responses in the Rorschach. *Journal of Projective Techniques and Personality Assessment*, 29, 228–231.

CHAPTER 14

THE RORSCHACH AND THE LIFE WORLD

Exploratory Exercises[1]

The life world is where we go about our lives. It is the world as we live it prior to scientific conceptualizing, theorizing, and measuring. This chapter describes exercises undertaken by doctoral students in a Rorschach course to help them to *explore* and appreciate the general relations between Rorschach data and the life world. Students also learn to work collaboratively with clients to explore how Rorschach data might provide access to their everyday lives and options.

Our guiding principle is that "If we can't describe our findings in terms of the client's everyday life, then literally we don't yet know 'what *in the world*' we're talking about." We regard an assessment account that restricts itself to reporting scores, ratios, symptoms, constructs, hypothetical dynamics, and diagnostic impressions as having stopped short, being unfinished. The next step would be to inquire into and then to describe how our derived data point back to a particular person's ways of participating in actual situations. For example, we might say "Just as Mary sometimes bypassed the instructions to say what the blots could be, and instead addressed the white space (S = 5), so too she sometimes has ignored her supervisor's instructions and completed tasks her own way." We also describe whatever the client and assessor have learned about the client's personally viable options – alternative ways to continue his or her course more satisfyingly. For example: "We eventually agreed that Mary might bypass irritating her boss, first by reiterating his goal to him and then by proposing *her* plan of action. Mary already has followed this tactic successfully with an office mate."

The students in the Rorschach course are enrolled in Duquesne University's human-science psychology graduate program. They have completed a prerequisite course in which they learned standardized administration of the Wechsler intelligence tests, the TAT, Draw-A-Person Test, and the Bender-Gestalt. In that course they also conducted collaborative, interventional assessments through which they developed tailored suggestions for clients and their helpers. Clients review the students' reports and write a "Client's Commentary" section on the last page. The textbook, *Individualizing Psychological Assessment* (Fischer, 1985/1994a), was developed for this prerequisite course. See also Finn (1996, 1998) and Fischer (1979).

For the Rorschach course, students learn Exner's (1993) Comprehensive System, first preparing summary sheets by hand (to better appreciate the constitution of the various ratios), and then by computer program. They administer and score five practice Rorschachs, exchanging them to check scoring and to discuss impressions, before turning them in to me. In addition each student serves as a Rorschach subject, and then scores his or her own protocol. Students videotape their standardized administrations and discuss possible impacts of their styles. They conclude the course with two clinical assessments utilizing the Rorschach and other assessment materials. Reports are based on multiply grounded impressions. They specify any impressions that were not discussed with the client or about which assessor and client have agreed to disagree.

Introducing Determinants Via Greeting Cards

In the first class I present an overview of the history and present status of the Rorschach. Then I say that we will do an exercise using greeting cards to demystify the scoring process. I have already written the names of all the parts of the "scoring sentence" across the top of a blackboard: location... developmental quality... determinants... form quality... pairs... content... popular... organization... special scores.

I show the class a series of greeting cards, one at a time. Each time, I ask "As the artist what would you have to attend to in order to produce this image?" or "What do you find that you've attended to as you perceived this image?" The first card depicts the American Psychological Association building in Washington, DC. Someone quickly mentions "perspective," and in response to my questioning says that he meant by that the coming closer together of lines and planes of windows and walls to indicate a receding into distance. Now on the blackboard I draw a line from "determinants," and begin what will become a list of all determinants, in this case beginning with "FV" for form seen as vista. Someone mentions that perspective is also indicated by the depiction of a person walking in front of the building. Now I write "FD" for form dimensionality and explain its criteria. Someone else says she was struck at first by the grayness of the building. I add "C'F" to the list, explain about achromatic color, and ask whether I have accurately indicated the student's attention to the gray as more important than the form of the building. I explain the alternative scores of "FC' " and of "C' " to reflect differing attunements to the card's grayness. I point out that in one of my own gray moments, I might perceive the entire card as more or less gray (C'), and that I might or might not be interested in noting shading variations (C'.Y). A student comments that in *his* dark moods, as an artist he would render the building as dark, not as the color gray. Now we discuss YF, FY and Y.

Next I display a card showing colorful flower beds, with individual flower clearly represented in the foreground. We discuss the attunement that would lead us to score CF to represent color dominating form, and FC for the inverse. Someone provides a fortuitous example of a deviant verbalization by referring to "daffolillies," and I list "DV1" under the special scores and give an example of a "DV2." I happily acknowledge another student's observation that we could also score FD and FV on this greeting card.

I hold up a card that is just red, with no illustration. The class agrees that viewer could only be attuned to color (C) on this greeting card. A brief discussion of the rarity of pure determinants, aside from F, ensues.

Now I hold up a children's Easter card with rabbits and chicks. We quickly score FCs and CFs, and then someone points out that on this card one could note fluffiness and softness. We go on to score FTs and TFs to represent texture. One person mentions that she could practically feel the silkiness of a tulip petal on the earlier greeting card. By now we can talk about how different cards invite or limit various attunements; I refer to Schachtel's (1966) book that discusses not only determinants but the differing stimulus qualities of each card. We note the just as we had not mentioned all that we saw, so too clients do not mention as that they see on Rorschach cards, even if the features stood out for them. We agree that "determinants" is a misnomer, that the card features themselves do not determine the response. "Determinants" might better be called "descriptors."

After we have noted examples of the remaining determinants, I point out how else we have been attending to the cards, such as mentioning the entire depiction (W), or an obvious feature noted by most of us (D), or a more obscure feature (Dd). I go back to write out the abbreviations for all the content that we have named.

By now we have shared some teasing and laughter as we recognize one another's styles of attending to and describing aspects of the greeting cards point out which of these features are scorable, which show up in later ratio and which can be otherwise noted.

A postcard photo of a New England seafood dinner draws pained expression of desire from a tired and hungry class. We note that our response would have been different that morning.

I conclude the first class with a demonstration of administering and enquiring Cards I and II. We write out the scoring sentences that characterize how the subject encountered and responded to the two cards. Our volunteer subject tells us that her first responses for each card were ones she had heard on a TV show, and that in her long pauses after that she was trying to censor the sexual and aggressive themes that leapt out at her. She wound up reporting benign percepts. I remark that clients too select which meanings to report. I encourage the students to retain the commonsense understandings we developed through the greeting cards and through our volunteer demonstration as they go on to work with the Rorschach blots.

Developing Life World Instances of Structural Summary Data

I emphasize that the summary sheet data do not present an X-ray of psychic structure, but rather, summary notations by a participant observer of how a person took up the Rorschach task. To extrapolate meaningfully into other situations, we must bear in mind the testing situation's characteristics: A seated person is presented with unfamiliar and ambiguous visual material and is asked to tell a psychologist what it might be. The person cannot be sure what the psychologist is looking for or finds significant. This interpersonal encounter is regarded as one scene in the person's ongoing life. About midway in our graduate course the students talk about how their own Rorschachs reflected not only their trans-situational ways of coping, but also what was happening at this stage and day in their lives, the time of day and setting, and their relationship with the classmate test administrator. After that we often preface interpretations with "*On this day*, the client..."

We build a repertoire of events in life that are similar to those that during a Rorschach administration resulted in various codings and ratios. As an introduction we review some of the statistical studies that Exner has summarized (e.g., 1993). For example, inanimate movement responses increased as medical students awaited results of their gross anatomy exams, while survivors awaited burial of loved ones, and while sailors weathered a dangerous storm.

We add to this review events from our own lives that seem structurally similar: treading water, being stuck in traffic, being in a holding pattern above your airport, enduring a repetitive bad dream. We note what all these instances have in common: having to wait alertly due to circumstances beyond our control, while wanting to get on with life. I share other instances that clients have readily provided when I have wondered with them whether they might be in circumstances like some of the aforementioned: awaiting a bank's decision on a mortgage application, getting through six weeks before comprehensive exams are graded, trying to plan for the future, although the company has not committed to preserving one's job.

Throughout the course, students share new items contributed to their repertoires by assessees. We speak in terms of collecting a range of possibilities that any score or ratio may point to. For example, one student had asked a client what it was like to attend to white space rather than to the ink in "a vase" (VII) and "islands" (III). The man spoke of relief in getting away from complexity and nuances, and went on to say that he had about had it with trying to figure out what people wanted from him. Other possible instances of responding to white space developed with other clients: being attuned to emptiness, taking one's own stand, being playful. Similar repertoires are developed for all entries in the summary sheet.

We practice exploring life world instances of summary sheet constellations by imagining what it would be like to be in the shoes of a person recently featured in the news (e.g., man perched on a bridge tower for three hours), and then attempting to sketch his or her living of that situation in Rorschach terms. Our life world orientation helps students to be patient about learning how to inquire and code; they already see the interpretive implications.

Discovering Dynamics Through Scoring Dilemmas

In discussing scoring questions, we first determine how to follow Exner's advice to score conservatively. Often we then explore tensions the client may have experienced while coping with the cards, now reflected in our conflicting scoring inclinations. Some examples follow:

Scoring Dilemma: Shall I score COP here: "Two people holding something"? *Answer*: No, because the client does not specify cooperative effort. *Possible Dynamic:* Perhaps, like us, the client sees potential for the people to be working together, but hesitates to develop that option. Likewise on Card VII she reported, "Two girls on a playground [They're jumping – hair up"], but she does not say that they are playing *together*. I wonder whether this woman similarly remains alongside of others, perhaps waiting to be invited in, or perhaps preferring the lesser involvement of "parallel play."

Scoring Dilemma: How do I code color in this response: (Card X) "Oh, I just love the color! – Much more pleasant (than Card IX). I'll say a painting of beautiful flowers [the petals – shaped like the ones in Torm prints. Stems. The rest would be leaves. (?) Pleasant because of the balance of the composition]"? *Answer*: We seem to have F, with no scorable color. *Possible Dynamic:* In other situations, too, this fellow may find himself pulled powerfully toward an emotional stance, but then after initially responding to this evocation, backing off to offer evaluative commentary. I'm reminded of a person erupting with, "John, you're here! I'm so glad you came!!," then incongruously evading a potential hug, and after a pause remarking, "Did you notice that Donninger's has those leather book covers again? They look as well stitched as the ones at Hickston's."

Scoring Dilemma: Do I score DQ_+ for "Animal climbing [its body is leaning this way. You can see it's straining because of the position of this bulging muscle in the back leg]"? *Answer*: Possibly FY or FV for "bulging," but DQ_O because what the animal is climbing is not mentioned. *Possible Dynamic:* I wonder if out in her daily life Charlene is focusing more on struggle and striving than on goals and context? I'll bet you could mention that you are wondering about this response, and directly ask her about that possibility. (See Fischer, 1994b, for further examples and discussion of how it is that scoring questions can provide access to possible dynamics.)

Describing One's Own Life Events in Rorschachese

As a take-home part of the final exam, students are asked to write a one- to two-page Rorschachese description of a recent personal event. Early in the course, I provided handouts describing several scenes from my own life. Knowing that this exercise is coming up, we all practice from time to time in our conversations: "Geez, my whole day has been Y, with hardly any F, and no S in sight." "You got the job?! Great! – Your CF must be way up!" "Let's take a break; our FM, m, and Fd are on the rise!"

In the following five excerpts[2], codes refer to the graduate student authors' experience as well as to the perceived scene:

1. About writing a late Rorschach report at 3 a.m.: "The formerly beautiful FV.FC MOR flowers are the only Bt in the room... As I realize how much more I still have to do, my Afr and Zd are sinking. My EA, which was so big this morning, is waning. My rising es seems to be looming in front of me. Isolate/R is climbing. I am aware mostly of shading blends. I want my EA back, so I can overcome the es that is oppressing me..."
2. A scored dream: "An H in the woods was M^aing toward me, his face illuminated with C' light. A C'.FD light beams from his eyes. Although the Hx during the scene had been W_v, I was now frightened by the AG/MOR capabilities of this H/(H)..."
3. An autumn walk to the river: "Every now and then m^a.FY (I feel compelled) to M^a (walk) down to the Na (river) to M^p (listen). Today is one of those decreased F+ %, increased Ls and Y, and wanting FD days. Cg (jeans, undershirt, flannel shirt, hiking boots) all TF FABCOM1 (feel like that spot down by the) Na (river). I M^a (go out) the Hh (door) and a certain Dd99 V.TF.m^p MOR (clogged heaviness) begins to FV.FT.M^a.m^a (flow productively again) as the slow descent m^p (draws) me to the Na... I M^a (turn) to W_+ (Autumn) and am C (awash) in it. The Cls blanket the YF Ls (sky) in a C'Yish glow... The Bt (trees) Mª FABCOM1 (shout) MOR (the end of another vital cycle) while FABCOM1 M^ping (basking) in Na's C'.YF (sky's iridescent glow)."
4. Preparing Thanksgiving dinner for an involved other, his family, and a sister: "As an ambitent, I don't even know how to begin cooking! I read recipes instructing how to combine Ds to make a W. Yet I vacillate between reading and being drawn out by the Cful Fd, desiring to learn by experimentation. As

I switch between INT and EXT styles, others become HVI wondering if I'll really Zf and Zd+ enough to achieve a delicious W_+ meal. Lots of Ds clutter the Hh: F recipes and spice containers, FC Fd, and Sc kitchen accessories. "'What a mess!' my sister says, Zf-ing the room to see what needs to be done. I don't Zf in a P way. I feel L escalate. But resistant, I provide no R, and put on my apron as a Cg shield. Now I feel protected. My sister asks to COP. I refuse her help, in S style, reluctant to COP after her R. Besides, in a 3r + (2)/R way I wish to covet credit. AGly, she M^as out of the kitchen? ... My D momentarily dips to a –3 and I feel a CDI developing. When someone PSVing about FM appetite for the fifth time, asks "When's dinner?", I grunt. After my DVs and DRs, no one asks again... My glorious fantasy evaporates. I feel MOR, and rub my soft Cg, yearning for T. "How will I get a W+ from all those Ds?," I weep to myself. What was my X+% when I aspired to the W? Can I M^a enough to reach my W?... I become OBS, meticulously stuffing each squash with a equal number of cranberries, painstakingly counted in PSV style. People are a longer (H) but Hd – helping hands counting cranberries for me... Attuned to my high es state, perhaps through my tears, my family provides a new FD, COP reassuring me that they've come to see me, not my Fd. I feel my EA rise, and M begins to flow, meeting the challenge of the W. Less HVI and OBS, I become appreciative of the EA provided by special Hs and begin to remember what I forgot when I was lost in Hds and Dds – simply to give thanks. Together, we achieve a W+ through COP and the Hx of Thanksgiving."

5. Shopping for a Christmas gift for a friend: "I decide to M^a my friends a practical Hh rather than a sparkling FC Art. My C is diminishing and shortly pure F takes hold. Now more attuned to W and Z, I notice several FC' Hh (Teflon pans) are on sale. As I inspect one Hh, I M^p its usefulness in preparing Fd. Ah, but an Hh is such an impersonal ideo."

   "Perhaps I can M^a her a book? I ALOG that she must enjoy reading because she studied English. In the bookstore I am confronted with AB and Dd books as well as FC INCOM figurines such as Santa wearing red swim trunks: FC (H), Cg. Tired of M^aing, my FM is quickly rising. I must M an ideo soon, for my X+% is dropping."

   "I approach a final D – Cg! After an H comments on the TF of a particular Cg, I try the Cg on my own Hds. The T, C, and F of the Cg are appealing. Why not M^a this Cg for myself? Ah, my must be up. As I focus my attention on W, Zf and Zd+ increase. I M^a the FC.TF Cg for my friend."

   "As I leave the Sc, I hear several Hs joyfully M^aing carols. Having finally found the appropriate ideo, I recognize with cheerful Hx a similar CP; I feel affected by the holiday spirit, Hx – AB."

Even after the course we still find ourselves scoring our situations and experiences. Our own lives thus serve as a continuously developing resource for understanding clients' Rorschachs. Our growing repertoires also provide us with concrete life world examples to offer to clients as the ground for collaborative exploration.

Collaborating with Clients

Students think their way through diagnostic ("thorough knowing") tasks by considering data in light of multiple developmental and personality theories and in light of researched patterns of pathology and well-being. Theories and categories come to life as we wonder how a particular person might have come to the place of taking up the Rorschach in particular ways. Students always regard life as primary data and theories and scores as derivations. Life events are our point of departure into tests and theories, and life events are also our point of return.

We engage the client as a coassessor, moving the assessment beyond nomothetic and other general characterizations to discussion of concrete instances in that particular person's life. Through discussion, contexts also become apparent, as do "when-nots" – the circumstances in which the client has experienced or behaved in contrasting ways. In that the assessor also observes and inquires about *how* clients participate in getting themselves in and out of various situations, alternatives can be explored directly. In this process, clients become more keenly aware that they are active agents in "what happens" to them. Collaboration of this sort occurs during the initial interview and throughout the assessment process – with the Bender, MMPI, and so on. This collaboration is a far cry from unilateral "feedback" after completion of an assessment. In the illustrations of assessors' shared impressions that follow, the client's remarks are in brackets:

1. (P = 8; F+% = 50) You know, there are things, like the bats, the bears, and the native dancers that most people notice. And you did too. I would guess that in your first scan of a situation, you read the scene the way most people do? [You mean like I get oriented first, like I'm good at maps, and like I can find the men's room in a new building without asking?] Good. That's more to the point than what I was thinking. Now, although I too could see everything you pointed out, because I'm familiar with the cards and because you helped me, a lot of the time what you said was unique, which leads me to wonder about times that other people find it difficult to follow you. [That's amazing! From this inkblot test?! Do you mean like my group not following my flip chart presentations? I have a hard time being patient when it's black and white to me.] Like you couldn't believe that I couldn't see your armadillo? [I wasn't impatient; I just couldn't believe you couldn't see it. Were you trying to test my patience?] No, I just needed you to "orient" *me* more, as you in fact did on the last card when you explained that the parachutist would either have to be seen as far away or as belonging to another scene. Should this be one of our suggestions for work? [Yes, write down that I should check with my "audience" to see if they need more orienting before I go on.]
2. (EB = 4:7.5; a:p = 8:2) It looks to me as though typically you've been a hands-on person – you like to figure things out by trying them out. Like with the blocks (WAIS–R), your hands just flipped the blocks until what you needed came up. Then when the designs became more difficult, you stopped and worked on figuring out a system. [What's wrong with that?] Nothing. I think that you enjoy that approach and that it works for you in most situations. When it wouldn't work is if you were to insist that some one solution *should* work, instead of backing off to see if a different system would work better. Oh, you told me that your wife says you get "obstinate." Tell me an example, and let's see if it fits. [Well, that was about Tim's curfew. But she was standing there, like testing me, to see if I'd check with her.] Ah, so it's been more difficult to check your own actions when someone's standing around judging you? [Yeah. – I guess that's what happens when Smitty's supervising.]

3. (P = 3; F+% = 74) [Yes, I don't like for people to think I'm just ordinary; you're right, I try not to be trite.] Could you think of some examples? [At work all the other secretaries have pictures of their children on their desks or the cubical cork board; I put up my "rogues gallery" of losers I've gone out with. It is really creative, but I've been getting pressure about it.] Whoops. Maybe sometimes you're not ordinary enough – maybe in this instance you didn't pick up on the kind of atmosphere your co-workers prefer? [I just don't care to. The place, the people, are just too dumbly bland and conformist.]

The preceding excerpt points to the importance of checking out life referents of characterizations. Often the client's provision of examples points in different directions from what the assessor had in mind, and the assessor changes his or her formulation. In other instances examples provide refinements and differentiating contexts. Sometimes client and assessor wind up acknowledging certain differences in their understandings.

In a later course, students conduct part of an assessment in the client's home where life contexts are more readily available for collaborative discussion. After that, students remain aware of the constraints imposed by office assessments.

Writing Reports that can be Read by Psychologists, Other Professionals, and Clients

The closing exercise in the Rorschach course is writing clinical reports. We endeavor to write with multiple readers in mind: clinicians, other helpers and decision makers, the client, and possible future readers. The author represents the understandings developed through the collaborative assessment, by *re-presenting* illustrative assessment events and similar life events that they evoked. The report therefore may be read by all the aforementioned parties, who are then "on the same page" in regard to the client's life. For example, instead of reporting that "The F -% and low P indicate that this person has poor reality testing," we might say, "Joe acknowledged that just as he didn't pay attention to what most people notice on the inkblots (P = 4), he often has found himself trying to find something pleasant even when he knows his family and co-workers don't share his Pollyannish view (F+% = 59, X+% = 48, T = 2, FC = 6).

The report's format is fairly standard, with the following exceptions:

1. The referral section contains not only the initial issue, but also the results of conferring with the referring party about the contexts in which the issue arose, and with the client about his or her understanding of the referral. The referral section also includes what the client said he or she would like to learn from the assessment. Example: "*Referral:* Dr. Monte requested a psychological assessment to aid in developing a differential diagnosis between schizoid personality disorder and schizophrenia in remission following an acute episode. Dr. Monte had found that medical records, family, and Mr. Jarak himself provided little history of help in deciding on medications and between individual psychotherapy and a group support program. The question is whether Mr. Jarak's present state is pretty much a life-long one, or whether neuroleptic medications might help him to regain a pre-episode level of interpersonal relating, which in turn

might allow him to make good use of psychotherapy. Mr. Jarak's interest in the assessment was additionally in learning why his cousins think he's 'crazy' and whether he could qualify for a job retraining program. When we reviewed Dr. Monte's referral and the DSM–IV diagnostic criteria, Mr. Jarak thought that he fit the schizoid and avoidant personality disorder characteristics better, although he said that when he has become very agitated, other people say he's 'paranoid.' "

2. Unless there are particular reasons to do so, the report is not organized by instruments, but rather by referral-relevant themes, often highlighted by subheadings, such as "'Doing the Job' in Familiar Situations," and "Retrenching in Unfamiliar Situations;" or "Watching From the Outside," "Rushing Toward Safety," and "Risking Successfully."
3. We attach a technical appendix that reports additional data and reflections to clinicians who may want to know more than was efficacious to include in the theme-oriented and already longish narrative report. (The appendix also lets me know how thoroughly the graduate student has studied the Rorschach and the other tests.) The form of the appendix is tailored for each case. Sometimes the appendix is a list of additional data that support themes, for example:

   "Concrete intellectual style:
   WAIS–R highest scale = Information (14);
   lowest scale = Similarities (8)
   Rorschach sequence: D, D, D; Approach: W = 2; D = 18
   R = 20; Zf= 8; Zd = –2
   16 P-F scale B (Concrete/Abstract Thinking) =7."

For other purposes, the author might comment on notable Rorschach summary sheet data, specifying how these items were discussed with the client. Excerpt:[3]

> "R: 41 responses contrasts with the expected range of 17–27 responses for adults. The assessee and I discussed this in terms of 'giving 110%.'
>
> "C': The assessee's elevated achromatic responses (4 in contrast to a mean of 1.53 for 23 responses) reflects affective constraint or a psychological 'biting of the tongue.' We discussed this in terms of the assessee's 'gritting her teeth.' "

4. The final section of the report is "Client Comments" or "Mr. Jarak's Comments," where the client writes remarks about the report and signs and dates it. We regard our reports as progress reports – reports of progress-to-date for both parties in coming to understand the person's participation in his or her world. The comments indicate the degree to which the person has comprehended and agreed with the author's written understandings. Often the review becomes an occasion for further clarification by both parties. Within reports, authors write in first person ("I" rather than "the examiner," or, "I administered the test,") rather than using the passive voice ("the test was administered"). This style reminds readers that assessments occur in interpersonal contexts, and that our findings are necessarily grounded in personal perspectives. We use past rather than present tense, to indicate that the conduct may change ("Thus Jayson has avoided situations in which he might fail," rather than "Jayson is

risk-avoidant"). This last example also illustrates another writing principle: we try to bypass constructs, and instead describe in terms of specific actions. For example, instead of, "His underlying hostility results in distorted human relationships," we might say, "When insisting on being treated fairly, Thomas has not noticed that some people would be willing to help him." We also try to own our impressions rather than attribute them to the tests. In place of "Despite her denial, the Rorschach indicates that this person is depressed," we might say, "Although Ms. Jamison said she was just tired, I saw her as being depressed as I witnessed her sighs and slouched posture, and when I reflected on her attunement to death and illness and to the dark and hidden aspects of the inkblots. This attunement was at the expense of noticing color and playful possibilities."

Finally, we regard the crafting of our reports as carefully grounded but creative exercises. We discover different meanings as we attempt to express our understandings to ourselves and to diverse readers. We carefully choose our language, images, juxtapositions, and inclusions to resonate with readers' lives so that those lives become a resource in evoking a sense of the client's life. Students find comparisons of Andrew Wyeth's disciplined representational art with the life-world assessment's disciplined description to be freeing and challenging (Fischer, 1980, 1994a).

Conclusion: The Rorschach Experience Lives On

Graduates retain a collaborative, exploratory attitude in all of their work – assessment, teaching, psychotherapy, consulting, research. Whether or not students again use the Rorschach, they continue to see depth and dynamics more readily than before the course. They understand more fully that all test data like other life tracks and outcomes, point to how a person took up a circumstance and traveled through it. Knowing that a person's journey through Rorschach cards (or other material) is part of that person's journey through life, they ask what other situations might have been like this one for the client. With all tests, graduates strive to get from statistics (static) back to a person in motion – a person en route to goals, perceiving and acting in accordance with attunement to landmarks, invitations, dangers. Graduates respect the access a person's life that a well-researched test provides, but they also respect its inherent ambiguity; they know that numbers are more precise than life. They continue to measure the validity of their work in terms of the extent to which it has assisted clients and their other helpers toward revising comportment and decisions. In short, the Rorschach students go forth from the course knowing "what in the world they are talking about."

Notes

1 Originally published as Fischer, C. T. (1998). The Rorschach and the life-world: Exploratory exercises. In L. Handler & M. Hilsenroth (Eds.). *Teaching and learning personality assessment* (pp. 347–358). Hillsdale, NJ: Lawrence Erlbaum.

2 Excerpts are drawn from papers by the following doctoral students (in alphabetical rather than sequential order): William Culley, Stacy Giguere, Alissa Perrucci, Rameshwari Rao, and Robert Sandford.

3 From a single-spaced one-and-a-half-page Rorschach Technical Appendix by Rameshwari Rao.

References

Exner, J. E. (1993). *The Rorschach: A comprehensive system: Vol. 3. Basic foundations* (3rd ed.). New York: Wiley.

Finn, S. E. (1996). *Manual for using the MMPI–2 as a therapeutic intervention.* Minneapolis: University of Minnesota Press.

Finn, S. E. (1998). Teaching Therapeutic Assessment in a required graduate course. In Handler, L., & Hilsenroth, M. (Eds.), *Teaching and learning personality assessment* (pp. 359–373). Mahwah, NJ: Erlbaum.

Fischer, C. T. (1979). Individualized assessment and phenomenological psychology. *Journal of Personality Assessment, 43*, 115–122.

Fischer, C. T. (1980). Phenomenology and psychological assessment: Re-presentational description. *Journal of Phenomenological Psychology, 11*, 79–105.

Fischer, C. T. (1994a). *Individualizing psychological assessment.* Hillsdale, NJ: Lawrence Erlbaum Associates. (Original work published 1985.)

Fischer, C. T. (1994b). Rorschach scoring questions as access to dynamics. *Journal of Personality Assessment, 62*, 515–525.

Schachtel, E. G. (1966). *Experiential foundations of Rorschach's test.* N.Y.: Basic Books.

APPENDIX

Complete Publications of Constance T. Fischer

BOOKS

Giorgi, A., Fischer, C. T., & Murray, E. L. (Eds.). (1975). *Duquesne studies in phenomenological psychology (Vol. 2)*. Pittsburgh: Duquesne University Press.

Fischer, C. T. & Brodsky, S. L. (Eds.). (1978). *Client participation in human services: The Prometheus principle*. New Brunswick, N. J.: Transaction.

Fischer, C. T. (1985). *Individualizing psychological assessment*. Monterey: Brooks-Cole. [Re-issued 1994, Mahwah, N. J.: Lawrence Erlbaum & Associates; now available through Routledge.]

Fischer, C. T. (2002). Guest Ed., Humanistic approaches to psychological assessment, *The Humanistic Psychologist, 30* (1–2, pp. 3–174; 3, pp. 178–236).

Fischer, C. T. (2006). (Ed.). *Qualitative research methods for psychologists: Introduction through empirical studies*. San Diego: Academic Press.

Finn, S. E., Fischer, C. T., & Handler, L. (Eds.) (2012). *Collaborative/Therapeutic Assessment: A casebook and guide*. Hoboken, NJ: Wiley.

Fischer, C. T. (2017). *On the way to collaborative psychological assessment: The selected works of Constance T. Fischer*. New York: Routledge.

Fischer, C. T., Laubscher, L., & Brooke, R. (Eds.) (2016). *An invitation to psychology as a human science*. Pittsburgh: Duquesne University Press.

CHAPTERS

Fischer, C. T. (1971). Toward the structure of privacy: Implications for psychological assessment. In A. Giorgi, W. F. Fischer, & R. von Eckartsberg (Eds.). *Duquesne studies in phenomenological psychology (Vol. 1)* (pp. 149–163). Pittsburgh: Duquesne University Press.

Fischer, C. T. (1974). Exit IQ: Enter the child. In G. Williams & S. Gordon (Eds.). *Clinical child psychology: Current practices and future perspectives* (pp. 333–348). New York: Behavioral Publications.

Fischer, C. T. (1975). Darrell Holderin (sample psychological report). In N. Tallent (Ed.). *Psychological report writing* (pp. 221–225). New York: Prentice-Hall. [reprinted in M. T. Nietzel & D. A. Bernstein (1987), *Introduction to clinical psychology* (2nd ed.), Englewood Cliffs, N. J.: Prentice-Hall.]

Fischer, C. T. (1978). Collaborative psychological assessment. In C. T. Fischer & S. L. Brodsky (Eds.). *Client participation in human services: The Prometheus principle* (pp. 41–61). New Brunswick, N. J.: Transaction.

Fischer, C. T., & Brodsky, S. L. (1978). Informed participation: Why now? In C. T. Fischer & S. L. Brodsky (Eds.). *Client participation in human services: The Prometheus principle* (pp. 1–10). New Brunswick, N. J.: Transaction.

Fischer, C. T., & Brodsky, S. L. (1978). On the way from Olympus. In C. T. Fischer & S. L. Brodsky (Eds.). *Client participation in human services: The Prometheus principle* (pp. 227–237). New Brunswick, N. J.: Transaction.

Fischer, C. T. (1978). Dilemmas in standardized testing. In J. Mearig (Ed.). *Working for children: Ethical issues beyond professional guidelines* (pp. 115–134). San Francisco: Jossey Bass.

Fischer, C. T. (1978). Personality and assessment. In R. Valle & M. King (Eds.). *Existential-phenomenological alternatives for psychology* (pp. 203–231). New York: Oxford University Press.

Fischer, C. T., & Wertz, F. J. (1979). Empirical phenomenological analyses of being criminally victimized. In A. Giorgi, R. Knowles, & D. Smith (Eds.). *Duquesne studies in phenomenological psychology (Vol. 3)* (pp. 135–158). Pittsburgh: Duquesne University Press.

Fischer, C. T. (1980). Privacy and human development. In W. C. Bier (Ed.). *Privacy: A vanishing value* (pp. 37–45). New York: Fordham University Press.

Fischer, C. T. (1982). Intimacy in assessment. In M. Fisher & G. Stricker (Eds.). *Intimacy* (pp. 443–460). New York: Plenum.

Fischer, C. T., & Fischer, W. F. (1983). Phenomenological-existential psychotherapy. In M. Hersen, A. E. Kazden, & A. S. Bellack (Eds.). *The clinical psychology handbook* (pp. 489–505). New York: Pergamon.

Fischer, C. T., & Alapack, R. (1987). Phenomenological approach to adolescent psychology. In V. B. Van Hasselt & M. Hersen (Eds.). *The handbook of adolescent psychology* (pp. 91–107). New York: Pergamon.

Fischer, C. T. (1987). A phenomenological approach to Mr. A. In M. T. Nietzel & D. Bernstein (Eds.). *Introduction to clinical psychology* (2nd ed.). Englewood Cliffs, N.J.: Prentice-Hall (pp. 59–62). Revised version in 3rd and 4th editions.

Fischer, C. T. (1989). Personality and assessment. In R. Valle & S. Halling (Eds.). *Existential phenomenological perspectives in psychology* (pp. 157–178). New York: Plenum.

Fischer, C. T. (1991). Phenomenological-existential psychotherapy. In M. Hersen, A. E. Kazdin, & A. S. Bellack (Eds.). *The clinical psychology handbook* (2nd ed.) (pp. 534–550). New York: Pergamon.

Fischer, C. T. (1992) Humanistic approaches to life-span development. In V. B. Van Hasselt & M. Hersen (Eds.). *Handbook of social development: A lifespan perspective* (pp. 113–128). New York: Plenum.

Fischer, C. T. (1994). Humanizing psychological assessment. In F. Wertz (Ed.), *The humanistic movement: Recovering the person in psychology* (pp. 202–214). Lake Worth, FL: Gardner Press.

Fischer, C. T. (1996). A humanistic and human science approach to emotion. In C. Magai, & S. H. McFadden (Eds.). *Handbook on emotion, adult development and aging* (pp. 67–82). Orlando: Academic Press.

Fischer, C. T. (1998). The Rorschach and the life-world: Exploratory exercises. In L. Handler & M. Hilsenroth (Eds.). *Teaching and learning personality assessment* (pp. 347–358). Hillsdale, NJ: Lawrence Erlbaum.

Fischer, C. T. (1998). Being angry revealed as deceptive protest: An empirical-phenomenological analysis. In R. Valle (Ed.). *Phenomenological inquiry in psychology: Existential and transpersonal dimensions* (pp.111–122). New York: Plenum.

Fischer, C. T. (1998). Phenomenological, existential, and humanistic foundations for psychology as a human science. In M. Hersen & A. Bellack (Series Eds.) & C. E. Walker (Vol. Ed.), *Comprehensive clinical psychology: Vol. 1: Foundations* (pp. 449–472). London: Elsevier Science.

Fischer, C. T. (1998). An existential-phenomenological analysis of Mr. B. In M. T. Nietzel, D. A. Bernstein, & R. Milich (Eds.), *Introduction to clinical psychology, 5th ed* (pp. 76–80). Englewood Cliffs, NJ: Prentice Hall.

Fischer, C. T. (1998). [untitled section on the use of touch in psychotherapy] In P. R. Clance & V. J. Petras, Therapists' recall of their decision-making process regarding use of touch

in ongoing psychotherapy. In Smith, E. W. L., Clance, P. R., & Imes, S. (Eds.), *Touch in psychotherapy: Theory, research, and practice* (pp. 105–107). New York: Guilford.
Fischer, C. T. (1999). Designing qualitative research reports for publication. In M. Kopala & L. Suzuki (Eds.). *Using qualitative research methods in psychology* (pp. 105–129). Thousand Oaks, CA: Sage.
Fischer, C. T., McElwain, B., & DuBose T. (2000). Existential psychotherapy. In C. R. Snyder & R. E. Ingram (Eds.), *Handbook of psychological change: Psychotherapy processes and practices for the 21st century* (pp. 243–257). New York: Wiley.
Fischer, C. T. (2001). Psychological assessment: From objectification back to the life world. In B. D. Slife, R. N. Williams, & S. H. Barlow (Eds.), *Critical issues in psychotherapy: Translating ideas into practice* (pp. 29–44). Thousand Oaks, CA: Sage.
Fischer, C. T., Embree, S., Eckenrod, J., & Jarzynka. J. (2001). Empirical phenomenological research in psychotherapy: Duquesne dissertations. In J. Frommer & D. L. Rennie (Eds.), *Qualitative psychotherapy research: Methods and methodology* (pp. 169–184). Lengerich, Germany: Pabst.
Fischer, C. T. (2001). Collaborative exploration as an approach to personality assessment. In K. J. Schneider, J. F. T. Bugenthal, & J. F. Pierson (Eds.), *The handbook of humanistic psychology: Leading edges in theory, research, and practice* (pp. 525–538). Thousand Oaks, CA: Sage.
Fischer, C. T., & Wertz, F. J. (2002). Empirical phenomenological analyses of being criminally victimized. Republished in M. Huberman & M. B. Miles (Eds.), *The qualitative researcher's companion* (pp. 275–304). Thousand Oaks: Sage.
Fischer, C. T., Georgievska, E., & Melczack, M. (2003). Collaborative exploration with projective techniques: A life-world approach. In M. Hersen (Ed.-in-Chief) and M. Hilsenroth & D. Segal, M. J. (Vol. Eds.), *Comprehensive handbook of psychological assessment: Vol. 2, Objective and projective assessment of personality and psychopathology* (pp. 586–594). Hoboken, NJ: John Wiley & Sons.
Fischer, C. T. (2005). Multifaceted Life Events Checklist. In L. VandeCreek (Ed.), *Innovations in clinical practice: Focus on adults* (pp. 155–160). Sarasota, FL: Professional Resource Press.
Fischer, C. T. (2006). Introduction. In C. T. Fischer (Ed.). *Qualitative research methods for psychologists* (pp. xv–xlii). Burlington, San Diego, & London: Elsevier.
Fischer, C. T. (2006). Questions & responses. In C. T. Fischer (Ed.). *Qualitative research methods for psychologists* (pp. 411–427). Burlington, San Diego, & London: Elsevier.
Fischer, C. T. (2006). Glossary. In C. T. Fischer (Ed.). *Qualitative research methods for psychologists* (pp. 429–441). London: Elsevier.
Fischer, C. T. (2007). Collaborative discussion with Marie. In S.R. Smith & L. Handler (Eds). *The clinical assessment of children and adolescents: A practitioner's handbook* (pp. 54–55). Mahwah, NJ: Erlbaum.
Fischer, C. T. (2007). Foreword, In S. E. Finn, *In our clients' shoes: Theory and techniques of Therapeutic Assessment* (pp. xv–xvi). Mahwah, NJ: Erlbaum.
Fischer, C. T., & Finn, S. E. (2008). Developing the life meaning of psychological test data: Collaborative and therapeutic approaches. In R. P. Archer & S. R. Smith (Eds.), *Personality assessment* (pp. 379–404). New York: Routledge.
Fischer, C. T. (2010). Actualization. In I. B. Weiner & W. E. Craighead (Eds.), *The Corsini encyclopedia of psychology, 4th Ed* (pp. 22–23). Hoboken, NJ: John Wiley & Sons.
Fischer, C. T. (2012). Collaboration throughout the assessment: A young man in transition. In Finn, S. E., Fischer, C. T., & Handler, L. (Eds.), *Collaborative/Therapeutic Assessment: A casebook and guide* (pp. 93–111). Hoboken, NJ: Wiley.
Fischer, C. T., & Finn, S. E. (2014). Developing the life meaning of psychological test data: Collaborative and therapeutic approaches. In Archer, R. P., & Smith. S. R. (Eds.), *Personality assessment, 2nd edition* (pp. 401–431). New York: Routledge.

ARTICLES

Fischer, C. T. (1968). Male-female differences in Catholic college students' attitudes toward the possibility of social change. *The Catholic Psychological Record*, 6, 30–34.

Fischer, C. T. (1968). Social schemas: Response sets or perceptual meanings? *Journal of Personality and Social Psychology*, *10*, 8–14.

Fischer, C. T. (1969). Intelligence defined as effectiveness of approaches. *Journal of Consulting and Clinical Psychology*, *33*, 668–674.

Fischer, C. T. (1969). Rapport as mutual respect. *Personnel and Guidance Journal*, *48*, 201–204. [Reprinted in C. E. Beck (Ed.). *Philosophical guidelines for counseling* (2nd. ed.) (pp. 149–153). Dubuque: Wm. C. Brown.]

Fischer, C. T. (1969). Relations among dynamic reading measures, Rokeach dogmatism scores, Personnel Test IQ, and reading experience protocols: Report to DEAR. *Summary in Research and Development Bulletin*, Diversified Education Research Corporation, New York, No. 16.

Fischer, C. T. (1970). Levels of cheating under conditions of informative appeal to honesty, public affirmation of value, and threats of punishment. *Journal of Educational Research*, *64*, 12–16.

Fischer, C. T. (1970). The testee as co-evaluator. *Journal of Counseling Psychology*, *17*, 70–76. [Reprinted in (1971) A. Giorgi, W. F. Fischer, & R. Von Ecksartsberg (Eds.). *Duquesne studies in phenomenological psychology*, (*Vol.* 1) (pp. 385–394). Pittsburgh: Duquesne University Press.

Fischer, C. T. (1970). Toward human research via a moratorium on IQ-testing. *Clinical Child Psychology Newsletter*, *10*, 4.

Fischer, C. T. (1972). Paradigm changes which allow sharing of results. *Professional Psychology*, *3*, 364–369.

Fischer, C. T. (1972). A theme for the child advocate: Sharable everyday life-events of the child-in-the-world. *Journal of Clinical Child Psychology*, *1*, 23–25.

Fischer, C. T. (1973). Behaviorism and behavioralism. *Psychotherapy: Theory, Research and Practice*, *10*, 2–4.

Fischer, C. T. (1973). Contextual approach to assessment. *Community Mental Health Journal*, *9*, 38–45.

Fischer, C. T. (1973). Intelligence contra IQ: A human-science critique and alternative to the natural science approach to man. *Human Development*, *16*, 8–20. [Reprinted in K. F. Riegel (Ed.). (1974). *Alternative views of a paradigm* (pp. 8–20). Basel, Switzerland: S. Karger.] [Reprinted in A. Giorgi, C. T. Fischer, & E. L. Murray. (Eds.) (1975). *Duquesne studies in phenomenological psychology* (*Vol.*2) (pp. 143–154). Pittsburgh: Duquesne University Press.]

Fischer, C. T., & Rizzo, A. A. (1974). A paradigm for humanizing special education. *Journal of Special Education*, *8*, 321–329.

Fischer, C. T. (1975). Privacy as a profile of authentic consciousness. *Humanitas*, *11*, 27–43.

Fischer, C. T. (1976). The meaning of phenomenological psychology. *Philosophical Psychologist*, *10*, 14–19.

Fischer, C. T. (1976). Undercutting the scientist-professional dichotomy: The reflective psychologist. *The Clinical Psychologist*, *29*, 5–7.

Fischer, C. T. (1977). Historical relations of psychology as an object-science and subject-science: Toward psychology as a human-science. *Journal of the History of the Behavioral Sciences*, *13*, 369–378.

Fischer, C. T. (1978). Graduate programs in clinical child psychology and related fields. *Journal of Clinical Child Psychology*, *7*, 87–88.

Fischer, C. T. (1979). Individualized assessment and phenomenological psychology. *Journal of Personality Assessment*, *43*, 115–122.

Fischer, C. T. (1980). Phenomenology and psychological assessment: Re-presentational description. *Journal of Phenomenological Psychology*, *11*, 79–105.

Mannarino, A. P. & Fischer, C. T. (1982). Survey of training programs in clinical child psychology. *Journal of Clinical Child Psychology*, *11*, 22–26.
Murphy, M. A. & Fischer, C. T. (1983). Styles of living with low back injury: The continuity dimension. *Social Sciences and Medicine*, *17*, 291–297.
Fischer, C. T. (1984). A phenomenological study of being criminally victimized: Contributions and constraints of qualitative research. *Journal of Social Issues*, *40*(1), 161–177.
Fischer, C. T. (1984). Being criminally victimized: An illustrated structure. *American Behavioral Scientist*, *27*, 723–738.
Fischer, C. T. (1987). Beyond transference. *Person-centered Review*, *2*, 57–164.
Fischer, C. T. (1987). The quality of qualitative research. *Theoretical and Philosophical Psychology*, *7*, 2–11.
Fischer, C. T. (1987). Empowering clients by deconstructing psychological reports. *Practice: The Journal of Politics, Economics, Psychology, Sociology, and Culture*, *5*, 134–139.
Fischer, C. T. (1989). A life-centered approach to psychodiagnostics: Attending to the life-world, ambiguity, and possibility. *Person-centered Review*, *4*, 163–170.
Fischer, C. T. (1993). Humanizing psychological assessment. *The Humanistic Psychologist*, *20*, 318–331.
Fischer, C. T. (1994). Rorschach scoring questions as access to dynamics. *Journal of Personality Assessment*, *62*, 515–525.
Fischer, C. T. (1994). Rigor in qualitative research: Reflexive and presentational. *Methods, Annual Edition*, 21–27.
Fischer, C. T. (1995). D-A-P Instructions: From "opposite sex" to "other gender." *SPA Exchange*, *5*(2), 3.
Barnard, S., & Fischer, C. T. (1998). A contemporary philosophical reading of the APA Memories of Childhood Abuse report. *Journal of Theoretical and Philosophical Psychology*, *18*, 127–134.
Elliott, R., Fischer, C. T., & Rennie, D. L. (1999). Evolving guidelines for publication of qualitative research in psychology and related fields. *British Journal of Clinical Psychology*, *38*, 215–229.
Fischer, C. T. (2000). Collaborative, individualized assessment. *Journal of Personality Assessment*, *74*, 2–14.
Fischer, C. T. (2003). Infusing humanistic perspectives into psychology. *Journal of Humanistic Psychology*, *43*, 93–105.
Fischer, C. T. (2003). What is individualized, collaborative assessment? *Bulletin of the Academy of Clinical Psychology*, *9*(1), 10–13.
Fischer, C. T. (2004). In what senses is collaborative assessment collaborative? Some distinctions. *SPA Exchange*, *16*, 14–15.
Fischer, C. T. (2004). Individualized assessment moderates the impact of HIPAA privacy rules. *Journal of Personality Assessment*, *81*, 35–38.
Fischer, C. T. (2006). Phenomenology, Bruno Klopfer, and individualized psychological assessment. *Journal of Personality Assessment*, *87*, 220–233. [SPA Bruno Klopfer Award presentation.]
Fischer, C. T. (2006). Humanistic psychology and qualitative research: Affinity, clarifications, and invitations. *The Humanistic Psychologist*, *34*, 3–11.
Fischer, C. T. (2006). Qualitative psychological research and individualized/collaborative psychological assessment: Implications of their similarities for promoting a life-world orientation. *The Humanistic Psychologist*, *34*, 347–356.
Fischer, C. T. (2009). Writing individualized psychological assessment reports. *Pennsylvania Psychological Association Bulletin*, *69*(3), 16, 18.
Fischer, C. T. (2009). Practical characterization of tests: Promoting the proposed retirement of the misleading "projective – objective" distinction. *SPA Exchange*, *21*(1), 2, 12, 13.
Fischer, C. T. (2009) Bracketing in qualitative research: Conceptual and practical matters. *Psychotherapy Research*, *19*, 1–8.

Fischer, C. T. (2010). Individualized assessment moderates the impact of HIPAA privacy rules. *Journal of Personality Assessment, 82*(1), 35–38.
Engelman, D. H., Allyn, J. B., Crisi, A., Finn, S. E., Fischer, C. T., & Nakamura, N. (2016). "Why am I so stuck?": A Collaborative/Therapeutic Assessment case discussion. *Journal of Personality Assessment, 98*(4), 360–373.

REVIEWS

Fischer, C. T. (1971). [Review of E. J. Keen, Three faces of being: Toward an existential clinical psychology]. *Journal of Phenomenological Psychology, 2*, 129–132.
Fischer, C. T. (1972). [Review of M. Zaner, The way of phenomenology: Criticism as a philosophical discipline]. *Journal of Phenomenological Psychology, 2*, 271–174.
Fischer, C. T. (1973). Foundations of fallible influence [Reviews of H. D. Christiansen, Ethics in counseling; W. C. Lewis, Why people change; and P. Morea, Guidance, selection, and training]. *Contemporary Psychology, 18*, 375–377.
Fischer, C. T. (1974) [Review of H. Misiak & V. S. Sexton, Phenomenological, existential, and humanistic psychologies: A historical survey]. *Journal of Phenomenological Psychology, 4*, 491–493.
Fischer, C. T. (1977). [Review of J. deRivera, Field theory as human science: Contributions of Lewin's Berlin group]. *Philosophical Psychologist, 11*, 4–6.
Fischer, C. T. (1980). [Review of R. J. Cohen, Malpractice: A guide for mental health professionals]. *Society, 17*, 90–93.
Fischer, C. T. (1980). [Review of Thines, Phenomenology and the science of behavior]. *Human Studies, 3*, 239–243.
Fischer, C. T. (1981). A special textbook on special children [Review of B. G. Surran & J. V. Rizzo, Special children: An integrative approach]. *Contemporary Psychology, 26*, 196–197.
Fischer, C. T. (1982). [Review of R. Naar, A primer of group psychotherapy]. *Newsletter of the Western Pennsylvania Group Psychotherapy Society, 1*(1), 7.
Fischer, C. T. (1996). Bridging many splits [Review of R. J. Muller, Anatomy of a splitting borderline: Description and analysis of case history]. *Contemporary Psychology, 41*, 263–264.
Fischer, C. T. (1998). A welcome alliance. [Review of R. J. Ganallen, Integrating the Rorschach and the MMPI-2 in personality assessment]. *Contemporary Psychology, 43*, 355.
Fischer, C. T. (2001). Review of L. S. Greenberg, J. C. Watson, & G. Lietaer (Eds.), Handbook of experiential psychotherapy. *Clinical Psychology Review, 21*, 491–2001.
Fischer, C. T. (2003). [Review of D. A. Dewsbury (Ed.), Unification through division: Histories of the divisions of the American Psychological Association (Vol. 5)]. *Contemporary Psychology, 48*, 351–353.
Fischer, C. T., & Adams, W. W. (2007, August 22). Alternative paths of awareness: For some of those so inclined [Review of the book Earth-based psychology: Path awareness from the teachings of Don Juan, Richard Feyman, and Lao Tse]. *Psych CRITIQUES–Contemporary Psychology: APA Review of Books, 52* (No. 34, Article 15).
Fischer, C. T. (2012). Comments on protecting clients about whom we write and speak. *Psychotherapy, 49*(1), 19–21.

COMMENTS

Fischer, C. T. (1968). Ethical issues in the use of human subjects. *American Psychologist, 23*, 532.
Fischer, C. T. (1970). Consent to release of what? *Professional Psychology, 1*, 424.
Fischer, C. T. (1973). Psychology as a human science contra humane behaviorism. *American Psychologist, 28*, 90–91.

Fischer, C. T. (1975). Barton's book is heuristic. *Contemporary Psychology*, *20*, 917.
Fischer, C. T. (1987). We do have standards for record-keeping. *The Independent Practitioner*, *70*, 30.
Fischer, C. T. (1988). Inhibiting public behavior [invited comment]. *The Independent Practitioner*, *8*(1), 3–4.
Barnard, S. & Fischer, C. T. (1994). "Gender" was correct the first time. *The Psychotherapy Newsletter*, *6*(1), 8.
Fischer, C. T. (1994). Remembering Renata Tesch. *International Human Science Newsletter*, Fall, 4.
Fischer, C. T. (1996). Fischer replies: Philosophical context and social responsibility. *SPA Exchange*, *5*(3), 10–11.
Ellliott, R., Fischer, C. T., & Rennie, D. L. (2000). Also against methodolatry: A reply to Reicher. *British Journal of Clinical Psychology*, *39*, 7–10.

INDEX

For Product Safety Concerns and Information please contact our EU representative GPSR@taylorandfrancis.com
Taylor & Francis Verlag GmbH, Kaufingerstraße 24, 80331 München, Germany

www.ingramcontent.com/pod-product-compliance
Ingram Content Group UK Ltd.
Pitfield, Milton Keynes, MK11 3LW, UK
UKHW021959180926
475701UK00003B/101
9781138310964